Quick & Easy

birmingham alabama what's cooking in birmingham phoenix arizona eat and
pepper to taste berkeley california the jewish cookbook beverly hills
beverly hills california from tro valley california what's c
california flavored with recipes san diego cali
california delectable nd helpings, please! r
health stamford co connecticut passo
leavened with lo a beach florida m
florida food fo recipes balabu
hallandale fl orites hollyw
gourmet de lle florida tr
this and ko ssee floric
jewish di cooker a
kitchen ort sheri
cookbo cooker
recipes chen t
louisia ootom
mass ht coo
cente y ma
sudt e hap
arbo ma
mag id t
trea ion
cou len
inoi ce
a s eat:
ess o se
jers ew j
new ork
bing okly
kosl v yor
new. ar be
elega lora w
enjoy n ma
inspir. rk nev
plainvi orite re
hadass alley ne
island ne ce west I
spice cha. ite recipes
cleveland rt of cookir
kitchen cinc ala cynwyd p
havertown pe plotz and par
with love philao d cookbook stai
women of brit sh asy cookbook cha
charleston with low speaking columbia
blountville tennessee vorite recipes dallas te
arthur texas bicentennia. favorite recipes from our
from soup to nosh lynchburg ushes newport news virginia a
virginia try it you'll like it parkersburg west virginia season to taste milwaukee w

Quick
& Easy

Edited by Shelley Melvin

TRIAD PUBLISHING COMPANY   GAINESVILLE, FLORIDA

BOOKS IN THE CHOSEN COOKBOOK SERIES

The Chosen: Appetizers & Desserts
Jewish Cooking Made Slim
Quick & Easy

Library of Congress Cataloging in Publication Data

Main entry under title:
Quick & Easy

(The Chosen cookbook series)
Includes index.
1. Cookery. I. Melvin, Shelley, 1944-
II. Title: Quick and easy. III Series.
TX652.Q46   1984   641.5'55   84-8886
ISBN 0-937404-56-X
ISBN 0-937404-55-1 (pbk.)

Printed in the United States of America

Published and distributed by Triad Publishing Company, Inc.
1110 Northwest Eighth Avenue
Gainesville, Florida 32601

Most Triad books are available at special quantity discounts for bulk purchases for sales promotions, premiums, or fundraising. For details contact Special Sales Department, Triad Publishing Company, 1110 Northwest Eighth Avenue, Gainesville, Florida 32601.

If your organization cookbook is not represented in this collection, and you feel it is suitable, we invite you to submit it for inclusion in future editions or cookbooks.

About the book

If you are like most busy, active people today, you like to serve meals that are delicious, unusual, attractively presented, and good for you and your family. Yet you probably have less time to spend in the kitchen than ever!

With the growing numbers of single parent households and women working outside the home, the task of getting dinner on the table has become extra demanding. A decade ago, one might have solved that problem by heading to a fast food restaurant. But today, an increased awareness of nutritional needs, including the need to avoid additives and preservatives, has led many people to search for faster ways to prepare fresh, wholesome foods without relying on packaged and canned ingredients.

With these needs in mind, *Quick & Easy* was developed — a book of family-oriented recipes that use fresh ingredients, can be prepared in up to 20 minutes of working time, and require only a minimum of technique and skill.

In the planning of the book, the question arose as to whether a 20-minute recipe should be actually ready to serve in 20 minutes or did it mean ready to freeze, put in the oven, etc. Choosing one definition of quick over the other would have meant leaving out too many good recipes, so I have included both. Therefore, you will find good recipes for either situation, whether you shop on the way home from work and must have dinner on the table instantly, or have only minutes to prepare a dish, but can allow it to simmer or bake while you run off to play tennis.

The one thing quick and easy doesn't mean here is cooking from jars, cans, packages, and bottles. The recipes are based primarily on fresh meat, fish, and vegetables. To give you the option of virtually eliminating prepared foods altogether, I have included recipes for some items that are traditionally store-bought, such as ketchup and mayonnaise. On the other hand, canned or frozen equivalents of fresh vegetables and fruits are given to accommodate those seasons and regions where fresh simply isn't available.

Quick & Easy can turn cooking into a pleasurable task. To that end I have included "quicker than quick" ideas that don't need a recipe. Those of you who own a microwave oven will be able to cut additional time off many recipes. Instructions and cooking times are given for both food processor and conventional method.

As with the first two Chosen cookbooks, *The Chosen: Appetizers & Desserts* and *Jewish Cooking Made Slim,* the recipe-selection process has been one of testing and retesting recipes from hundreds of Jewish fund-raising cookbooks to find those that best met the book's criteria. Most of the recipes have been altered slightly to eliminate prepared canned ingredients, to clarify instructions, or to follow a single format. All can be made by anyone observing Jewish dietary laws. I am grateful to all the contributing organizations who permitted us to excerpt from their books.

SHELLEY MELVIN
October, 1984

ABOUT THE AUTHOR

Shelley Melvin is a cooking instructor, caterer, and a consumer advisor for a leading manufacturer of food processing equipment. She studied cooking with Simone Beck at l'Ecole des Trois Gourmandes in France.

Contents

Notes to the cook

Here are some suggestions that will help you get the best results, in taste and efficiency, from *Quick & Easy*. As in using any cookbook, you should read the recipe completely before you begin cooking and measure all ingredients accurately.

IN GENERAL

Cook uncovered unless the directions say to cover.

Never fill a pan more than half full of oil when deep frying.

Check the beginning of each chapter for hints, new ideas, and some exceedingly quick recipes.

Eggs. Use large eggs in all recipes.

Flour. Use unbleached all-purpose flour unless recipe calls for another type.

Salt. If you double a recipe, do not double the salt. You may use less salt in almost all recipes except for recipes for baked goods.

Brown sugar. Always measure packed firmly in the measuring cup.

USING YOUR MICROWAVE OVEN

I did not test these recipes with a microwave oven. I have tried, however, to suggest when you can save time by using your microwave. I'll remind you when it is faster to melt, sauté, or blanch in a microwave than on top of the stove. Since cooking times vary a great deal from one brand of microwave to another, I have not given instructions for microwave cooking. Your best

---

Ingredients followed by an asterisk (*) indicate that there is a recipe in *Quick & Easy*. These are mostly for foods that you usually buy at the store, such as ketchup and mayonnaise.

guide is your owner's manual and the cookbook that comes with your microwave.

WHEN USING YOUR FREEZER

Many cooks don't realize how many staples can be frozen so that meal preparation can be faster. Here is a list of items that I keep in my freezer.

Cooked rice
Small and large quantities of sauces and gravies
Egg whites
Fresh bread crumbs
Grated cheeses and an emergency pack of cream cheese
Nuts (chopped and ground)
Chicken and beef stocks
Casseroles and entrees
Coffee cakes, muffins, and waffles
Homemade applesauce
Slices of lemon, lime, and orange
Chopped parsley
Celery leaves (add to soups and stocks)

USING YOUR FOOD PROCESSOR

You do not have to use a food processor to make or enjoy most of the recipes in this book. However (as you will see if you compare preparation times given for processor and conventional methods), when you can use a processor, you can save a great deal of time.

The recipes in the book were tested with a large capacity food processor (7" diameter, 6" tall work bowl). If your processor is smaller, you may need to process food in batches, emptying the work bowl between batches. The recipes will indicate when to use this procedure.

You'll get the best results from your food processor if you follow the manufacturer's instruction manual. The hints that follow apply to all processors and will help you prepare the recipes in this book regardless of the type of equipment you have.

When chopping or mixing, use pulse lever or use the On-Off manually to control the consistency. Arrange even-sized chunks of food around the work bowl and pulse until desired texture is reached. Generally, you should cut onions and green peppers into quarters, carrots and celery into 2-inch lengths, sticks of butter and 8-ounce packages of cream cheese into 8 pieces, and so on. Do not overprocess when chopping.

Cheese. Chop Parmesan with the metal blade; grate other cheeses. Or, even better, chop any cheese by first cutting into 1-inch cubes and pulsing until desired texture is reached. If you are using the slicing blade or grating blade, use light pressure on the pusher. Softer cheeses will grate better after spending a few minutes in the freezer.

Cream cheese and butter. It is not necessary to soften before processing, although cutting into pieces will make processing faster.

Garlic, gingerroot and onions. Drop through the feed tube with the machine running and process until chopped. Or add to a dip or spread which is already in the work bowl and process until well incorporated.

Mayonnaise. When a recipe calls for mayonnaise, make it first. Then you can add and process the remaining ingredients without having to wash work bowl.

Oil. Add oil with the machine running in order to make a good emulsion in a dip or dressing.

Vegetables. Slice using pressure on the pusher to correspond with texture of vegetable, i.e., medium pressure for carrots and potatoes, light for tomatoes and green peppers.

Appearance. For beautiful slices, cut both ends of vegetables or fruit flat and then pack feed tube tightly so that pieces cannot tilt sideways. Experiment with grating and julienning for interesting combinations of textures and colors.

To slice meat and poultry: (1) Arrange on a cookie sheet and freeze for about 40 minutes. You should still be able to penetrate the meat with the tip of a knife. Stack in feed tube and slice against the grain. (2) Cut to fit the feed tube. You can do this by placing on foil and making a neat package that will fit the feed tube. Freeze until solid, then wrap in more foil (and label). About 30 minutes before beginning a recipe, pull out of freezer and thaw at room temperature until knife tip penetrates. Then unwrap and slice with the slicing blade. (3) Pepperoni and hard sausages should be peeled and tightly packed into feed tube to slice neatly.

For baked goods: Process dry ingredients (flour, salt, baking powder and/or soda, spices) for 2 to 3 seconds or pulse to aerate and combine. Remove to a paper plate or bowl and reserve. Process sugar and eggs 1 minute. Then add the room temperature shortening (cut into pieces to save processing time) and process for 1 minute. Add dry ingredients and pulse until just combined.

Beaten egg whites. Have at room temperature and process for 7 to 8 seconds. With machine running, add 1 tablespoon water mixed with 1 tablespoon vinegar and process for about 1½ to 2 minutes or until whipped and stiff.

Nuts. Add to a recipe at the end; pulse several times to chop and incorporate.

Ingredients followed by an asterisk (*) indicate that there is a recipe in *Quick & Easy*. These are mostly for foods that you usually buy at the store, such as ketchup and mayonnaise.

appetizers & beverages

llinois world of our flavors south bend indiana the cookery cedar rapids
wa specialties of the house alexandria louisiana kitchen treats cookboo
es to noshes lewiston maine sisterhood cookbook potomac maryland p
nelting pot lexington massa   'hought cookbook newton
ok norwood massachus   ody massachusetts co
etts in the best of tast   e happy cooker of te
s with temple beth   a used to make f
igan all the recip   'o ask saint pau
souri deborah d   o generation l
rry hill new je   'eating east
son new jersi   with love so
vle tinton fa   y the spice
poking? al   onderful
k cookie '   york the
g brook   osher ki
like it cli   east no
new yo   great r
york th   it vern
na had   sher c
osher   iester
scarsc   what
od ta   d new
carol   l ohi
ount t   nd ol
io in t   nia th
ania th   n per
ia pen   penr
n wynr   south
charles   rolina
e recip   ) years
nnial co   oks fall
nchburg   n good
ke it parke   sin from
gham alab   eat and en
ste berkele   ills califor
california fr   hat's cookir
flavored with   iego californ
lectable collect   ease! rockvill
d connecticut foc   passover made
earwater florida cle   a measures and tr
ght gainesville florid   alabustas' more favc
o it in the kitchen hollywc   s hollywood florida nit
ksonville florida what's coc.   ville florida try it you'll like
atellite beach florida our favorite recipes tallahassee florida knishes gefil
a georgia golden soup atlanta georgia the happy cooker augusta georgi
bis portal to good cooking great lakes illinois the fort sheridan and great l

Hot appetizers

Fried Artichoke Hearts

MADE TO ORTER DAY, EVENING, JAMES RIVER CHAPTERS OF WOMEN'S AMERICAN ORT   RICHMOND, VA

2 cans (14 oz. each) artichoke
  hearts
1 cup Italian dressing*
¼ cup grated Parmesan or
  Romano cheese
1½ cups Italian flavored
  seasoned bread crumbs*

Preparation time: 5 to 10 minutes
Marinating time: 8 hours
Baking time: 12 to 15 minutes
Makes about 2 dozen

1. Drain artichoke hearts and cut in half. Marinate in Italian dressing for at least 8 hours. Drain well.

2. Preheat oven to 375°.

3. Place grated cheese and bread crumbs in a plastic bag. Add artichokes and shake gently to coat well. Arrange on a baking sheet and bake 12 to 15 minutes.

Artichoke-Chili Dip

ALL THAT SCHMALTZ AUGUSTA CHAPTER OF HADASSAH AUGUSTA, GEORGIA

1 can (14 oz.) artichoke
hearts
1 can (4 oz.) green chili
peppers
1 cup grated Parmesan
cheese
1 cup mayonnaise or salad
dressing*

Preparation time/processor: 5 minutes
Preparation time/conventional: 10 minutes
Baking time: 20 minutes
Makes about 2⅔ cups

1. Preheat oven to 350°.
2. Drain artichoke hearts; chop. Rinse chili peppers, remove seeds, and chop.
3. Combine all ingredients and turn into an 8-inch round baking dish. Bake for 20 minutes or until heated through.
4. Serve warm with tortilla chips or breadsticks.

=== **Quick Ideas** ===

NACHOS. Place tortilla chips on a platter. Cover with grated Cheddar cheese, diced chili peppers, and sliced black olives. Heat in microwave on low for about 2 minutes or place in a 350° oven until hot.

NACHOS II. Line the bottom of a 9″ round cake pan with Dorito chips. Spread with a layer of refried beans and a layer of grated Monterey Jack or sharp Cheddar cheese. Place under broiler until cheese melts. Garnish with shredded lettuce and diced tomatoes. Serve with sour cream, hot sauce, and more chips. Serves 4.

KABOBS. Place vegetables on skewers, brush with Kennedy Center Mustard Dressing (see recipe) and grill or broil until hot.

HOT BITES. Broil bite-size bits of lamb, beef, chicken, or fish on small skewers. Serve with your favorite dipping sauce.

PITA BREAD APPETIZER. Split pita bread and spread halves with butter seasoned with Worcestershire sauce and sprinkle with Parmesan cheese. Bake in 350° oven until crisp. Break into small pieces.

Artichoke Bars
BEGINNING AGAIN   ROCKDALE TEMPLE SISTERHOOD   CINCINNATI, OHIO

1 clove garlic
1 small onion
2 tablespoons oil
½ pound Swiss cheese
1 can (14 oz.) artichoke
  hearts, drained
4 large eggs
¼ cup dry bread crumbs*
2 tablespoons minced
  parsley
½ teaspoon salt
1½ teaspoons chopped
  oregano (or ½ tsp. dried)
⅛ teaspoon Tabasco sauce
⅛ teaspoon pepper

Preparation time/processor: 10 to 15 minutes
Preparation time/conventional: 15 to 20 minutes
Baking time: 25 to 30 minutes
Makes 35

Food processor
1. Preheat oven to 325°.

2. Insert metal blade; drop garlic through feed tube with the machine running. Add onion (cut into quarters), and pulse to chop.

3. Remove to a small skillet and sauté in oil until translucent (or cook in microwave).

4. Insert grating blade and grate the Swiss cheese. Remove to a mixing bowl. Insert the metal blade and chop artichoke hearts; add to the cheese. Place eggs, bread crumbs, and all seasonings in the work bowl and process for 10 seconds to mix well. Add the onion, cheese, and artichokes and pulse once or twice to combine.

5. Transfer the mixture to a greased 7 x 11 baking dish and bake for 25 to 30 minutes, or until set when lightly touched. Let cool slightly, then cut into 1½-inch squares.

Conventional
In step 2, mince garlic and chop onion. In step 4, grate cheese and chop artichoke hearts. Combine all ingredients. Proceed to step 5.

Note: This recipe can be made ahead and refrigerated, then reheated at 325° for 10 minutes.

Glazed Garlic Chicken Wings

PALATE TREATS   MOUNT ZION TEMPLE SISTERHOOD   ST. PAUL, MINNESOTA

3 pounds chicken wings
4 cloves garlic
1 piece gingerroot
  (1" x 1½")
2 teaspoons dry mustard
½ cup soy sauce
½ cup red wine vinegar
2 cups dark brown sugar

Preparation time/processor: 10 minutes
Preparation time/conventional: 15 to 20 minutes
Pre-preparation: bake chicken
Makes 36 pieces

Food processor

1. Preheat oven to 350°.

2. Clean and trim wings; cut each in half to make 2 portions. Place on rack in a roasting pan and bake for about 35 minutes.

3. Meanwhile, prepare sauce: Insert metal blade and drop garlic and gingerroot through feed tube with the machine running. When finely chopped, add remaining ingredients and process until smooth.

4. Transfer to a saucepan and cook 3 to 5 minutes. Add cooked chicken wings to the sauce and toss to coat evenly.

5. Serve in a chafing dish.

Conventional
In step 3, chop garlic and ginger, and mix ingredients with a wire whisk. Or use a blender for chopping and mixing. Proceed to step 4.

Geftedes (Greek Meatballs)

FROM SOUP TO NOSH   NORTH VIRGINIA CHAPTER OF HADASSAH   FALLS CHURCH, VA

2 pounds ground chuck
2 medium onions, minced
⅔ cup dry bread crumbs*
2 eggs, lightly beaten
1 tablespoon chopped
  oregano (or 1 tsp. dried)
⅛ teaspoon cinnamon
1½ teaspoons chopped mint
  (or ½ tsp. dried)
Salt and pepper to taste

Sauce
1 cup ketchup*
2 teaspoons Dijon mustard
½ cup red wine

Preparation time/processor: 10 to 15 minutes
Preparation time/conventional: 15 to 20 minutes
Cooking time: 5 to 20 minutes
Makes 60

1. Combine ground chuck with all other meatball ingredients, mixing lightly but thoroughly. Shape into bite-size balls.

2. Cook in hot oil or bake in a 350° oven for about 20 minutes; or microwave until done.

3. Combine sauce ingredients and bring to a boil; pour over the cooked meatballs. Serve in a chafing dish.

Variations: Serve meatballs cold without the sauce, or serve over rice as an entrée.

South of the Border Meatballs

KOSHER GOURMET II   SISTERHOOD OF TEMPLE BETH-EL   NORTH BELLMORE, NEW YORK

½ cup chopped onion
½ cup coarsely chopped
  raisins
½ cup chopped parsley
2 pounds ground veal or beef
2 eggs
2 cloves garlic, minced
1 can (6 oz.) tomato paste
2 tablespoons cider vinegar
¾ teaspoon cinnamon
½ teaspoon ground cumin
3 to 4 drops Tabasco sauce
½ teaspoon salt
⅛ teaspoon pepper

Preparation time/processor: 15 minutes
Preparation time/conventional: 20 minutes
Cooking time: 15 minutes
Makes 3 dozen

1. Combine all ingredients and shape into 1-inch balls.

2. Broil until brown (or cook in a microwave until done).

Note: Can be frozen and reheated in oven or microwave.

Water Chestnuts and Pastrami Hors d'Oeuvres

SEASONED WITH LOVE   WHITE MEADOW TEMPLE SISTERHOOD   ROCKAWAY, NEW JERSEY

1 can (8 oz.) water chestnuts
¼ pound pastrami slices
Brown sugar

Preparation time: 10 minutes
Soaking time: 30 minutes
Cooking time: 5 to 10 minutes
Serves 6 to 8

1. Drain water chestnuts and soak in water for 30 minutes. Drain; dry on paper towels. Cut in half.

2. Cut pastrami slices in half. Wrap a slice of pastrami around each chestnut half. Fasten with a toothpick and dip in brown sugar.

3. Broil until brown or microwave until hot (will not be brown).

Mushroom and Sour Cream Dip

ALL THAT SCHMALTZ   AUGUSTA CHAPTER OF HADASSAH   AUGUSTA, GEORGIA

1 medium onion, chopped
½ stick margarine or butter
1 pound mushrooms
1 cup sour cream
1 tablespoon dry sherry
1 teaspoon salt
Pepper to taste

Preparation time/processor: 10 to 20 minutes
Preparation time/conventional: 15 to 20 minutes
Serves 6 to 8

1. Cut mushrooms in half if they are very large.

2. Sauté onion in margarine until soft. Add mushrooms. Cover and cook slowly for 5 minutes. Add remaining ingredients. Simmer until thoroughly heated and mushrooms are tender.

Note: Can also be served as a vegetable side dish.

Cold appetizers

Chutney-Glazed Cheese Pâté
COOK WITH TEMPLE BETH EMETH   TEMPLE BETH EMETH SISTERHOOD   ANN ARBOR, MICHIGAN

4 ounces sharp Cheddar cheese
6 ounces cream cheese
3 tablespoons dry sherry
¾ teaspoon curry powder
¼ teaspoon salt
½ cup mango chutney, finely chopped
4 green onions, finely chopped

Preparation time/processor: 5 minutes
Preparation time/conventional: 15 to 20 minutes
Chilling time: 1 hour
Makes 1 cup

Food processor
1. Insert grating blade and grate Cheddar cheese. Insert metal blade and add cream cheese, sherry, curry powder, and salt. Process until smooth.

2. Spread mixture in a one-half inch layer on a serving platter. Chill until firm.

3. Before serving, cover with a layer of chutney and garnish with green onion. Serve with sesame or other crackers.

Conventional
Soften cream cheese. In step 1, chop Cheddar cheese coarsely; combine ingredients and mix well until smooth. Proceed to step 2.

Quick Ideas

● Serve a dip in a hollow green pepper or red cabbage.

● Make individual "dishes" with red cabbage leaves — put dip in one and raw vegetables in other.

● Scoop out a round pumpernickel loaf, leaving a 1-inch wall. Fill with favorite dip and serve with chunks of bread.

● To freshen a wooden chopping board, rub it with lemon or lime halves. Use the reverse side for chopping foods that discolor the wood.

QUICK DIP 1. Sour cream, cream cheese, plain yogurt, or well-beaten cottage cheese mixed to taste with:
Chopped garlic and dill weed
Grated horseradish and chopped parsley
Anchovy paste and chopped onion
Almost any leftover fish or tasty sauce, seasoned to taste

QUICK DIP 2. Combine and beat until smooth: 12 ounces cream-style cottage cheese, 2 tablespoons mayonnaise, 1 tablespoon lemon juice, 1½ teaspoon paprika, ¾ teaspoon garlic salt, and a dash of pepper.

DIPPERS: Carrot, celery, yellow squash, zucchini, cucumbers, turnips, asparagus, cauliflower, radishes, snow peas, Brussels sprouts, broccoli.

STUFFED CELERY. Use any stiff cream cheese based dip mixture.

AVOCADO BITES. Cut avocado into bite-size pieces and dip in mayonnaise thinned with lemon juice, roll in crushed corn chips, and serve on toothpicks.

TOAST CUPS. Trim crusts from sliced sandwich bread, brush bread with butter, press into muffin tins and toast until golden at 350°. Fill with your favorite sandwich spread.

DEVILED EGGS. Add mashed ripe avocado and a dash of Tabasco to egg yolks.

Dilly Cheese Dip

WORLD OF OUR FLAVORS — CERTIFIED TA'AM   BETH HILLEL SISTERHOOD   WILMETTE, IL

½ cup grated Cheddar
 cheese
½ cup sour cream
2 teaspoons prepared
 horseradish*
¾ teaspoon snipped dill
 weed (or ¼ tsp. dried)

Preparation time: 5 minutes
Chilling time: 1 hour
Makes 1 cup

1. Blend ingredients together; place in a small bowl. Cover and chill.

Tomato Cheese Log

IN THE BEGINNING   ROCKDALE TEMPLE SISTERHOOD   CINCINNATI, OHIO

1½ cups walnuts
½ pound Cheddar cheese
1 package (8 oz.) cream
 cheese
⅓ cup tomato paste
1 stick butter or margarine
2 cloves garlic
1 small onion
1 teaspoon salt
⅛ to ¼ teaspoon ground
 red pepper

Preparation time/processor: 5 minutes
Preparation time/conventional: 15 to 20 minutes
Chilling time: 1 hour
Serves 10

Food processor
1. Insert metal blade and chop walnuts; reserve. Insert grating blade and grate the Cheddar cheese; leave in work bowl. Insert metal blade and process cream cheese, tomato paste, butter, and garlic until smooth. Add onion (quartered), salt and pepper and pulse until onion is very finely chopped.

2. Spoon out onto a large sheet of wax paper or plastic wrap and roll to form a log. Place in freezer for 1 hour or until firm.

3. Roll in chopped walnuts and serve very cold with crackers.

Conventional
Soften cream cheese and butter. Grate Cheddar cheese. Chop garlic and onion. Chop walnuts or use packaged chopped nuts. Combine all ingredients except nuts. Proceed to step 2.

Liptauer Cheese

1 package (8 oz.) cream
  cheese
1 stick butter
½ pound cream-style cottage
  cheese
1 teaspoon dry mustard
2 tablespoons caraway seeds
2 tablespoons Hungarian
  sweet paprika
½ teaspoon salt
¼ teaspoon pepper
2 tablespoons gin

Preparation time/processor: 5 to 10 minutes
Preparation time/conventional: 10 to 15 minutes
Chilling time: 24 hours
Makes 2 to 2½ cups

Food processor
1. Insert metal blade; place cream cheese and butter in work bowl and process until smooth. Add remaining ingredients and mix well. Turn into a bowl and cover.

2. Let ripen in the refrigerator for 1 to 7 days.

3. Form into a ball or place in a crock. Serve with crackers.

Conventional
Soften cream cheese and butter. Combine all ingredients.

Cheddar Bon Bons

FAMILY FAVORITES TEMPLE SOLEL SISTERHOOD HOLLYWOOD, FLORIDA

2½ to 3 ounces Cheddar
  cheese
¼ teaspoon chili powder
½ teaspoon dry mustard
1 to 2 tablespoons dry sherry
Nuts, parsley, or chives

Preparation time/processor: 5 minutes
Preparation time/conventional: 5 to 10 minutes
Cooling time: 30 minutes
Makes 3 dozen

Food processor
1. Insert grating blade and grate the cheese. Change to the metal blade, add chili powder, mustard, and sherry to the work bowl, and process until smooth.

2. Cover and place in freezer for 30 minutes or until firm (or chill in refrigerator for 2 hours).

3. Form into balls and roll in finely chopped nuts, chopped parsley, or chopped chives.

Conventional
Grate cheese coarsely. Add other ingredients and beat until smooth. Proceed to step 2.

Salsa Dip

FAVORITE RECIPES   JEWISH WOMEN'S CLUB OF BRYAN COLLEGE STATION   BRYAN, TEXAS

2 cups plain, low-fat yogurt
½ cup mild green chili salsa*
½ cup chopped cucumber
1¼ tablespoon chopped
   cilantro (or ¾ tsp. dried)
   (optional)

Preparation time: 5 minutes
Chilling time: 4 hours
Makes about 2¾ cups

1. Combine all ingredients and chill for at least 4 hours.

2. Serve with tortillas, corn chips, or fresh vegetables.

Note: Cilantro is also known as coriander or Chinese parsley; there will be some difference in taste. Parsley can be substituted.

Pesto Spread

1 package (8 oz.) cream
   cheese
2 tablespoons sour cream
1 tablespoon Pesto Sauce*
1 tablespoon lemon juice

Soften cream cheese. Process until smooth. Serve as a spread for rye crackers or bread.

Pesto-Cheese Dip

1 carton (8 oz.) cottage
   cheese
2 tablespoons sour cream
1 tablespoon Pesto Sauce*

Mix well and chill. Serve with raw vegetables or crackers.

Marvelous Dip

COOK UNTO OTHERS   HILLEL JEWISH STUDENT CENTER, U. OF CINCINNATI, CINCINNATI, OH

2 cups mayonnaise*
1 cup sour cream
1 package (3 oz.) cream
  cheese
2 cloves garlic
¼ teaspoon curry powder
1 teaspoon Worchestershire
  sauce
2 tablespoons lemon juice
2 teaspoons Italian herbs*
¼ cup parsley sprigs
1 red onion
1 jar (3½ to 4 oz.) capers,
  drained

Preparation time/processor: 5 minutes
Preparation time/conventional: 15 to 20 minutes
Makes 4 cups

Food processor

1. Insert metal blade; place mayonnaise, sour cream, cream cheese, garlic, curry powder, Worcestershire sauce, lemon juice, Italian herbs, and parsley in the work bowl and process until smooth, scraping down sides of bowl. Add red onion (quartered) and pulse until finely chopped. Add capers to work bowl and pulse once to combine.

Conventional

Soften cream cheese. Chop parsley, onion, and garlic. Combine cream cheese with all ingredients and beat well.

Variation: Can be thinned with vinegar and used as a salad dressing.

Chopped Liver

OUR FAVORITE RECIPES   SISTERHOOD OF TEMPLE BETH SHOLOM   SATELLITE BEACH, FLORIDA

½ pound beef or chicken
  liver
1 medium onion
2 hard-cooked eggs
2 tablespoons chicken fat*
½ teaspoon salt, or to taste

Preparation time/processor: 10 to 15 minutes
Preparation time/conventional: 20 minutes
Serves 3 to 4

Food processor

1. Broil liver and cool; cut into 2-inch pieces.

2. Insert metal blade. Place liver, onion (quartered), eggs, fat, and salt in the work bowl and pulse to chop until desired consistency is reached.

Conventional

In step 2, use a meat grinder or chopping bowl.

Gertrude's Chopped Herring

NOT FOR NOSHERS ONLY   BETH ISRAEL SISTERHOOD   LEBANON, PENNSYLVANIA

2 jars (8 oz. each) herring
  tidbits in wine sauce,
  drained
2 small onions, halved
2 medium-sized tart apples,
  peeled
2 stalks celery
2 hard-cooked eggs
7 or 8 sweet midget pickles
1 tablespoon sugar
¼ teaspoon salt
¼ cup bread crumbs*
  (optional)

Preparation time/processor: 10 minutes
Preparation time/conventional: 20 minutes
Makes 4 cups

Food processor
1. Cut apples into quarters and cut celery into 2-inch lengths.

2. Insert metal blade. Place all ingredients in work bowl and pulse until finely chopped. Add bread crumbs last. (Do in batches in a small processor.)

Conventional
Chop or grind all ingredients and mix together.

Chopped Herring

GARDEN OF EATING   TEMPLE BETH O'R   CLARK, NEW JERSEY

1 jar (16 oz.) herring in
  wine sauce, drained
1 slice bread, white or rye
2 apples
4 hard-cooked eggs
1 tablespoon sugar,
  or to taste
Salt and pepper to taste

Preparation time/processor: 5 minutes
Preparation time/conventional: 10 to 15 minutes
Chilling time: several hours
Serves 6 to 8

Food Processor
1. Remove crusts from bread. Peel apples and cut into quarters.

2. Insert metal blade and place herring in work bowl. Add remaining ingredients evenly around the work bowl. Pulse until desired consistency is reached.

3. Transfer to a covered container. Refrigerate for several hours before serving.

Conventional
In step 2, chop or grind all ingredients and mix together. Proceed to step 3.

Salmon Mousse

THE COOKS' BOOK TEMPLE ISRAEL SISTERHOOD TULSA, OKLAHOMA

1 can (1 lb.) salmon
1 envelope unflavored
  gelatin
1 tablespoon lemon juice
½ small onion
½ cup boiling water
½ cup mayonnaise*
¼ teaspoon paprika
1 tablespoon dill weed
  (or 1 tsp. dried)
1 cup heavy cream

Preparation time: 5 to 10 minutes
Chilling time: several hours
Makes about 4 cups

Food processor/blender
1. Drain salmon and pick over.

2. Place gelatin, lemon juice, and onion in food processor (metal blade) or blender and add boiling water with the machine running.

3. Add salmon and pulse several times. Add mayonnaise, paprika, and dill and pulse again several times. Add the cream and pulse to incorporate.

4. Rinse a 4-cup decorative mold in cold water. Pour in the mousse mixture and chill several hours until firm (place in freezer if in a hurry). Unmold and serve with crackers.

Olive-Anchovy Canapés

WITH LOVE AND SPICE SHOSHANA CHAPTER, AMERICAN MIZRACHI WOMEN WEST HEMPSTEAD, NY

1 package (3 oz.) cream
  cheese
12 large stuffed green olives
1 can (2 oz.) anchovy fillets,
  drained
2 hard-cooked eggs
½ cup walnuts
Chopped parsley, chopped
  olives, or paprika

Preparation time/processor: 5 to 10 minutes
Preparation time/conventional: 10 to 15 minutes
Makes about 15

Food processor
1. Insert metal blade and beat cream cheese until fluffy. Add olives, anchovies, eggs, and nuts. Pulse several times to chop, being careful not to overprocess.

2. Make small balls and roll in parsley, olives, or paprika. Chill.

Conventional
Soften cream cheese. Chop olives, anchovies, eggs, and walnuts finely and combine with cream cheese. Proceed to step 2.

Tuna-Filled Cucumber Slices

TRADITION IN THE KITCHEN   NORTH SUBURBAN BETH EL SISTERHOOD   HIGHLAND PARK, ILLINOIS

2 large cucumbers, peeled
1 can (7 oz.) tuna, drained
2 tablespoons or more
  mayonnaise*
1 tablespoon minced onion
⅛ teaspoon lemon juice
⅛ teaspoon Worcestershire
  sauce
⅛ teaspoon salt
⅛ teaspoon paprika

Preparation time: 10 minutes
Soaking time: 1 hour
Chilling time: about 1 hour
Makes about 24 slices

1. Cut cucumbers in half crosswise and use an apple corer to remove seeds from center. (You will later slice into rings.) Cut off ends. Soak for 1 hour in cold water. Drain and dry well.

2. Blend remaining ingredients together and fill cucumbers. Chill well and cut into ½-inch slices.

Mushroom Pâté

EDITOR'S CHOICE

2 tablespoons butter,
  softened
2 green onions, finely
  chopped
½ pound mushrooms, finely
  chopped
½ teaspoon fresh lemon
  juice
¼ cup walnuts, finely
  chopped
½ teaspoon Tabasco sauce
2½ tablespoons butter
Salt and pepper to taste

Preparation time/processor: 5 to 10 minutes
Cooking time: 10 to 20 minutes
Makes about 1 cup

1. Sauté green onion in butter for 30 seconds. Add mushrooms and cook until all the liquid has evaporated. Stir in the remaining ingredients and season with salt and pepper.

2. Serve at room temperature with melba toast or use as a stuffing for artichokes, tomatoes, fish, or crêpes.

Egg Salad Deluxe

THE WONDERFUL WORLD OF COOKING   BALDWIN HADASSAH   BALDWIN, NEW YORK

2 stalks celery
1 small onion
2 sweet pickles
6 stuffed olives
8 hard-cooked eggs
1 teaspoon prepared mustard
Mayonnaise*

Preparation time/processor: 5 to 10 minutes
Preparation time/conventional: 10 to 15 minutes
Makes 2 cups

1. Chop celery, onion, pickles, olives, and eggs. Add mustard and mayonnaise to moisten. Chill. Serve as a sandwich spread or dip.

Eggs and Caviar

SALT AND PEPPER TO TASTE   SISTERHOOD OF CONGREGATION ANSHEI ISRAEL   TUCSON, ARIZONA

6 hard-cooked eggs
3 small onions
Salt and pepper to taste
½ cup mayonnaise*
½ cup or more sour cream
1 jar (2 oz.) caviar

Preparation time/processor: 5 to 10 minutes
Preparation time/conventional: 10 to 15 minutes
Makes about 1 ½ cups

Food processor

1. Insert metal blade. Place eggs, onions (quartered), salt and pepper in the work bowl and pulse to chop.

2. Moisten with mayonnaise. Remove to serving platter, forming a flattened mound. Spread with a layer of sour cream. Just before serving spread with caviar. Serve with crackers.

Conventional
Use prepared mayonnaise. Chop eggs and onion; add seasoning. Proceed to step 2.

Hummous

SISTERHOOD COOKERY SISTERHOOD OF BROOKLYN HEIGHTS SYNAGOGUE BROOKLYN, NEW YORK

1 can (16 oz.) garbanzos
  (chick peas)
¼ cup liquid from garbanzos
Juice of 1 lemon (about 3
  Tbsp.)
½ teaspoon salt
2 tablespoons chopped
  parsley
2 tablespoons sesame seeds
  or tahini
2 cloves garlic

Preparation time: 5 minutes
Makes about 1 ½ cups

1. Place all ingredients in a food processor, blender, or chopping bowl and process or chop until very smooth.

2. Serve with pita bread as a dip or mound on a lettuce leaf as an appetizer.

Note: Tahini is available in health food stores.

Spiced Pecans

SPECIALTY OF THE HOUSE TEMPLE ISRAEL SISTERHOOD BOSTON, MASSACHUSETTS

½ stick butter
1 tablespoon Worcestershire
  sauce
1 tablespoon minced garlic
½ teaspoon Tabasco sauce
2 cups large pecans

Preparation time: 5 minutes
Baking time: 20 minutes
Makes about 2 cups

1. Preheat oven to 375°.

2. Melt butter and combine with seasonings. Toss nuts with this mixture.

3. Place nuts on a cookie sheet and toast for about 20 minutes or until browned, shaking occasionally. (Or use microwave.) Drain on paper towels before serving. Salt if desired.

Beverages

Banana Yogurt Shake
MADE TO ORTER   DAY, EVENING, JAMES RIVER CHAPTERS OF WOMEN'S AMERICAN ORT   RICHMOND, VA

1 cup milk
½ cup vanilla or fruit yogurt
1 ripe banana
1 teaspoon honey or sugar
¼ teaspoon nutmeg

Preparation time: 5 minutes
Serves 1 or 2

1. Place all ingredients in a food processor or blender and process until very smooth.

Variation: Orange, apple, or pineapple juice may be substituted for the milk.

Tomato Juice Cocktail
SHARING OUR BEST   CANTON CHAPTER OF HADASSAH   CANTON, OHIO

1 can (48 oz.) chilled tomato
  juice
¼ cup fresh lemon juice
1 teaspoon sugar
1 tablespoon minced onion
1 teaspoon Worcestershire
  sauce
1 teaspoon prepared
  horseradish*
Salt to taste

Preparation time: 5 minutes
Serves 6 to 8

1. Combine all ingredients and refrigerate. Stir before serving.

Variation: Add vodka to make Bloody Marys or add sour cream to make a summer soup.

Spiced Iced Tea

HISTORICALLY COOKING — 200 YEARS OF GOOD COOKING   K. K. BETH ELOHIM SISTERHOOD   CHARLESTON, SC

6 cups water
1 teaspoon whole cloves
1-inch piece cinnamon stick
3 tea bags
½ cup sugar
¾ cup orange juice
1 tablespoon lemon juice

Preparation time: 5 minutes
Cooking time: 10 minutes
Makes 1 ½ quarts

1. Combine water, cloves, and cinnamon in a saucepan and bring to a boil; remove from heat and add tea bags. Cover and let steep for 10 minutes.

2. In another saucepan, bring the sugar, orange juice, and lemon juice to a boil. Strain tea mixture into the juice mixture. Refrigerate. Serve over ice.

Lime Daiquiri

COLLECTABLE DELECTABLES   RODEF SHALOM TEMPLE SISTERHOOD   HAMPTON, VIRGINIA

6 ounces (1 can) frozen
  limeade concentrate
6 ounces 7-Up
6 ounces rum
¼ cup confectioners' sugar
  (optional)
2 drops green food coloring
  (optional)
Crushed ice

Preparation time: 5 minutes
Serves about 6

1. Use limeade can to measure 7-Up and rum. Place all ingredients in a blender, fill with crushed ice, and blend 30 seconds. Pour into a pitcher and keep frozen until needed.

- To frost glasses, dip rim in beaten egg white or fruit juice, then into granulated sugar. Chill until ready to serve.

- Freeze lemon, orange, and lime slices on a cookie sheet and store in a plastic bag. Use in iced drinks.

- When squeezing lemons, place in microwave for 10-15 seconds or in boiling water for 10 seconds. They will yield twice as much juice.

- Freeze fruit and fruit juice in a ring mold for a punch bowl. Mint leaves or small fruits may be frozen into individual ice cubes.

WINE SPRITZER. Combine equal amounts of wine (red or white) and soda water. Serve over ice.

ORANGE BLOSSOM. Combine equal parts of white wine and orange juice. Serve over ice.

VERMOUTH ORANGE BLOSSOM. Combine a 6-ounce can frozen orange juice concentrate (thawed), 1½ cups cold water, 1 cup dry vermouth, and 1 tablespoon fresh lemon juice. Makes about 1 quart.

MIMOSA. Combine equal parts of cold champagne and orange juice.

ROSÉ SPARKLING PUNCH. Combine four 12-ounce packages frozen strawberries (thawed), 1 cup sugar, and 1 bottle rosé wine. Let stand 1 hour. Add four 6-ounce cans frozen lemonade concentrate and stir until thawed. Just before serving, add 3 more bottles rosé wine and 2 large bottles chilled sparkling water.

SANGRIA. Combine 1 quart red wine, ½ quart soda, ½ lemon with peel (sliced), ½ orange with peel (sliced), 1 tablespoon confectioners' sugar, and a few drops brandy (optional). Serve with ice.

MULLED WINE: Combine in a pot: 1 quart burgundy, about ¼ pound dark brown sugar (to taste), 2 cinnamon sticks, 5 whole cloves, 3 slices lemon, and ½ cup raisins. Bring to a boil and simmer 30 minutes.

PUNCH FOR 50. Break up 3 quarts of sherbet in a punch bowl. Add 5 quarts chilled gingerale. Garnish with maraschino cherries and mint leaves. Variation: substitute 4 bottles of champagne for the gingerale.

MICROWAVE COCOA. Place ¼ cup sugar and ¼ cup unsweetened cocoa powder in a 1½ quart mixing bowl. Add 1 cup water and cook on high for 1½ minutes, stirring once. Add 3 cups milk and heat until piping hot, but not boiling, about 3 minutes.

TOMATO SLUSH. Freeze Tomato Juice Cocktail (see recipe) to a slush and serve in a stemmed glass.

Fast Whiskey Sour in a Pitcher

FROM THE BALABUSTA'S TABLE   SISTERHOOD OF TEMPLE ISRAEL   NATICK, MA

1 can (6 oz.) frozen lemonade
6 ounces whiskey (rye,
   scotch, or bourbon)
12 ounces water, or to taste
Orange slices
Maraschino cherries

Preparation time: 5 minutes
Serves 4 to 6

1. Use lemonade can to measure whiskey and water. Mix ingredients well, adding about 1 tablespoon juice from jar of maraschino cherries, if desired, for color. Chill or serve over ice. Garnish with a cherry and orange slice on a toothpick.

Kir

PORTAL TO GOOD COOKING, VOL. IV   WOMEN'S AMERICAN ORT, DISTRICT VIII   CHICAGO, ILLINOIS

1 bottle Chablis, chilled
¼ to ⅓ cup crème de Cassis
Lemon peel

Preparation time: 5 minutes
Serves 6 to 8

1. Combine wine and crème de Cassis and stir well. Chill. Serve in large wine glasses with a twist of lemon.

Note. For a single serving use 4 ounces of Chablis and ½ teaspoon crème de Cassis.

Homemade "Kahlua"

PALATE TREATS   MOUNT ZION TEMPLE SISTERHOOD   ST. PAUL, MINNESOTA

3 cups sugar
1 cup water
2 ounces instant coffee
  powder
2 cups vodka
1 vanilla bean

Preparation time: 15 minutes
Storage time: 1 month
Makes 2 quarts

1. Place sugar and water in a large saucepan over medium heat and stir until sugar dissolves. Add coffee and stir until well mixed. Remove from heat and allow to cool.

2. Add vodka and stir well. Break vanilla bean into 4 pieces and place in two sterilized 1-quart bottles (2 each). Pour liquid into the bottles and seal. Store in a cool place for 30 days before using.

soups, salads & sauces

Soups

Tomato and Cucumber Cold Soup
EDITOR'S CHOICE

2 cups tomato juice, chilled
1 cup sour cream
½ teaspoon salt
Dash Tabasco sauce
1 large cucumber
½ cup coarsely chopped
   chutney
2 tablespoons snipped chives
   or chopped green onions

Preparation time: 5 to 10 minutes
Chilling time: 1 hour
Serves 5 to 6

Food processor/blender
1. In a food processor (metal blade) or blender, place tomato juice, sour cream, salt, and Tabasco. Process until smooth.

2. Peel cucumber, seed, and cut into chunks; add to work bowl and pulse until finely chopped. Transfer to a covered bowl and chill.

3. Whisk before serving. Ladle into chilled bowls or mugs and top each with a heaping tablespoon of chutney and a sprinkling of chives.

- If soup is too salty, add a slice of potato and cook for 5 to 10 minutes.

- Add a little dry sherry to perk up almost any soup. Garnish with croutons, parsley, lemon slices.

- Remove vegetables or other solids from soup with slotted spoon. Place in food processor or blender and process until smooth. Return purée to soup.

- To remove excess fat from soup: (1) place a lettuce leaf on the surface of the liquid; it will soak up all the fat that comes to the surface. (2) Refrigerate after cooking; fat will rise and congeal.

BORSCHT. Combine and cook for 15 minutes: 2 cans beets, grated, with juice, 6 cups water, 6 tablespoons sugar (or to taste), 1 teaspoon sour salt (or to taste), and 1½ teaspoons salt (or to taste).

CASTILIAN GARLIC SOUP. Place 1 slice French bread in a soup bowl. Top with lots of minced garlic and add boiling broth or stock. Add an egg if desired.

MAIN COURSE SOUP

For each serving:
1 cup chicken broth or beef broth or stock (see recipe)
¼ lb. meat, poultry, or fish
⅓ cup "starch" — pasta, potatoes, legumes, barley, or rice
1 cup any combination of vegetables

Order of cooking:
1. Broth or stock, starches, onions, carrots, root vegetables, cabbage, meat
2. Raw chicken, peas, leeks, asparagus, green beans
3. Zucchini, yellow squash, bean sprouts, precooked starches, mushrooms
4. Salad greens, spinach, lettuce

BASIC CREAM SOUP

2 tablespoons butter or margarine
2 tablespoons flour
2-4 cups warm liquid (milk or stock)
Vegetables

Method 1. Melt butter, add flour and cook several minutes. Remove from heat. Slowly whisk in liquid. Place over heat and stir in finely chopped or puréed vegetables and seasonings (do not boil, simply simmer). Thin, if desired, with more stock.

Method 2. Cook vegetables in stock or water. Remove cooked vegetables with slotted spoon and place in food processor or blender. Purée, add cream and butter and a little stock. Bring back to simmer. Do not let boil.

Bulgarian Cucumber Soup

FAVORITE RECIPES FROM HADASSAH   MID-MISSOURI DEBORAH CHAPTER OF HADASSAH   COLUMBIA, MO

1 clove garlic
2 large cucumbers, peeled
  and seeded
2 tablespoons olive oil
1 teaspoon salt
¼ teaspoon pepper
3 tablespoons chopped dill
  weed (or 1 Tbsp. dried)
½ to 1 cup walnut pieces
½ to 1½ cups plain yogurt or
  sour cream

Preparation time/processor: 5 to 10 minutes
Preparation time/conventional: 10 to 15 minutes
Chilling time: 2 hours
Serves 4

Food processor
1. Insert metal blade; drop garlic through the feed tube with the machine running. Cut cucumbers into chunks; add to work bowl and pulse several times to chop coarsely. Blend in olive oil, salt, pepper, and dill and remove to a bowl. Refrigerate for 2 to 6 hours.

2. Just before serving, stir in walnuts and yogurt.

Conventional
Mince garlic. Either work in batches with a blender or chop the cucumbers by hand.

Carrot Orange Cream Soup

EDITOR'S CHOICE

6 tablespoons butter or
  margarine
2 medium onions, chopped
2 cups chopped carrot
1½ cups dry white wine
4 cups light cream or half
  and half
2 tablespoons frozen orange
  juice concentrate
1 teaspoon nutmeg
1 tablespoon curry powder,
  or less to taste

Preparation time/processor: 5 to 10 minutes
Preparation time/conventional: 10 to 15 minutes
Cooking time: 1 hour
Serves 6 to 8

1. Place all ingredients in a large saucepan. Bring to a boil and simmer gently for 1 hour (soup will look curdled). Stir frequently while cooking.

2. Purée in a food processor or blender in batches. Return to pan and reheat, tasting and adjusting seasoning as desired.

Gazpacho

INSPIRATIONS ... FROM RENA HADASSAH   RENA GROUP HADASSAH, MT. VERNON CHAPTER, MT. VERNON, NY

1 clove garlic
1 medium onion
3 tomatoes
1 medium green pepper
1 large cucumber
1½ to 2 cups tomato juice
¼ cup olive oil
¼ cup wine vinegar
1 teaspoon salt
⅛ teaspoon pepper
Chopped cucumber, tomato,
  and green pepper for
  garnish
Croutons*

Preparation time/processor: 5 to 10 minutes
Preparation time/conventional: 20 minutes
Serves 6

Food processor

1. Insert metal blade. Drop garlic through the feed tube and process until chopped. Cut onion, tomatoes, and green pepper into quarters, and cut cucumber into 2-inch chunks; place in work bowl and pulse several times to chop.

2. Add about 1 cup tomato juice and the remaining ingredients and pulse until desired consistency is reached. Add the remaining tomato juice and refrigerate.

3. Serve in bowls, garnished with chopped vegetables and croutons.

Conventional

Mince garlic and chop vegetables. Proceed to step 2; use blender for fine texture or mix by hand.

Variation: Can also be served hot as a soup or as a sauce for pasta, rice, egg dishes, and other vegetables.

Curry Tomato Soup

FROM CHARLESTON, WITH LOVE   SYNAGOGUE EMANU-EL SISTERHOOD   CHARLESTON, SOUTH CAROLINA

1 pound ripe tomatoes
2 tablespoons butter or
  margarine
2 tablespoons flour
½ teaspoon curry powder
2 cups milk
1 teaspoon salt
1 to 2 tablespoons light
  brown sugar

Preparation time/processor: 20 minutes
Preparation time/conventional: 20 to 25 minutes
Serves 4

Food processor

1. Insert metal blade. Place tomatoes in work bowl and purée. Force through a fine mesh strainer to remove seedy residue.

2. Pour into a 1-quart saucepan and heat to boiling. Keep hot over low heat.

3. In a medium saucepan, melt butter; stir in flour and curry powder. Remove from heat and gradually whisk in the milk. Return to moderately low heat and cook, stirring constantly, until thickened and boiling. Whisk in hot tomato purée. Stir in salt and brown sugar. Serve at once.

Conventional

Put tomatoes through a food mill, or cook cut-up tomatoes and then purée. Proceed to step 2.

Cantaloupe Soup

FROM SOUP TO NOSH   NORTH VIRGINIA CHAPTER OF HADASSAH   FALLS CHURCH, VIRGINIA

1 large ripe cantaloupe
  (about 3 lbs.), chilled
½ cup dry sherry or Port
¼ cup sugar, or to taste
1 tablespoon lime juice

Preparation time: 10 minutes
Chilling time: 1 hour
Serves 5 to 6

Food processor/blender
1. Scoop out fruit and place in a food processor or blender. Add remaining ingredients and purée until very smooth. Adjust seasoning. Chill until serving time.

Broccoli Cream Soup

EDITOR'S CHOICE

1 large bunch broccoli
1 small onion, cut up
1 cup water
½ stick butter or margarine
2 tablespoons flour
2 cups half and half (or milk)
Salt and pepper to taste

Preparation time/processor: 10 minutes
Preparation time/conventional: 15 to 20 minutes
Cooking time: 30 minutes
Serves 4

1. Cut broccoli into small pieces. As soup cooks, steam a few pieces for garnish.

2. Place broccoli, onion, and water in a large saucepan. Cover and cook for 20 minutes until mushy. Place in a food processor (metal blade) or blender and purée until smooth. May also press through a sieve.

3. In a medium saucepan, melt butter. Add flour and cook, stirring, for several minutes. Whisk in the half and half and simmer for 5 minutes. Stir in the broccoli mixture and adjust seasoning. Heat soup well but do not boil. Garnish with the steamed broccoli pieces.

Note: The broccoli and onion mixture can be cooked in the microwave and the soup finished on the stovetop.

Quick Vermicelli Soup

ALL THAT SCHMALTZ   AUGUSTA CHAPTER OF HADASSAH   AUGUSTA, GEORGIA

1 quart chicken broth
½ cup snipped dill weed
¼ cup chopped parsley
Salt and pepper to taste
¼ cup broken vermicelli

Preparation time: 15 to 20 minutes
Serves 4

1. Combine the chicken broth, dill, parsley, salt and pepper in a large saucepan and bring to a boil. Stir in the vermicelli and return to a boil. Reduce heat and simmer 4 minutes. Serve immediately.

Lentil Soup

COOKING WITH CHUTZPAH CARLISLE JEWISH WOMEN'S COUNCIL OF CARLISLE CARLISLE, PA

½ cup parsley leaves
1 large clove garlic
1 medium carrot
1 large stalk celery
1 medium onion
2 cups lentils, rinsed and
  drained
2 quarts water
1½ teaspoons chopped
  oregano (or ½ tsp. dried)
2 teaspoons salt, or to taste
¼ teaspoon pepper
1 pound tomatoes, peeled
  and chopped
2 to 3 frankfurters, sliced
  (optional)
1 can (6 oz.) tomato paste
2 to 3 tablespoons red wine
  vinegar

Preparation time/processor: 10 to 15 minutes
Preparation time/conventional: 15 to 20 minutes
Cooking time: 2 hours
Serves 5 to 6

Food processor
1. Insert metal blade. With the machine running, drop parsley and garlic through the feed tube to chop. Cut carrot and celery into 2-inch pieces and cut onion in half; place in work bowl and pulse several times to chop finely.

2. Transfer to a large pot. Add lentils, water, oregano, salt and pepper and bring to a boil. Reduce heat; cover and simmer for 1½ hours.

3. Add tomatoes, frankfurters, tomato paste, and vinegar. Cover and simmer for another 30 minutes. Adjust seasonings.

Conventional
Mince garlic. Chop parsley, carrot, onion, and celery. Proceed to step 2.

Cheddar Cheese Soup

FROM THE BALABUSTA'S TABLE SISTERHOOD OF TEMPLE ISRAEL NATICK, MASSACHUSETTS

⅓ cup shredded carrot
2 tablespoons chopped onion
½ stick margarine
⅓ cup flour
1 teaspoon salt, or to taste
Dash pepper
1 quart milk
8 ounces sharp Cheddar
  cheese

Preparation time/processor: 20 minutes
Preparation time/conventional: 20 to 25 minutes
Serves 6

1. Sauté carrot and onion in margarine. Stir in flour, salt, and pepper. Gradually add milk and cook, stirring, until thickened. Coarsely grate Cheddar cheese and add, stirring until melted. Do not boil.

Note: A bowl of popcorn makes a nice accompaniment.

Quick Meat Ball Vegetable Soup

FAMILY FAVORITES   TEMPLE SOLEL SISTERHOOD   HOLLYWOOD, FLORIDA

1 pound ground beef
⅛ teaspoon pepper
1 egg
¼ cup cracker crumbs or
   matzo meal
1 tablespoon water
1 teaspoon salt
3 cups beef stock
3 cups tomato juice
2 to 3 medium onions
3 carrots
1 large potato (or 2 Tbsp.
   rice or ¼ cup barley)
Any leftover vegetables
½ tablespoon sugar
1 teaspoon salt
1 bay leaf
¾ teaspoon chopped
   marjoram or thyme
   (or ¼ tsp. dried)

Preparation time: 15 to 20 minutes
Cooking time: 30 minutes
Serves 6 to 8

1. Combine beef, salt, pepper, egg, crumbs, and water. Mix lightly and form into about 25 bite-size balls.

2. Cut onions into quarters; cut carrots into 1-inch pieces. Dice the potato.

3. Place vegetables and remaining ingredients in a large stock pot and bring to a boil. Reduce heat and gently drop in the meat balls. Cook, covered, for 30 minutes. Remove bay leaf before serving.

Variation: Remove the meat balls and bay leaf from the soup with a slotted spoon and purée the vegetable mixture in a food processor or blender. Return meat balls to soup before serving.

Chicken Soup

A BOOK FOR THE COOK   BRANDEIS UNIVERSITY N.W.C.   WESTCHESTER, NEW YORK

2 to 3 pound chicken
4 carrots, peeled
4 stalks celery
1 large onion
Parsley sprigs
Salt and pepper to taste
Thyme sprigs, dill sprigs,
   extra chicken bones
   (optional)

Preparation time: 5 to 10 minutes
Cooking time: 2½ to 3 hours
Makes about 2 quarts

1. Place chicken in stock pot and add water to cover. Bring to a boil and skim residue. Add remaining ingredients and simmer until the chicken is tender, 2½ to 3 hours.

2. Strain and use as soup, stock, or broth. The chicken may be used in recipes calling for cooked chicken.

Basic Beef Broth

SHARING OUR BEST   CANTON, OHIO CHAPTER OF HADASSAH   CANTON, OHIO

3 to 5 pounds meaty beef
  bones
3 quarts water
1 medium onion
2 carrots
2 stalks celery with leaves
1 tomato (optional)
3 to 4 sprigs parsley
Salt and pepper
1 tablespoon minced thyme

Preparation time: 15 to 20 minutes
Cooking time: 2 to 4 hours
Makes 6 to 8 cups

1. Cover bones with cold water and bring to a boil.

2. Skim any residue as it appears. Reduce heat and add vegetables and remaining ingredients. Simmer, partially covered, until meat is tender, 2 to 3 hours. Remove meat for another use.

3. Continue cooking bones for several hours if desired. Strain broth and skim off fat. Use as a clear soup, or chill or freeze for future use.

Variation

Brown Beef Stock: Place beef and bones in a shallow roasting pan. Add vegetables and bake in a 450° oven for about 40 minutes, stirring frequently. Empty into a large stock pot and proceed as above.

Cauliflower Soup

PORTAL TO GOOD COOKING, VOL. IV   WOMEN'S AMERICAN ORT, DISTRICT VIII   CHICAGO, ILLINOIS

1 medium cauliflower
4 ounces sharp Cheddar
  cheese, grated
¼ cup chopped onion
1 stick butter or margarine
2 tablespoons flour
1 quart milk
1 teaspoon salt
Dash pepper
Dash nutmeg

Preparation time: 20 minutes
Serves 4 to 6

1. Cut cauliflower into flowerettes and cook until tender (may use microwave). Drain.

2. While cauliflower is cooking, sauté onion in butter in a large saucepan until translucent. Add the flour and cook, stirring, for 3 to 4 minutes without browning.

3. Chop the cauliflower. Add to the onion with the milk, salt, pepper, and nutmeg. Cook, stirring, until slightly thickened.

4. Just before serving, add cheese and stir until melted. Do not boil.

Sweet Cabbage Soup

THE WAY TO A MAN'S HEART   BETH ISRAEL CONGREGATION   WASHINGTON, PENNSYLVANIA

1 small head cabbage,
  shredded
1 cup beef stock or water
2 tablespoons tomato paste
1 small onion, chopped
½ stick margarine (pareve)
2 tablespoons flour
1 tablespoon brown sugar
1 tablespoon vinegar
¼ cup water
Salt and pepper to taste

Preparation time/processor: 10 minutes
Preparation time/conventional: 15 to 20 minutes
Cooking time: 25 to 30 minutes
Serve 4

1. Place cabbage in a large saucepan with beef stock, tomato paste, and water to just cover. Bring to a boil; reduce heat and simmer 20 minutes until cabbage is tender.

2. While cabbage is cooking, sauté onion in margarine until browned; stir in flour and sugar. Add vinegar and water; stir well. Add to cabbage mixture. Season to taste.

3. Simmer about 5 minutes. Taste and very carefully adjust seasoning, adding pepper and more sugar or vinegar as necessary.

Cream of Zucchini Soup

COLLECTABLE DELECTABLES   RODEF SHALOM TEMPLE SISTERHOOD   HAMPTON, VIRGINIA

3 cups sliced zucchini
3 tablespoons minced onion
1 teaspoon seasoned salt
½ clove garlic, minced
  (optional)
⅓ cup water
½ teaspoon chopped parsley

Cream Sauce
2 tablespoons margarine or
  butter
2 tablespoons flour
1 cup milk
½ cup light cream
Dash pepper

Preparation time/processor: 10 minutes
Preparation time/conventional: 20 minutes
Cooking time: 20 to 30 minutes
Serves 4 to 6

Food processor/blender
1. Place all the soup ingredients in a saucepan and cook until tender and very little liquid is left. Place in a food processor or blender and purée.

2. Melt margarine; stir in flour and cook several seconds to blend. Add milk and cream and cook, stirring constantly, until thickened. Blend in zucchini purée and season with pepper. Thin with a little milk if desired, and adjust seasonings. Reheat to serve.

Salads

Meal-in-One-Salad

PORTAL TO GOOD COOKING, VOL. 2 WOMEN'S AMERICAN ORT, VIII CHICAGO, ILLINOIS

4 small red potatoes, cooked
½ pound green beans, cut in
  half and cooked
2 medium onions
2 cups Italian dressing*
1 quart salad greens
1 can (6½ oz.) tuna, drained
1 can (6 oz.) black olives,
  drained
1 can (16 oz.) artichoke
  hearts, drained
3 or 4 tomatoes
4 hard-cooked eggs

Preparation time: 20 minutes
Pre-preparation:cook vegetables
Chilling time: several hours
Serves 4

1. Dice potatoes and slice onions thinly.

2. Place potatoes, green beans, and onions in a large bowl with the Italian dressing and toss to blend. Cover and refrigerate several hours or overnight.

3. To serve, tear greens into bite-size pieces and arrange in a large salad bowl. Drain potatoes and green beans well, reserving the dressing, and arrange over salad with tuna, olives, and artichoke hearts. Toss very lightly and garnish with tomato wedges and egg quarters. Serve with reserved dressing.

Variation: Substitute chicken for the tuna and add other vegetables as desired — marinated mushrooms, cauliflower, or zucchini.

Quick Ideas

BASIC VINAIGRETTE DRESSING. Combine 1 part vinegar, 3 parts oil, and seasoning (salt, pepper, garlic, herbs).

SALAD COMBINATIONS:

1. Mixed greens, strips of gruyere cheese, sliced green onions, cut cooked asparagus.

2. Sliced avocado, cherry tomatoes, croutons, black olives, with Italian dressing and sprinkled with Parmesan cheese.

3. Romaine and Bibb lettuce, toasted pine nuts, sliced radishes, capers, Italian dressing.

4. Watercress tossed with a dressing of oil, vinegar, and grainy mustard.

A DOZEN SALADS

Here are a dozen fruit salad combinations, all of which are delightful. Choose from a wide variety of salad greens to enhance the beauty of the salad. (From *Glennwood's Gourmets*, Women's American ORT—Glennwood Chapter, Southfield, MI.)

1. Sliced fresh peaches, blueberries, and cottage cheese.

2. Diced pineapple, strawberries, cream cheese balls rolled in chopped walnuts.

3. Orange sections, grapes, diced pears.

4. Assorted melon balls, red raspberries.

5. Diced unpeeled red apples, diced bananas, sliced nectarines.

6. Diced oranges, diced pears, and pitted cherries in orange cups.

7. Peeled and sliced Golden Delicious apples, coarsely chopped walnuts, sliced nectarines.

8. Blackberries, sliced bananas, toasted slivered almonds.

9. Cubed honeydew melon, sliced fresh peaches, grapes.

10. Blackberries, pineapple cubes, cottage cheese.

11. Sliced plums, blueberries, cubed cream cheese.

12. Cantaloupe halves filled with blueberries and red raspberries.

Cold Pasta and Chicken Primavera

THE COOK'S BOOK   TEMPLE ISRAEL SISTERHOOD   TULSA, OKLAHOMA

½ pound green spaghetti
½ pound vermicelli or plain
  spaghetti
1 cup green peas
1 cup broccoli flowerettes
4 or 5 cloves garlic
1½ teaspoons Dijon mustard
2 tablespoons red wine
  vinegar
1 teaspoon salt
1 cup olive oil
10 mushrooms
12 to 14 cherry tomatoes
⅓ cup pine nuts, toasted
  (optional)
3 tablespoons chopped basil
  (or 1 Tbsp. dried)
2 cups cubed cooked chicken

Preparation time: 15 to 20 minutes
Chilling time: 3 hours or more
Pre-preparation: cook chicken
Serves 4

1. Cook spaghetti and vermicelli according to instructions; drain. Cook peas. Blanch broccoli in boiling water for 1 minute, or microwave. Drain vegetables.

2. Meanwhile, make dressing by dropping garlic through feed tube of food processor or blender while machine is running. Add mustard, vinegar, and salt. Pour oil in slowly with the machine running. Remove and reserve. Slice the mushrooms.

3. Transfer pasta to a large bowl and toss with ½ cup of dressing. Cool and chill at least 3 hours (or place in freezer about ½ hour). Toss the remaining ingredients with the rest of the dressing. Refrigerate.

4. Just before serving, toss vegetables and chicken with the pasta.

Variation: Cooked fish or other meats may be substituted for the chicken. Other pastas can be substituted for the spaghetti.

Osaka Chicken Salad

FIDDLER IN THE KITCHEN   NATIONAL COUNCIL OF JEWISH WOMEN, GREATER DETROIT SECTION   DETROIT, MI

½ cup vegetable oil
1½ tablespoons lemon juice
1 tablespoon soy sauce
2 tablespoons sesame seeds
¾ teaspoon sugar
½ teaspoon dry mustard
½ teaspoon cinnamon
½ teaspoon ground
 coriander
Pinch ginger

1 head lettuce
4 cups cooked chicken or
 turkey, cubed
6 green onions, sliced
1 can (3 oz.) rice noodles

Preparation time: 10 to 15 minutes
Serves 4 to 6.

1. Combine oil, lemon juice, soy sauce, seeds, sugar, mustard, cinnamon, coriander, and ginger in a jar or bowl and mix well.

2. Tear lettuce into bite-size pieces. Combine lettuce, chicken, and green onions in a large bowl. Just before serving, toss with dressing and sprinkle with rice noodles.

Italian Fish Salad

KOSHER PARTIES UNLIMITED   WOMEN'S LEAGUE FOR CONSERVATIVE JUDAISM   NEW YORK, NEW YORK

½ pound small shell pasta
½ cup mayonnaise*
¾ cup milk
½ cup French dressing*
½ teaspoon salt
¼ teaspoon pepper
1 cup cooked or canned
 salmon, flaked
1 cup sliced celery
2 small onions
3 hard-cooked eggs
2 cups shredded cabbage

Preparation time: 20 minutes
Chilling time: 1 hour
Serves 4

1. Cook shells according to package directions; drain and chill.

2. While shells are cooking, combine mayonnaise, milk, French dressing, salt and pepper in a large bowl. Slice onions and eggs, and prepare other ingredients.

3. Combine pasta and dressing and toss well. Add remaining ingredients and toss again to mix. Chill until serving time.

Deli Pasta Salad

FOOD FOR SHOW/FOOD ON THE GO   MOUNT SINAI HOSPITAL AUXILIARY   MINNEAPOLIS, MINNESOTA

1 pound spiral pasta (rotelle)
¼ pound hard salami, sliced
1¼ cups black olives
1 cup chopped green pepper
1 small red onion, sliced thin
¼ cup finely chopped
   parsley
1 jar (2½ oz.) sliced or diced
   pimento, drained
¾ cup Italian dressing*

Preparation time/processor: 15 minutes
Preparation time/conventional: 15 to 20 minutes
Serves 8 to 10

1. Cook pasta according to package instructions; drain well. Cut salami slices into thin strips. Separate onion slices into rings.

2. Combine all ingredients in a large bowl and toss to mix well. Serve at room temperature or chilled.

Note: May be made a day ahead.

Curry Rice

MADE TO ORTER   DAY, EVENING, JAMES RIVER CHAPTERS OF WOMEN'S AMERICAN ORT   RICHMOND, VIRGINIA

4 cups cooked rice (cold)
½ pound green peas, shelled
   (or 10 oz. pkg. frozen)
1 cup thinly sliced celery
   (about 2 stalks)
1 cup sliced or slivered
   almonds, toasted
½ cup mayonnaise*
½ cup sour cream
5 tablespoons mango
   chutney
2 teaspoons curry powder
Salt and pepper to taste

Preparation time: 10 to 15 minutes
Pre-preparation: cook rice
Chilling time: overnight
Serves 6 to 8

1. Cook peas (or thaw frozen).

2. Combine rice, peas, celery, and almonds in a large bowl. In another bowl, combine mayonnaise, sour cream and seasonings; add to rice and toss lightly until well blended. If too dry, add more mayonnaise or sour cream.

3. Chill overnight.

Tabbouleh

1 to 2 cups cracked wheat
(bulgur)
2 cups parsley sprigs (tightly
packed)
½ cup minced onion
2 green peppers
1 clove garlic
Salt and pepper to taste
⅓ cup lemon juice
⅓ cup olive or peanut oil
1 large tomato (optional)
Chopped green onion

Preparation time/processor: 20 minutes
Preparation time/conventional: 20 to 25 minutes
Serves 8

1. Soak the cracked wheat in warm water for 15 minutes; drain.

2. While wheat is soaking, chop parsley, onion, green peppers, and garlic; add salt and pepper and toss gently with the wheat. Mix in the lemon juice and oil. Toss well.

3. Just before serving, add tomato and garnish with green onion. Serve on lettuce leaves.

Tomato-Corn Salad

EDITOR'S CHOICE

½ cup parsley sprigs
1 clove garlic
2 tablespoons white wine
vinegar or lemon juice
1 tablespoon tomato paste
½ teaspoon salt, or to taste
¼ teaspoon ground cumin
Freshly ground black pepper
⅓ cup olive oil

½ cup sliced green onion,
including some tops
1 jar (4 oz.) diced pimento,
drained
2 cups crisp-cooked corn
kernels

Preparation time: 5 to 10 minutes
Serves 4

Food processor/blender

1. In a food processor (metal blade) or blender, drop in parsley and garlic with the machine running. Add vinegar, tomato paste, and seasonings. With the machine running, add olive oil and process several seconds.

2. Combine green onion, corn, and pimento. Toss with dressing and serve immediately, or cover and chill for an hour or so.

Cauliflower and Egg Salad

KOSHER GOURMET II SISTERHOOD OF TEMPLE BETH-EL NORTH BELLMORE, NEW YORK

1 small red onion, sliced thin
3 hard-cooked eggs, chopped
3 cups raw cauliflower
 pieces
1 cup sliced celery
½ cup green pepper
½ to ¾ cup vinaigrette
 dressing or Italian
 dressing*

Preparation time/processor: 5 to 10 minutes
Preparation time/conventional: 10 to 15 minutes
Chilling time: 1 hour
Serves 6 to 8

1. Combine all ingredients. Cover and chill for at least 1 hour. Serve on a bed of lettuce.

Cauliflower Relish

NOT FOR NOSHERS ONLY BETH ISRAEL SISTERHOOD LEBANON, PENNSYLVANIA

1 cauliflower (about 2 lbs.)
1 green pepper
⅔ cup vegetable oil
⅓ cup white wine vinegar
1 teaspoon salt
1 tablespoon chopped
 oregano (or 1 tsp. dried)
½ teaspoon sugar
¼ teaspoon pepper
1 clove garlic, crushed
1 can (6 oz.) pitted large
 ripe olives, drained

Preparation time: 15 minutes
Chilling time: several hours
Serves 12

1. Cut cauliflower into small sections or flowerettes. Cut green pepper into ½ inch strips.

2. Combine oil, vinegar, salt, oregano, sugar, pepper, and garlic in a large saucepan; bring to a boil. Add cauliflower pieces; cover and simmer for about 8 minutes or until crisp-tender. Stir occasionally.

3. Discard garlic; add olives and green pepper. Transfer to a bowl and cool. Cover and chill for several hours or overnight. Drain well before serving.

Garbanzos Italienne

EDITOR'S CHOICE

1 can (16 oz.) garbanzos
  (chick peas)
3 tablespoons chopped onion
1 small clove garlic, minced
⅓ cup red wine vinegar
¼ cup olive oil
1 tablespoon chopped
  parsley
1 teaspoon salt
1 teaspoon sugar
¾ teaspoon chopped oregano
  (or ¼ dried)
Dash pepper

Preparation time: 5 to 10 minutes
Chilling time: several hours
Serves 4

1. Drain garbanzos and place in a bowl. Combine all other ingredients and pour over the garbanzos. Chill for several hours or overnight before serving.

Dilled Zucchini Salad

EDITOR'S CHOICE

⅓ cup cider vinegar
⅔ cup oil
¾ teaspoon salt
1 clove garlic
½ teaspoon sugar
6 small thin zucchini
1 small onion
1 green pepper
1 tablespoon snipped dill
  weed (or 1 tsp. dried)

Preparation time/processor: 5 to 10 minutes
Preparation time/conventional: 10 to 15 minutes
Chilling time: overnight
Serves 8

Food processor

1. Insert metal blade and process vinegar, oil, salt, garlic, and sugar until garlic is finely chopped. Remove. Insert slicing blade and slice zucchini, onion, and green pepper as thinly as possible.

2. Place in a large bowl with the dill. Toss with dressing and marinate overnight in the refrigerator.

Israeli Eggplant Salad

TO STIR WITH LOVE SISTERHOOD AHAVATH ISRAEL KINGSTON, NEW YORK

1 large eggplant
1 small onion
1 small dill pickle
2 hard-cooked eggs
2 garlic cloves
¼ cup mayonnaise*
3 tablespoons olive oil
2 tablespoons lemon juice
Salt and pepper to taste
Chopped parsley
Toasted sesame seeds

Preparation time/processor: 5 to 10 minutes
Preparation time/conventional: 15 to 20 minutes
Cooking time: 30 minutes
Chilling time: several hours
Makes about 2 cups

Food processor

1. Prick skin of eggplant; cook until soft — about 5 minutes in a microwave or 30 minutes in a 400° oven. Cool, drain off excess moisture, and remove skin.

2. Insert metal blade. Cut onion into quarters and cut pickle in half; place in work bowl with eggs and garlic and pulse several times to chop. Remove. Place eggplant, mayonnaise, olive oil, and lemon juice in the work bowl and process into a smooth purée. Fold this mixture into the onion-egg mixture. Adjust seasoning.

3. Chill several hours. Garnish with chopped parsley and toasted sesame seeds. Serve with thin slices of toasted rye bread.

Conventional

In step 2, use a blender and work in batches. Or chop onion, garlic, etc. by hand and purée with a mixer. Proceed to step 3.

Minted Artichoke Hearts

2 packages (10 oz. each)
  frozen artichoke hearts
½ cup olive oil
1 medium onion, minced
2 tablespoons sugar
Salt and pepper to taste
¼ cup white wine vinegar
2 tablespoons water
3 tablespoons minced mint
  leaves (or 1 Tbsp. dried)

Preparation time: 10 minutes
Cooking time: 20 to 30 minutes
Serves 6 to 8

1. Thaw artichoke hearts and pat dry; sauté in olive oil until golden brown. Add onion and sauté for about 3 minutes. Sprinkle with sugar and season with salt and pepper.

2. Add vinegar and water and bring to a boil. Simmer until tender and the liquid is syrupy. Sprinkle with mint and serve at room temperature.

Mardi Gras Salad

TRADITION IN THE KITCHEN   NORTHERN SUBURBAN BETH EL SISTERHOOD   HIGHLAND PARK, ILLINOIS

½ pound shelled green peas
  (or 10 oz. pkg. frozen)
½ pound green beans (or
  10 oz. pkg. frozen)
1 green pepper, diced
1 small onion, diced
1½ cups diced celery
1 jar (2 oz.) chopped pimento

½ cup sugar, or to taste
½ cup vegetable oil
1 tablespoon salt
¾ cup vinegar

Preparation time: 15 to 20 minutes
Chilling time: 12 hours
Serves 6

1. Cook peas and green beans (or thaw frozen); drain.

2. Place all vegetables in a large mixing bowl.

3. Combine sugar, oil, salt, and vinegar. Pour over vegetables and toss. Cover and marinate in the refrigerator for at least 12 hours. Drain.

Kay's Salad
FROM CHARLESTON, WITH LOVE   SISTERHOOD SYNAGOGUE EMANU-EL   CHARLESTON, SOUTH CAROLINA

1¼ pounds green peas,
  shelled (or 2 - 10 oz. pkg.
  frozen)
1 Bermuda onion
1 can (8 oz.) water chestnuts
1 head iceberg lettuce

Topping
⅔ cup sour cream
1⅓ cups mayonnaise*
Sugar to taste
¼ cup slivered almonds,
  toasted

Preparation time/processor: 10 minutes
Preparation time/conventional: 10 to 15 minutes
Chilling time: 2 hours
Serves 6 to 8

1. Cook peas lightly (defrost frozen peas). Slice onion and water chestnuts. Break up the lettuce.

2. In a glass casserole, layer lettuce, onion, peas, and water chestnuts. End with lettuce.

3. Combine sour cream, mayonnaise, and sugar. Spread over salad and sprinkle with toasted almonds. Refrigerate at least 2 hours before serving.

Beet Salad with Horseradish Cream
COOK'S DELIGHT   SISTERHOOD OF CONGREGATION OHEV SHALOM   ORLANDO, FLORIDA

1 can (16 oz.) beets, chilled
½ cup sour cream
¼ cup prepared
  horseradish*
½ teaspoon salt, or to taste
2 tablespoons sugar
1 cup sliced celery
1 cup sliced onion
Lettuce leaves

Preparation time: 10 to 15 minutes
Serves 4 to 5

1. Drain beets. Combine sour cream, horseradish, salt, and sugar. Refrigerate.

2. Separate onion slices into rings. Just before serving, toss beets with celery and onion. Arrange on plates lined with lettuce leaves and top with sour cream dressing.

Marinated Salad

WORLD OF OUR FLAVORS — CERTIFIED TA'AM BETH HILLEL CONGREGATION WILMETTE, ILLINOIS

1 large cucumber, peeled
2 large tomatoes
1 green pepper
1 stalk celery
4 green onions, including
tops
4 to 6 mushrooms
Chopped parsley

Dressing
2 tablespoons vegetable oil
½ teaspoon celery salt
1 clove garlic, minced
Juice of 1 lemon (2½ to
3 Tbsp.)
¼ teaspoon salt
½ teaspoon black pepper
1 tablespoon cider or white
wine vinegar

Preparation time/processor: 5 to 10 minutes
Preparation time/conventional: 10 to 15 minutes
Chilling time: 6 hours
Serves 6

1. Chop or cut up all vegetables and place in a 2-quart bowl.

2. Mix dressing ingredients together in a jar and shake well.

3. Toss dressing with vegetables and chill at least 6 hours before serving.

Cucumber and Onion Salad

CREATIVE COOKERY SISTERHOOD TEMPLE SHAARE TEFILAH NORWOOD, MASSACHUSETTS

1 cucumber, sliced thin
1 medium onion, sliced thin
1 teaspoon salt
½ cup water
½ cup white vinegar
½ cup sour cream

Preparation time: 5 to 10 minutes
Chilling time: several hours
Serves 4

1. Salt cucumber and onion and let stand for 5 minutes. Combine with water and vinegar and chill for several hours or overnight.

2. Drain and toss with sour cream.

Vegetable Dill Combo

NOSHES, NIBBLES, AND GOURMET DELIGHTS   TEMPLE IN THE PINES SISTERHOOD   HOLLYWOOD, FLORIDA

¼ cup creamy French
  dressing*
¼ cup mayonnaise or salad
  dressing*
2 tablespoons chili sauce
2 teaspoons lemon juice
1 teaspoon salt
Dash pepper

½ small head cauliflower
  (about 1½ cups)
1½ cups sliced carrots
½ pound green peas, shelled
  (or 10 oz. pkg. frozen)
½ cup sliced celery
¼ cup chopped onions
1 tablespoon chopped dill
  weed (or 1 tsp. dried)

Preparation time: 20 minutes
Chilling time: 1 hour
Serves 8 to 10

1. Combine French dressing, mayonnaise, chili sauce, lemon juice, salt and pepper. Cover and chill several hours or overnight.

2. Cut cauliflower into bite-size pieces. Cook cauliflower, carrots, and peas. May microwave. (If using frozen peas, thaw.) Drain all vegetables and place in a large bowl. Cool in refrigerator or run under cold water.

3. Add dressing and toss gently to combine well. Chill until serving time. Sprinkle with dill weed just before serving.

Aloha Salad

SEASONED WITH LOVE   WHITE MEADOW TEMPLE SISTERHOOD   ROCKAWAY, NEW JERSEY

1 pound bean sprouts
  (or 16 oz. can)
1 large head iceberg lettuce
¼ cup minced green onions
1 cup sliced celery
½ pound snow peas (or 6 oz.
  pkg. frozen)

Dressing
1 cup mayonnaise*
2 teaspoons curry powder
¼ cup soy sauce
2 teaspoons lemon juice

Preparation time/processor: 10 to 15 minutes
Preparation time/conventional: 15 to 20 minutes
Chilling time: 1 hour
Serves 6 to 8

1. Blanch bean sprouts for 1 minute in boiling water; drain (or drain canned sprouts). Blanch snow peas (or thaw and pat dry frozen). Tear lettuce into bite-size pieces.

2. Combine lettuce, bean sprouts, green onions, celery, and snow peas; chill until ready to serve.

3. Combine dressing ingredients in a jar and shake well. Just before serving, toss with salad greens in a large bowl.

Foo Yung Toss and Dressing

NOT FOR NOSHERS ONLY   BETH ISRAEL SISTERHOOD   LEBANON, PENNSYLVANIA

1 head Romaine lettuce
1 pound bean sprouts (or
  16-oz. can)
1 can (8 oz.) water chestnuts
2 hard-cooked eggs

Dressing
1 small onion
2 teaspoons Worcestershire
  sauce
¼ cup vinegar
⅓ cup ketchup*
½ cup sugar
1 cup vegetable oil

Preparation time: 5 to 10 minutes
Serves 6 to 8

Food processor

1. Blanch fresh bean sprouts for 1 minute in boiling water; drain (or drain canned sprouts). Rinse and slice water chestnuts. Slice eggs.

2. Combine lettuce, bean sprouts, water chestnuts, and eggs in a large salad bowl.

3. Insert metal blade. Cut onion in half and place in work bowl with Worcestershire sauce, vinegar, ketchup, and sugar; process about 10 seconds or until well combined. Add oil through the feed tube with the machine running.

4. Toss salad with dressing just before serving.

Conventional

In step 3, chop onion. Use blender or wire whisk to mix.

Lemon Olive Coleslaw

INSPIRATIONS ... FROM RENA HADASSAH   RENA GROUP HADASSAH, MT. VERNON CHAPTER   MT. VERNON, NY

1 small head cabbage, grated
  or shredded
1 small onion, chopped fine
½ cup stuffed green olives,
  sliced

½ cup mayonnaise*
½ teaspoon celery salt
¼ cup lemon juice
¼ teaspoon dry mustard

Preparation time/processor: 5 to 10 minutes
Preparation time/conventional: 15 to 20 minutes
Chilling time: 1 hour
Serves 6 to 8

1. Combine cabbage, onion, and olives.

2. Combine the remaining ingredients and toss with the cabbage mixture. Chill and serve.

Potato Salad

SHARING OUR BEST   CANTON, OHIO CHAPTER OF HADASSAH   CANTON, OHIO

2 pounds baking potatoes
(unpeeled)
2 tablespoons Italian
dressing*
4 to 6 hard-cooked eggs
2 stalks celery
1 small onion
1½ cups mayonnaise*
Salt, pepper, and paprika to
taste
Relish or chopped pickle to
taste

Preparation time/processor: 20 minutes
Preparation time/conventional: 25 to 30 minutes
Serves 8 to 10

1. Cut potatoes into quarters (or smaller pieces). Cook in boiling water to cover until tender.

2. While potatoes are cooking, chop the eggs, celery, and onion; combine.

3. Peel and thinly slice the hot potatoes, and sprinkle with Italian dressing. Allow to cool, stirring from time to time.

4. Combine potatoes with remaining ingredients. Cover and chill. Before serving, adjust seasoning, and garnish with chopped green pepper, grated carrot, dill weed, or pickles.

To mold: Pack lightly into an oiled ring mold and chill. Unmold and decorate with pimento, olives, green pepper rings, and chopped parsley.

Chinese Cole Slaw

UNDER THE CHEF'S H.A.T.   HEBREW ACADEMY OF TOLEDO   TOLEDO, OHIO

1 can (8 oz.) water chestnuts
4 cups Chinese cabbage,
  shredded
1 cup chopped parsley
1 can (8 oz.) crushed
  unsweetened pineapple,
  drained
¼ cup chopped onion
¼ cup mayonnaise* or cole
  slaw dressing
1 teaspoon grated gingerroot
  (or ½ tsp. ground)

Preparation time/processor: 10 minutes
Preparation time/conventional: 20 minutes
Chilling time: several hours
Serves 10 to 12

1. Slice water chestnuts and combine with cabbage, parsley, pineapple, and onion in a large bowl. Cover and chill.

2. In a small bowl, combine mayonnaise and gingerroot. Cover and chill.

3. Just before serving, toss the dressing with the vegetables.

Cabbage Slaw

MRS. COOPER'S ENCORE   B'NAI JACOB SYNAGOGUE AUXILLIARY   CHARLESTON, WEST VIRGINIA

1 medium head cabbage,
  chopped or sliced finely
1 medium onion, chopped
1 green pepper, chopped
1 large carrot, grated

Dressing
½ to 1 cup sugar
1 cup vinegar
1 cup vegetable oil
1 teaspoon celery seed
1 teaspoon dry mustard
1 teaspoon salt

Preparation time/processor: 15 minutes
Preparation time/conventional: 20 minutes
Serves 8 to 10

1. Combine vegetables in a large bowl.

2. Combine dressing ingredients in a saucepan. Bring to a boil and simmer 3 to 4 minutes. Pour hot dressing over vegetables. Refrigerate until ready to serve.

Note: May be kept in refrigerator for up to 3 weeks.

Green Salad

1 large egg
¼ cup red wine vinegar
2 teaspoons Worcestershire sauce
1 large clove garlic
Dash pepper
¼ teaspoon salt
½ cup olive oil

1 head Romaine lettuce
1 pint cherry tomatoes
½ cup grated Parmesan cheese
1 ounce blue cheese
Seasoned croutons*

Preparation time: 10 to 15 minutes
Serves 4 to 6

Food processor

1. Insert metal blade. Place egg in work bowl; process for 10 seconds. Add vinegar, Worcestershire, garlic, salt and pepper. Process several seconds, then add oil very slowly with the machine running.

2. Tear up lettuce. Combine with tomatoes, Parmesan cheese, and blue cheese. Just before serving, add dressing and toss.

Conventional

In step 1, whisk egg for 10 seconds; add vinegar, Worcestershire, garlic, salt and pepper. Whisking constantly, add oil slowly. Or omit the egg and shake ingredients in a jar.

Romaine Salad with Cashews

FIDDLER IN THE KITCHEN   NATIONAL COUNCIL OF JEWISH WOMEN, GREATER DETROIT   DETROIT, MICHIGAN

3 heads Romaine lettuce
½ cup garbanzo beans (chick peas)
½ cup thinly sliced red onion
1 cup salted cashews

¼ cup cider vinegar
1 generous tablespoon Dijon mustard
Salt to taste
Freshly ground pepper to taste
Pinch ground cumin
Pinch ground cardamom
¾ cup light olive oil

Preparation time: 10 to 15 minutes
Serves 8 to 10

1. Tear lettuce into bite-sized pieces. Rinse and drain garbanzos. Combine lettuce, garbanzos, onion, and cashews.

2. In a food processor or blender, place vinegar and seasonings. Add olive oil with the machine running. (Could also shake in a jar or beat with a whisk.)

3. Just before serving, pour dressing over salad and toss.

Mrs. Johnson's Spinach Salad

THE KOSHER KITCHEN TEMPLE SHAAREY ZEDEK SISTERHOOD AMHERST, NEW YORK

½ cup sugar
Dash salt
½ cup ketchup*
1 teaspoon Worcestershire
  sauce
¼ cup white vinegar
1 small onion

1 cup oil
1 bag (1 lb.) fresh spinach
1 can (8 oz.) water chestnuts
¼ to ½ pound bean sprouts
  (or 14 oz. can)
2 hard-cooked eggs, chopped
Baco-bits (optional)

Preparation time: 15 to 20 minutes
Serves 4 to 6

Food processor/blender

1. Place sugar, salt, ketchup, Worcestershire, vinegar, and onion (quartered) in a food processor (metal blade) or blender and process 10 seconds; add oil with the machine running.

2. Remove stems from spinach and break into pieces. Drain and rinse water chestnuts; slice. Blanch fresh bean sprouts in boiling water for 1 minute, or drain and rinse canned sprouts.

3. Place spinach, water chestnuts, bean sprouts, and chopped egg in a large salad bowl. Pour dressing over and toss (you may not need all of dressing). Sprinkle with Baco-bits and serve.

Conventional

In step 1, chop onion, place dressing ingredients in a jar, and shake well.

Creamy Caesar Salad

FROM SOUP TO NOSH NORTH VIRGINIA CHAPTER OF HADASSAH FALLS CHURCH, VIRGINIA

1 medium onion
½ cup mayonnaise*
3 tablespoons vinegar
2 tablespoons anchovy paste
1 tablespoon olive oil
1 teaspoon dry mustard
1 teaspoon salt
1 teaspoon paprika

1 large head Romaine lettuce
3 hard-cooked eggs, chopped
1 cup croutons*

Preparation time/processor: 5 to 10 minutes
Preparation time/conventional: 10 to 15 minutes
Chilling time: 1 hour
Serves 6

Food processor

1. Insert metal blade. Chop onion; add remaining dressing ingredients and process until smooth. Chill until serving time.

2. Tear lettuce into bite-sized pieces; combine with eggs and croutons. Just before serving, pour dressing over salad and toss.

Conventional

Use blender to chop onion and combine dressing ingredients. Or chop onion by hand and combine ingredients with a wire whisk.

Greek Salad

ALL THIS AND KOSHER, TOO BETH DAVID SISTERHOOD MIAMI, FLORIDA

2 cloves garlic
⅓ cup white wine vinegar
3 tablespoons chopped
  oregano (or 1 Tbsp. dried)
1 teaspoon salt
1 cup oil (olive and corn oil)

1 head iceberg lettuce
1 cucumber
1 green pepper
1 large onion
5 ounces Feta cheese,
  crumbled
2 tomatoes, quartered
4 Greek or black olives

Preparation time/processor: 10 to 15 minutes
Preparation time/conventional: 15 to 20 minutes
Serves 4

Food processor

1. Insert metal blade. With the machine running, drop garlic through feed tube. Add vinegar, oregano, and salt. Add oil with the machine running. Process until well combined. Remove. Do not wash bowl.

2. Tear lettuce into bite-size pieces and place in a salad bowl. Insert slicing blade and slice the cucumber, green pepper (rings), and onion (rings); add vegetables to salad bowl.

3. Add Feta, tomatoes and olives. Toss salad with the dressing. Arrange in 4 bowls or plates, garnishing with onion rings and an olive.

Conventional

In step 1, use a blender or place crushed garlic in a jar and add other ingredients. Cut up vegetables by hand in step 2. Proceed to step 3.

Salad dressings

Mayonnaise

FOOD FOR SHOW/FOOD ON THE GO   MOUNT SINAI HOSPITAL AUXILIARY   MINNEAPOLIS, MINNESOTA

1 large egg
1 teaspoon fresh lemon juice
1 teaspoon red wine vinegar
1 to 2 teaspoons Dijon
  mustard
1 teaspoon salt
Freshly ground white pepper
1 cup safflower oil
¼ cup olive oil

Preparation time: 5 minutes
Makes about 1 ½ cups

Food processor/blender

1. In a food processor (metal blade) or blender, combine egg, lemon juice, vinegar, mustard, salt, and pepper. Process for 5 seconds.

2. Combine oils and slowly pour through feed tube with the machine running. When mixture becomes thick you can add oil more quickly.

Variation: Other oils or oil combinations may be used.

Kennedy Center Mustard
Salad Dressing

FROM SOUP TO NOSH   NORTH VIRGINIA CHAPTER OF HADASSAH   FALLS CHURCH, VIRGINIA

½ cup Dijon mustard
½ cup red wine vinegar
2 teaspoons salt
1 teaspoon sugar (optional)
¼ teaspoon white pepper
1 cup olive or vegetable oil

Preparation time: 5 minutes
Makes about 2 cups

Food processor/blender

1. Combine all ingredients except oil in a food processor or blender. Add oil with the machine running.

2. Serve over chilled greens, hearts of palm, endive, or cooked vegetables (hot or cold).

Conventional

Combine all ingredients in a covered jar and shake well.

Favorite Salad Dressing

HISTORICALLY COOKING — 200 YEARS OF GOOD EATING   K.K. BETH ELOHIM SISTERHOOD   CHARLESTON, SC

1 cup mayonnaise*
¼ cup mustard (Dijon preferred)
¼ cup honey
¼ cup white vinegar
2 tablespoons chopped parsley (optional)
1 small onion, chopped fine
Pinch salt
½ teaspoon sugar (optional)

Preparation time: 10 to 15 minutes
Makes about 1 ½ cups

1. Combine all ingredients and mix well.

Note: This also makes a good dip.

Creamy Italian Dressing

NOT FOR NOSHERS ONLY   BETH ISRAEL SISTERHOOD   LEBANON, PENNSYLVANIA

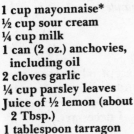

1 cup mayonnaise*
½ cup sour cream
¼ cup milk
1 can (2 oz.) anchovies,
  including oil
2 cloves garlic
¼ cup parsley leaves
Juice of ½ lemon (about
  2 Tbsp.)
1 tablespoon tarragon
  vinegar
1 tablespoon Worcestershire
  sauce
Salt and pepper to taste
1 tablespoon snipped chives
  (optional)

Preparation time: 5 to 10 minutes
Makes about 2¼ cups.

Food Processor

1. Insert metal blade. Place all ingredients (except chives) in work bowl and process until smooth (you may have to work in batches). Add chives and process briefly to fold in.

Conventional

Combine ingredients in blender or mix by hand.

Italian Dressing

FIDDLER IN THE KITCHEN   NATIONAL COUNCIL OF JEWISH WOMEN   DETROIT, MICHIGAN

¼ cup vinegar
1 clove garlic
1 teaspoon salt
½ teaspoon white pepper
½ teaspoon celery salt
¼ teaspoon ground red
  pepper
¼ teaspoon dry mustard
Dash Tabasco sauce
1 cup oil

Preparation time: 5 minutes
Makes about 1¼ cups

Food processor/blender

1. Combine vinegar, garlic, and seasonings in a food processor (metal blade) or blender. Add oil slowly with machine running.

w Cholesterol French Dressing

0 YEARS IN THE KITCHEN   SISTERHOOD TEMPLE EMANU-EL   DALLAS, TEXAS

1 medium onion
¾ cup sugar, or to taste
1 cup ketchup*
1 cup vinegar
1 teaspoon dry mustard
1 teaspoon salt
2 teaspoons Worcestershire
sauce
1 clove garlic (optional)
1 cup corn oil

Preparation time: 5 to 10 minutes
Makes about 1 quart

Food processor/blender

1. Place all ingredients except oil in food processor (metal blade) or blender and process until very smooth. Add corn oil with the machine running. Work in batches if necessary.

Conventional

Chop onion and mince garlic. Combine with wire whisk or mixer.

Note: This dressing keeps for months in refrigerator.

Quick Ideas

- To peel citrus fruits, soak whole fruit in hot water 5 or 10 minutes. White fibers and membrane will slip off.

- To ripen an avocado, place in a plastic or paper bag with flour to cover.

- Substitute lemon juice for vinegar in dressings for a fresher, livelier taste.

- Mince watercress stems and add to salads, soups, or omelets for a peppery flavor.

- Make sure salad ingredients are dry or dressing will dilute and run off.

- Toss greens with dressing just before serving.

- Do not cut lettuce — tear into bite-size pieces.

Sauces

Cucumber Dill Sauce

PORTAL TO GOOD COOKING   WOMEN'S AMERICAN ORT, DISTRICT VIII   CHICAGO, ILLINOIS

1 cup mayonnaise*
1 large cucumber,
  peeled and seeded
1 cup plain yogurt or sour
  cream
1 tablespoon minced dill
  weed or (1 tsp. dried)
½ teaspoon salt
½ teaspoon white pepper

Preparation time: 5 to 10 minutes
Makes about 2 cups

Food processor

1. Insert metal blade. Cut cucumber into chunks; add to work bowl and pulse several times to chop finely. Add remaining ingredients and process until almost smooth.

2. Refrigerate in a covered container for several hours. Serve with poached fish or use as a dressing.

Conventional

In step 1, chop cucumber and combine with other ingredients. Use blender for a smooth mixture.

● Store Tabasco sauce and other "red seasonings" such as paprika, chili powder, and red pepper in the refrigerator. They will keep their flavor and color much longer.

● Ground red pepper used to be called cayenne pepper.

● To locate spices easily, keep them in alphabetical order.

● Rub dried herbs between fingers to release flavor.

● To keep herbs fresh: rinse, shake off excess moisture, and place in a glass of water, root ends down, Place container in a plastic bag and store in the refrigerator. Will keep several weeks.

● When substituting dried herbs for fresh, use one-third the amount.

● When cooking chopped onions, make more than you need. Add sliced or chopped mushrooms, tomatoes, green peppers to the extra quantity and cook together. Freeze in portions. To use, thin to desired consistency with wine, tomato juice, stock, or water and season to taste. Use as a sauce on fish, meat, pasta, eggs, or rice.

BASIC SEASONING. Combine 1 part pepper to 5 or 6 parts salt. Store in a large shaker.

ITALIAN HERBS. Combine equal quantities dried oregano, basil, sage, marjoram, summer savory, and rosemary. Keep in an airtight container. Try to use within 3 months.

Texas Barbecue Sauce

MADE TO ORTER DAY, EVENING, JAMES RIVER CHAPTERS, WOMEN'S AMERICAN ORT RICHMOND, VA

1 cup tomato juice
½ cup water
¼ cup ketchup*
¼ cup vinegar
2 tablespoons
  Worcestershire sauce
2 tablespoons dark brown
  sugar
1 tablespoon paprika
1 teaspoon salt
1 teaspoon dry mustard
¼ teaspoon chili powder
⅛ teaspoon ground red
  pepper

Preparation time: 5 to 10 minutes
Cooking time: 15 to 20 minutes
Makes about 2 cups

1. Place all the ingredients in a large saucepan and bring to a boil. Simmer for 15 minutes or until thickened.

Hollandaise Sauce

IN THE BEGINNING ROCKDALE TEMPLE SISTERHOOD CINCINNATI, OHIO

6 large egg yolks
¼ cup lemon juice
½ teaspoon salt
Few grinds pepper
Pinch ground red pepper
2 sticks unsalted butter

Preparation time: 10 minutes
Makes about 1 ½ cups

Food processor

1. Insert metal blade. Place egg yolks, lemon juice, salt and both peppers in the work bowl and process for 5 seconds.

2. Heat butter until almost boiling; add slowly through the feed tube with machine running, so that all the butter is incorporated. Serve immediately.

Note: May be kept for an hour or so in a wide-mouth Thermos.

Tabasco Tartare Sauce

FROM GENERATION TO GENERATION B'NAI AMOONA SISTERHOOD ST. LOUIS, MISSOURI

1 cup mayonnaise*
½ teaspoon Tabasco sauce
1 teaspoon white wine
  vinegar
½ small onion
5 or 6 green olives
½ medium pickle

Preparation time: 5 minutes
Makes about 1 cup

Food processor/blender

1. Place all ingredients in a food processor (metal blade) or blender and pulse until finely chopped.

Conventional

Chop onion, olives, and pickle finely. Combine all ingredients.

Lamaze Sauce

OUR COOKBOOK BETH SHOLOM CONGREGATION ELKINS PARK, PENNSYLVANIA

1 cup mayonnaise*
1 cup chili sauce
¼ cup dill relish
1 hard-cooked egg, chopped
1 teaspoon snipped chives
½ tablespoon Dijon mustard
Dash Tabasco sauce
Salt and pepper to taste

Preparation time: 5 to 10 minutes
Makes about 2 cups

1. Combine all ingredients and chill several hours before serving. Serve with fish or as a salad dressing.

Ketchup

EDITOR'S CHOICE

1 medium onion
½ clove garlic
5 tablespoons frozen apple
  juice concentrate
1 can (6 oz.) tomato paste
½ cup malt or cider vinegar
½ teaspoon ground red
  pepper
¼ teaspoon cinnamon
⅛ teaspoon ground cloves

Preparation time: 5 minutes
Makes about 1 ½ cups

Food processor/blender

1. Purée onion (quartered), garlic, and apple juice. Add remaining ingredients and process until smooth. Store tightly covered in a jar in the refrigerator. Will keep several months.

Home Prepared Horseradish

LOVE, JEWISH STYLE TEMPLE SHAREY TEFILO/ISRAEL SOUTH ORANGE, NEW JERSEY

1 horseradish root
1 to 2 tablespoons white
  vinegar, or to taste
1 to 2 tablespoons sugar, or
  to taste

Preparation time: 10 to 15 minutes

1. Scrape or cut thick peel from horseradish root. Grate or chop very fine with a food processor or blender. Blend in vinegar and sugar to taste. Keep tightly covered.

Variation: Add finely chopped beets and beet juice to add color.

Fresh Tomato Sauce

SEASONED WITH LOVE SISTERHOOD OF WHITE MEADOW TEMPLE ROCKAWAY, NEW JERSEY

1 large onion
2 cloves garlic
½ cup parsley sprigs
½ cup olive oil
2 pounds ripe tomatoes
1½ teaspoons salt
½ teaspoon sugar
½ teaspoon pepper
1½ teaspoons chopped fresh
  oregano (½ tsp. dried)

Preparation time/processor: 10 to 15 minutes
Cooking time: 25 to 30 minutes
Makes about 1½ cups

Food processor

1. Insert metal blade and chop onion, garlic, and parsley. Sauté in olive oil until soft. Return to work bowl, add remaining ingredients, and process until smooth (you may have to work in batches).

2. Turn into a large saucepan and simmer for 25 to 30 minutes, stirring often. Cool. Strain if desired.

Quick Chinese Orange-Ginger Sauce

5000 YEARS IN THE KITCHEN SISTERHOOD TEMPLE EMANU-EL DALLAS, TEXAS

1 clove garlic
1-inch piece gingerroot
  (or ¾ tsp. ground)
⅓ cup orange marmalade
2 tablespoons sweet relish
1½ tablespoons vinegar
¼ teaspoon Dijon mustard
  (optional)
Salt and pepper to taste

Preparation time/processor: 5 minutes
Preparation time/conventional: 10 to 15 minutes
Makes ½ cup

Food processor

1. Insert metal blade. Drop garlic and gingerroot through feed tube with the machine running. Add remaining ingredients and pulse once or twice to combine; do not overprocess.

2. Adjust seasonings; may want to add more ginger. Use with Chinese dishes or as a meat glaze or sauce.

Conventional

Mince garlic and gingerroot. Combine all ingredients with a whisk.

Mushroom Cream Sauce

A TASTE OF TRADITION   TEMPLE ADATH ISRAEL SISTERHOOD   LEXINGTON, KENTUCKY

5 tablespoons margarine
¼ cup flour
3 cups warm milk, half and
   half, or stock
Salt and pepper to taste
Dash paprika
¼ to ½ pound mushrooms,
   sliced

Preparation time: 15 minutes
Serves 4 to 6

1. In a large saucepan, melt 3 tablespoons margarine. Add flour and stir with a wire whisk until smooth and blended, 2 to 3 minutes. Do not brown. Slowly whisk in the milk and cook, stirring constantly, until smooth and thick.

2. Sauté mushrooms in remaining 2 tablespoons margarine until lightly browned. Add to sauce and heat well. Serve with fish, egg dishes, and vegetables.

Sesame Butter Sauce

EDITOR'S CHOICE

3 tablespoons sesame seeds,
   toasted
6 tablespoons butter
Juice of ½ lemon
½ teaspoon Worcestershire
   sauce
¼ cup chopped parsley
2 drops Tabasco sauce

Preparation time: 5 minutes
Makes about ½ cup

Food processor/blender

1. Process all ingredients until smooth and well combined. Serve on fish or vegetables.

Mustard Applesauce

APPLES ALL WAYS   SANTA CRUZ CHAPTER OF HADASSAH   SANTA CRUZ, CALIFORNIA

2 cups applesauce
¼ cup Dijon mustard
1 tablespoon celery seed

Preparation time: 5 minutes
Makes 2 ¼ cups

1. Combine ingredients and chill. Serve with cold cuts or corned beef.

main dishes & side dishes

Meats

Tournedos Arlesienne

THE HAPPY COOKER   WOMEN'S COMMITTEE OF TEMPLE SINAI   ATLANTA, GEORGIA

1 large eggplant
1 egg, lightly beaten
Flour
6 slices French bread
 (1" thick), or 12 slices
 if small
2 cloves garlic
2 tablespoons oil
Olive oil
6 slices tomato, ½" thick
6 slices tender steak, 1 inch
 thick
French fried onion rings,
 heated
Salt and pepper to taste

Preparation time: 15 to 20 minutes
Cooking time: 10 to 15 minutes
Serves 6

1. Preheat oven to 200°.

2. Slice eggplant about ¾ inch thick, dip in beaten egg, then into flour; set aside. Lightly salt and pepper the tomatoes.

3. Rub bread with garlic on both sides. Heat oil and sauté bread until golden; drain on paper towels and keep warm in the oven. Add olive oil to pan and sauté the eggplant slices until browned; keep warm in oven. Sauté the tomato slices and keep warm.

4. Cook steaks to taste. Season well with salt and pepper.

5. To assemble, top each bread slice (or 2 small) with an eggplant slice, then a steak, then a tomato slice. Top with onion rings, and serve immediately.

Note: This may look complicated but is very fast to cook once you get organized.

• Make individual meat loaves — they take less time to cook. They can be baked in muffin tins or in a large shallow baking dish.

• Brush cut surface of a leftover roast or thick steak with drippings before refrigerating to keep meat from drying out.

• To soften cabbage leaves for stuffed cabbage, freeze entire head of cabbage overnight. Thaw before using.

• When broiling steaks, place a slice of bread in the pan. The bread soaks up fat and reduces the chance of a fat fire.

• Lightly oil hands when making meatballs to keep meat from sticking to your hands.

• You can tenderize any meat or poultry by marinating in vinaigrette dressing. It will also add flavor.

BASIC STIR-FRY. Combine 1 tablespoon each soy sauce, dry sherry, cornstarch, 1 teaspoon finely chopped gingerroot, and 1 clove minced garlic. Marinate 1 pound boneless meat or chicken (thinly sliced) or tofu (cut into cubes) for 15 minutes. Heat about 2 tablespoons peanut oil in a wok or skillet until very hot. Add meat and stir until it loses its red color. Remove. Add a little more oil to pan and stir-fry any or all of the following vegetables for about 2 minutes:

1 onion (sliced)
3 stalks celery (sliced on diagonal)
½ lb. broccoli flowerettes (blanched until crisp tender) or
½ lb. cauliflower (blanched)
½ to 1 lb. bean sprouts, bamboo shoots, or sliced water chestnuts

Return meat to pan. Add ¼ cup water mixed with 1 tablespoon soy sauce. Cook, stirring, until sauce is thick and glossy.

SLOW ROAST. Place any oven roast, fat side up, on a rack in a shallow pan. Insert a meat thermometer. Turn oven to 200°. Cooking time varies with the size of the roast, with the average being about 1 hour per pound. The slowness of the cooking allows maximum flexibility for serving time; the meat will not overcook if dinnertime is later than planned. Season to taste, if desired.

KNOCKWURST AND POTATO SALAD. Toss hot cooked potatoes with Kennedy Center Mustard Dressing (see recipe), ½ teaspoon celery seed, and 1 teaspoon sugar. Combine with hot cooked knockwurst slices.

BEEF AND ASPARAGUS SALAD. Slice leftover steak or roast beef; add lightly cooked asparagus and some chopped onion, bamboo shoots, or water chestnuts. Make Ginger Dressing by adding minced fresh gingerroot to your favorite garlicky vinaigrette. Marinate at least 15 minutes, sprinkle with sesame seeds, and serve.

STEAK AND NOODLES. Place cooked noodles in a metal serving dish and cover with a thin steak. Broil on both sides. Top with tomato sauce and broil for a few seconds until hot.

ROULADEN. Place a flavorful stuffing on thin slices of round, strip, or flank steak. Roll up and tie or skewer. (1) Brown on all sides and then simmer in equal quantities of red wine and beef stock flavored with herbs. Thicken gravy if desired. (2) Brush with oil and ½ teaspoon dried rosemary (or other seasonings). Broil until just done.

STUFFED HAMBURGERS. Make large, thin patties. Place ½ cup stuffing on half the patties and top with another patty. Secure with toothpicks and bake at 350° for about 35 to 40 minutes. Serve with favorite sauce.

LAMB SHANKS POLYNESIAN. Bake shanks at 400° for 1 hour. Top with pineapple juice and water (equal amounts, combined) and cover. Bake at 325° for 1 hour. Add a little curry powder to juices and thicken with cornstarch or by boiling down.

LAMB CHOPS DIABLO. Spread rib chops with Dijon mustard before broiling.

Beef and Asparagus

FROM GENERATION TO GENERATION B'NAI AMOONA SISTERHOOD ST. LOUIS, MISSOURI

¾ pound fresh asparagus
1½ pounds beef shoulder or
  chuck
1 clove garlic, minced
6 tablespoons oil (approx.)
3 tablespoons minced onion
2 teaspoons salt, or to taste
⅛ teaspoon pepper
1½ cups chicken stock or
  broth
½ pound mushrooms, sliced
2 tablespoons cornstarch
⅓ cup cold water

Preparation time: 20 minutes
Serves 4 to 6

Food processor

1. Peel asparagus and cut diagonally into 2-inch pieces. Insert slicing blade and slice partially frozen meat into strips 3" x 1" x ¼".

2. Heat 3 to 4 teaspoons oil in a wok or skillet. Add meat, garlic, and onion and cook, stirring constantly, until meat is brown. Add asparagus, salt, pepper, and chicken broth. Heat to boiling; lower heat, cover, and simmer 8 to 10 minutes or until asparagus is tender.

3. Sauté the mushrooms in 2 tablespoons oil.

4. Blend cornstarch with water and add to the beef mixture. Add mushrooms. Cook, stirring frequently, until thickened. Serve over hot rice.

Spareribs with Sauce

GARDEN OF EATING SISTERHOOD OF TEMPLE BETH O'R CLARK, NEW JERSEY

4 pounds beef short ribs
½ cup soy sauce
½ cup dry sherry
½ cup water
¼ cup brown sugar or honey
2 large cloves garlic, minced
½ cup chopped green pepper
½ cup chopped green onion
1 tablespoon lemon juice
1 teaspoon ground ginger
½ cup tomato sauce*
Dash Worcestershire sauce
Pinch minced tarragon

Preparation time: 5 to 10 minutes
Baking time: 1 hour
Serves 4 to 6

1. Preheat oven to 350°.

2. Place meat in a shallow pan. Combine other ingredients and add to pan. Cover with foil and bake for about 1 hour or until tender; turn once. Serve with sauce.

Glazed Corned Beef

SUPER CHEF BETH ISRAEL TEMPLE SISTERHOOD WARREN, OHIO

1 to 5 pounds corned beef
3 slices onion
1 bay leaf
1 stalk celery
1 clove garlic
½ teaspoon rosemary
8 whole cloves

Glaze
2 tablespoons oil
5 tablespoons ketchup*
1 tablespoon prepared
  mustard
3 tablespoons white vinegar
⅓ cup dark brown sugar

Preparation time: 10 minutes
Cooking/baking time: 4 to 4½ hours
Serves about 3 people per pound

1. In a large stock pot, place meat, onion, bay leaf, celery, garlic, and rosemary. Add enough water to cover by 2 inches. Bring to a boil and simmer until tender, about 3½ to 4 hours.

2. Preheat oven to 350°. Drain corned beef and place in a baking pan. Dot with whole cloves.

3. Bring the glaze ingredients to a boil and immediately pour over the beef. Bake for 35 to 40 minutes, basting occasionally, until brown.

Sweet and Sour Beef Chunks

FAVORITE RECIPES FROM OUR BEST COOKS TEMPLE BETH SHALOM SISTERHOOD DANVILLE, VIRGINIA

2 pounds lean stewing beef
1 tablespoon oil
1 large onion, chopped or
  sliced
1 large green pepper, cut
  into strips
2 cups thinly sliced carrots
  (optional)
2 cups tomato sauce*
½ cup vinegar
⅓ cup dark brown sugar (or
  ½ cup molasses)
2 teaspoons chili powder
1 teaspoon paprika
1 teaspoon salt

Preparation time/processor: 5 to 10 minutes
Preparation time/conventional: 10 to 15 minutes
Cooking time: 2½ hours
Serves 4 to 6

1. Preheat oven to 325°.

2. Cut beef into cubes and brown in oil; work in batches. Remove to an ovenproof baking dish. Add remaining ingredients and stir well. Cover and bake for about 2½ hours or until tender. Taste and adjust seasoning.

3. Thicken sauce, if desired, with a paste made of equal quantities of flour and margarine, or with cornstarch dissolved in cold water.

Oriental Beef Pot Roast

FROM CHARLESTON WITH LOVE   SYNAGOGUE EMANU-EL SISTERHOOD   CHARLESTON, SOUTH CAROLINA

3 to 4 pounds beef pot roast
8 cloves garlic
4 tablespoons vegetable oil
3 cups tomato sauce*
2 tablespoons white vinegar
½ teaspoon cinnamon
½ teaspoon allspice
1 teaspoon nutmeg

Preparation time: 10 to 15 minutes
Baking time: 1½ to 2 hours
Serves 4 to 6

1. Cut slits in the meat and insert garlic cloves. Heat oil in a large Dutch oven. Brown the meat on all sides. End with garlic side up.

2. Combine tomato sauce, vinegar, and spices; pour over meat. Cover and simmer for 1½ to 2 hours or until very tender. (Or bake for same time in a 325° oven). Check from time to time, adding a little more tomato sauce or water if necessary. Taste and adjust seasoning, adding salt and pepper if desired.

Beef Brisket with Horseradish Sauce

THE MJCC PRESENTS OUR FAVORITE RECIPES   JEWISH COMMUNITY CENTER   MEMPHIS, TENNESSEE

4 to 6 pounds beef brisket
2 medium onions, sliced
2 ribs of celery with tops
1 bay leaf
1 tablespoon salt, or to taste
½ teaspoon pepper

Sauce
1 medium onion, chopped
  fine
1 tablespoon oil
1 tablespoon flour
1 cup liquid from roast
½ cup prepared
  horseradish*
½ cup vinegar
⅓ cup dark brown sugar
2 cloves garlic, minced
1 bay leaf
½ teaspoon salt
⅛ teaspoon pepper

Preparation time: 20 minutes
Baking time: 3 to 4 hours
Serves 8 to 10

1. Preheat oven to 325°.

2. Place meat, onions, celery, bay leaf, salt and pepper in a roaster or large casserole. Add water to the top of the meat. Cover and bake until tender, about 3 or 4 hours.

3. To make the sauce: Sauté onion in oil; gradually add flour and liquid from meat. Mix well. Add remaining ingredients and heat to boiling. Reduce heat and simmer for 10 minutes.

4. Serve sliced roast with hot sauce.

Hungarian Goulash

3 medium onions, chopped
¼ cup oil
2 pounds beef cubes
1 tablespoon sweet paprika
1 medium green pepper,
  sliced
1 medium tomato, peeled
  and chopped
1 clove garlic, minced
1 tablespoon tomato paste
Salt and pepper to taste
1½ cups water

Preparation/food processor: 15 to 20 minutes
Cooking time: 2 hours
Serves 4 to 6

1. Sauté onions in oil until brown. Stir in meat and paprika. Cover skillet and simmer 10 minutes, stirring several times and adding water if necessary.

2. Add green pepper, tomato, and remaining ingredients. Cover and simmer on low heat until done, about 2 hours. Stir occasionally while cooking. Adjust seasoning. Serve with rice or noodles.

Italian Pot Roast

TO STIR WITH LOVE   SISTERHOOD AHAVATH ISRAEL   KINGSTON, NEW YORK

3 pounds beef brisket or
  other pot roast
2 tablespoons oil
2 medium onions, chopped
2 cloves garlic, chopped
1½ tablespoons chopped
  oregano (or 1½ tsp. dried)
1 tablespoon chopped thyme
  (or 1 tsp. dried)
1½ teaspoons chopped basil
  (or ½ tsp. dried)
½ teaspoon sugar
⅛ teaspoon cinnamon
1 teaspoon salt
¼ teaspoon pepper
2 cans (6 oz. each) tomato
  paste
3 cups water
Chopped chives

Preparation time/processor: 10 to 15 minutes
Preparation time/conventional: 15 to 20 minutes
Cooking time: 2 to 3 hours
Serves 5 to 6

1. Brown meat slowly on all sides in hot oil. Remove meat and lower heat. Add onion, garlic, and seasonings to pan. Cook about 5 minutes, being careful not to burn.

2. Return meat to pan. Combine tomato paste and water and pour over meat. Bring to boil, lower heat, and simmer until tender, about 2 to 3 hours.

3. Slice roast and serve on a platter with thin noodles. Cover with sauce and sprinkle with chives.

London Broil I

QUICK QUISINE   GREATER RED BANK SECTION NCJW   RED BANK, NEW JERSEY

1 London Broil
2 tablespoons sugar
2 tablespoons dry sherry
2 tablespoons soy sauce
½ teaspoon cinnamon

Preparation time: 5 minutes
Marinating time: 1½ hours
Cooking time: 10 to 15 minutes
Serves 3 or 4

1. Place meat in a shallow dish. Combine remaining ingredients and pour over meat. Marinate in the refrigerator for at least 1½ hours, turning occasionally.

2. Broil or grill the steak as desired. Warm any leftover marinade and pan juices and pour over sliced steak.

London Broil II

COOK'S DELIGHT   CONGREGATION OHEV SHALOM   ORLANDO, FLORIDA

1½ pounds London Broil
1 clove garlic, minced
½ cup vinegar
½ cup vegetable oil
½ teaspoon pepper
3 tablespoons brown sugar
3 tablespoons soy sauce
2 medium onions, sliced thin

Preparation time/processor: 20 minutes
Preparation time/conventional: 20 to 25 minutes
Marinating time: 8 hours
Cooking time: 12 to 15 minutes
Serves 4

1. Place steak in shallow dish. Combine remaining ingredients (except onions). Pour over steak, cover, and refrigerate at least 8 hours or overnight, turning occasionally. Drain off marinade and reserve.

2. Grill 2 inches from prepared coals (or under broiler) until done: for medium rare, cook 6 minutes on each side, then another minute or two on each side.

3. Cook onions in the marinade, and serve with the steak.

Picadillo

FAVORITE RECIPES FROM OUR BEST COOKS TEMPLE BETH SHOLOM SISTERHOOD DANVILLE, VIRGINIA

1½ lbs. lean ground beef
2 large onions, thinly sliced
2 stalks celery, thinly sliced
¼ cup thinly sliced green
  olives
¼ cup olive juice (from jar)
¼ cup dry sherry
3 tablespoons lime juice
1½ cups tomato juice
¼ cup golden raisins
2 cloves garlic, minced
1 teaspoon ground cumin
Salt and pepper to taste

Preparation time/processor: 10 to 15 minutes
Preparation time/conventional: 20 minutes
Cooking time: 20 to 30 minutes
Serves 6

1. Brown ground meat in a large skillet. Drain and discard fat. Add all remaining ingredients and simmer, uncovered, stirring from time to time until most of the liquid has been absorbed, 20 to 30 minutes.

2. Serve with yellow rice and a green salad.

Unstuffed Cabbage

COOK'S DELIGHT SISTERHOOD OF CONGREGATION OHEV SHALOM ORLANDO, FLORIDA

2 pounds sauerkraut
1 can (25 oz.) tomato purée
½ cup dark brown sugar
2 cups beef broth or bouillon
½ to ¾ cup raisins
Salt and pepper to taste
2½ pounds ground beef
½ cup raw rice
Onion slices (optional)
Caraway seeds (optional)

Preparation time: 15 minutes
Cooking time: 1½ hours
Serves 6 to 8

1. Drain sauerkraut (rinse if very sour) and combine with tomato purée, brown sugar, broth, raisins, salt and pepper in a large pot. Mix well and bring to a simmer over moderate heat.

2. Combine beef, rice, salt and pepper in a mixing bowl. Form into meatballs (about the size of golf balls) and add to the sauce. Cover; simmer gently, stirring occasionally, for about 1½ hours.

3. Add sliced onion and caraway seeds to the sauce, if desired.

Mexican Noodles

THE MJCC PRESENTS OUR FAVORITE RECIPES   MEMPHIS JEWISH COMMUNITY CENTER   MEMPHIS, TN

1 pound broad noodles
1 large green pepper
1 large onion
1 garlic clove
1 pound ground beef
1 can (16 oz.) whole kernel corn, drained
2 cans (6 oz. each) tomato paste
1 can (6 oz.) sliced ripe olives (with liquid)
1 tablespoon chili powder
Dash ground red pepper
Dash Tabasco sauce
Salt and pepper to taste

Preparation time: 20 minutes
Baking time: 30 minutes
Serves 4 to 6

1. Preheat oven to 350°.

2. Cook noodles according to package instructions.

3. While noodles are cooking, chop green pepper and onion, mince garlic, and sauté together in a little oil. Remove. Brown ground beef in same skillet. Remove excess fat and return vegetables to skillet. Add all other ingredients, including noodles. Place in a 3-quart baking dish.

4. Bake for about 30 minutes or until hot.

Note: You can cook the beef and vegetables in a microwave while the noodles are cooking. This dish keeps well and reheats well.

Texas Chili

EAT, DARLING — AND ENJOY!   BETH ISRAEL SISTERHOOD   FLINT, MICHIGAN

Oil
2 pounds coarsely ground beef
3 large onions, chopped
3 large cloves garlic, minced
1 pound tomatoes (or 1½ c. canned)
5 tablespoons chili powder, or to taste
1 can (16 oz.) kidney beans (optional)
1 cup hot water
2 tablespoons chopped oregano (or 2 tsp. dried)
2 teaspoons ground cumin
1 teaspoon sugar
2 to 6 dashes Tabasco sauce
Salt to taste

Preparation time/processor: 15 minutes
Preparation time/conventional: 15 to 20 minutes
Cooking time: 1 hour
Serves 8

1. Heat oil in heavy skillet. Add meat, onions, and garlic. Cook until browned, adding oil as necessary.

2. Peel, seed, and chop tomatoes. Add with remaining ingredients and bring to a boil. Lower heat and simmer 1 hour.

Meat Balls in Apple Barley Ring
UNDER THE CHEF'S H.A.T.   HEBREW ACADEMY OF TOLEDO   TOLEDO, OHIO

2 cups apple juice
2 tablespoons cornstarch
¼ cup chopped green pepper
1 pound ground beef
¼ pound ground veal
1 cup quick or old-fashioned
  oats (uncooked)
¼ cup finely chopped onion
1 egg, beaten
1½ teaspoons salt
¼ teaspoon pepper
¾ teaspoon chopped oregano
  (or ¼ tsp. dried)
½ cup water

Preparation time/processor: 15 to 20 minutes
Preparation time/conventional: 20 to 25 minutes
Cooking time: 25 to 30 minutes
Serves 6 to 8

1. Combine apple juice, cornstarch, and green pepper in a heavy saucepan.

2. Combine remaining ingredients and shape into 24 balls. Place in saucepan with apple juice mixture. Cover and simmer for 25 to 30 minutes.

3. Serve with Apple Barley Ring.

Note: Meat balls may be browned in hot oil before adding to sauce.

Apple Barley Ring

3 cups water
3 cups apple juice
1½ teaspoons salt
¼ teaspoon nutmeg
2 cups quick barley
2 red apples (unpeeled)
Lemon juice
6 tablespoons margarine
  (parve)

Preparation time: 20 minutes
Serves 6 to 8

1. Combine water, apple juice, salt, and nutmeg in a 3-quart saucepan. Bring to a boil and stir in the barley. Cover and simmer for 10 to 12 minutes, stirring occasionally.

2. Cut each apple in 8 wedges and dip in a little lemon juice. Sauté the apple wedges in 2 tablespoons margarine. Cover and cook over low heat until tender (or cook in microwave). Line the bottom of an ungreased 6-cup ring mold with the apple wedges, skin side down.

3. Drain barley and stir in the remaining ½ stick of margarine. Pack into ring mold. Let stand 5 minutes, then invert onto serving platter to unmold. Fill center with meat balls and sauce. Serve extra sauce in a bowl.

Applesauce Meatloaf

MRS. COOPER'S ENCORE   B'NAI JACOB SYNAGOGUE AUXILIARY   CHARLESTON, WEST VIRGINIA

3 slices good-textured bread
1 small onion
1 stalk celery
1 pound ground beef
½ cup applesauce
1 egg
1 teaspoon Dijon mustard
½ teaspoon salt
Dash pepper

Topping
½ cup applesauce
1 tablespoon brown sugar
1½ teaspoons vinegar
½ teaspoon Dijon mustard

Preparation time/processor: 10 to 15 minutes
Preparation time/conventional: 20 minutes
Baking time: 1 hour
Serves 4 to 5

Food processor

1. Preheat oven to 350°.

2. Insert metal blade. Make bread crumbs and remove to a large mixing bowl. Add the onion and celery (cut up) to the work bowl and pulse to chop; remove and add to the bread crumbs. Add remaining ingredients and mix well.

3. Form into a round loaf and place in a shallow 8 x 8 baking dish.

4. Combine topping ingredients. Make a crater-like depression in the top of the meatloaf and pour in the topping mixture. Bake for 1 hour.

Beef and Eggplant Casserole

LOVE, JEWISH STYLE   TEMPLE SHAREY TEFILO/ISRAEL   SOUTH ORANGE, NEW JERSEY

1 large eggplant
2 pounds ground beef
1 large onion, chopped
1 large green pepper, chopped
1 or 2 cloves garlic, minced
½ teaspoon salt
Freshly ground black pepper
½ teaspoon oregano or Italian herbs*
1 cup tomato sauce* or juice

Preparation time/processor: 5 to 10 minutes
Preparation time/conventional: 10 to 15 minutes
Baking time: 45 minutes
Serves 4 to 6

1. Preheat oven to 350°.

2. Peel eggplant if desired; dice.

3. In a large skillet, brown the ground beef and onion until the beef loses its pink color. Combine with remaining ingredients and place in a 9 x 13 baking dish. Bake uncovered for about 45 minutes. Serve with rice or noodles or crisp French bread.

Layered Meat Loaf

QUICK AND EASY COOKBOOK   MAIN LINE REFORM TEMPLE SISTERHOOD   WYNNEWOOD, PENNSYLVANIA

1½ pounds ground beef
1 egg
½ cup seasoned bread
  crumbs*
½ cup tomato juice
Tomato sauce, optional*

Dressing
1 cup soft bread crumbs*
3 cups cornflakes
½ cup chopped celery
1 egg
1 tablespoon minced onion
1 tablespoon minced parsley
1 tablespoon oil
3 tablespoons water
1 teaspoon salt
⅛ teaspoon pepper

Preparation time/processor: 10 to 15 minutes
Preparation time/conventional: 15 to 20 minutes
Baking time: 50 to 60 minutes
Serves 6

1. Preheat oven to 350°.

2. Combine beef, egg, bread crumbs, and to-mato juice and set aside. Combine all dressing ingredients.

3. In a 9 x 5 x 3 loaf pan, layer half the meat, all the dressing, then the remaining meat. Bake for 50 to 60 minutes. Serve with tomato sauce if desired.

Hamburger Corn Casserole

FROM CHARLESTON, WITH LOVE   SYNAGOGUE EMANU-EL SISTERHOOD   CHARLESTON, SOUTH CAROLINA

4 tablespoons oil
¾ cup chopped onion
2 green peppers, sliced
2 cloves garlic
1 pound ground beef
1½ teaspoons salt
½ teaspoon pepper
2 eggs, beaten
2 cups cooked corn
2 large tomatoes, sliced
½ cup dry bread crumbs*
Margarine

Preparation time/processor: 10 to 15 minutes
Preparation time/conventional: 15 to 20 minutes
Cooking time: 35 minutes
Serves 6

1. Preheat oven to 375°.

2. Sauté onion and green peppers in oil. Add ground meat, salt and pepper and cook until meat is lightly browned. Remove from heat and allow to cool for several minutes. Stir in the beaten eggs.

3. Place 1 cup corn in a 1¾ to 2-quart casserole. Add half the meat mixture and a layer of tomato slices. Repeat for the second layer. Top with bread crumbs and dot with margarine. Bake for 35 minutes.

Gingered Beef and Broccoli

EDITOR'S CHOICE

1 pound beef
1 tablespoon cornstarch
1 tablespoon sherry
1 tablespoon soy sauce
1½ teaspoons minced
  gingerroot (or ½ tsp.
  gound)
1 clove garlic, minced
½ pound broccoli
  flowerettes
2 tablespoons peanut oil
¼ cup water mixed with
  1 tablespoon soy sauce

Preparation time/processor: 10 minutes
Preparation time/conventional: 20 minutes
Marinating time: 15 minutes
Serves 6

Conventional

1. Slice beef very thin.

2. Combine cornstarch, sherry, soy sauce, ginger, and garlic and stir well. Add beef and marinate for 15 minutes.

3. In a wok or large skillet, heat 1 tablespoon oil; stir-fry the broccoli for 5 minutes or until crisp-tender. Remove with a slotted spoon.

4. Heat the remaining oil in the wok and stir-fry the beef until the beef loses its red color. Stir in the broccoli and the water-soy sauce. Cook until sauce is glossy and thick.

Food processor

Place cornstarch, sherry, soy sauce, gingerroot, and garlic in work bowl with metal blade inserted and process until gingerroot is finely chopped. Change to slicing blade and slice partially frozen meat. Toss with marinade and allow to stand in work bowl for 15 minutes. Proceed to step 3.

Esau's Pottage (Sukkoth Dish)

UNDER THE CHEF'S H.A.T.   HEBREW ACADEMY OF TOLEDO   TOLEDO, OHIO

3 medium onions, sliced
Oil
1 pound ground lamb
1 large green pepper, sliced
4 carrots, sliced
2 stalks celery, sliced
2 parsnips, sliced
3 cups chopped tomatoes
1 quart water
1 pound lentils, rinsed
2 teaspoons salt, or to taste
½ teaspoon pepper

Preparation time/processor: 20 minutes
Preparation time/conventional: 20 to 25 minutes
Cooking time: 1 ½ hours
Serves 4 to 6

1. Sauté onions in oil in a large saucepan. Add lamb and brown, stirring to crumble the meat. Stir in remaining ingredients. Cover and simmer over low heat for about 1½ hours.

Note: quantities of vegetables can be varied and need not be exact.

Orange Lamb Chops

EDITOR'S CHOICE

6 shoulder lamb chops, ¾"
   thick
½ teaspoon grated orange
   peel*
¼ cup orange juice
1 tablespoon chopped thyme
   (or 1 tsp. dried)
1 tablespoon oil
¼ to ½ pound mushrooms,
   sliced
2 tablespoons orange
   marmalade
2 tablespoons cornstarch
¼ cup cold water
Salt and pepper to taste

Preparation time: 5 to 10 minutes
Marinating time: 3 hours
Cooking time: 40 minutes
Serves 6

1. Combine orange peel, orange juice, and thyme in a shallow dish and marinate chops for at least 3 hours. Drain and pat dry; reserve marinade.

2. Sauté chops in oil. Add mushrooms, marinade, and marmalade. Cover and simmer for about 40 minutes or until chops are tender. Dissolve cornstarch in water and add. Add salt and pepper. Simmer uncovered until sauce is thick and glossy.

Note: Extra orange peel or marmalade may be added as desired.

Curried Lamb Steaks

COOK UNTO OTHERS   HILLEL JEWISH STUDENT CENTER, UNIV. OF CINCINNATI   CINCINNATI, OHIO

2½ pounds lean ground lamb
¾ cup pine nuts
2 teaspoons curry powder
¼ teaspoon ground
  coriander
1 teaspoon Hungarian sweet
  paprika
1 tablespoon kosher salt, or
  to taste
¾ cup chicken stock or
  broth, chilled
Mango chutney

Preparation time: 20 minutes
Chilling time: 2 hours
Serves 4 to 6

1. Combine all ingredients (except chutney); do not overmix or mixture will become pasty. Divide into 8 equal portions and form each into an oval patty. Cover and chill at least 2 hours.

2. Grill or broil to desired doneness (about 5 minutes per side for medium rare). Patties can also be sautéed.

3. Serve with chutney and accompany with wild rice and a green salad.

Variation: Ground beef can be substituted for the lamb.

Lamb Shanks Sangria

TRADITION IN THE KITCHEN   NORTH SUBURBAN SYNAGOGUE, BETH EL SISTERHOOD   HIGHLAND PARK, ILLINOIS

6 lamb shanks
1 lemon, sliced
1 orange, sliced
¾ cup red wine
½ cup orange juice
1 large clove garlic, minced
½ teaspoon salt, or to taste
⅛ teaspoon pepper, or to
  taste
Minced parsley

Preparation time: 5 to 10 minutes
Baking time: 1 hour 45 minutes
Serves 6

1. Preheat oven to 325°.

2. Arrange lamb shanks in a shallow baking dish. Cover with sliced lemon and orange. Bake for 45 minutes.

3. Combine remaining ingredients, except parsley, and pour over the shanks. Cover and bake for about 60 minutes or until tender. Sprinkle with parsley before serving. Serve with rice.

Veal Marsala

1 pound veal, very thinly
  sliced (4 escalopes)
2 to 3 tablespoons flour
3 tablespoons chopped
  oregano (or 1 Tbsp. dried)
Dash salt
Dash pepper
Oil
½ pound mushrooms, sliced
⅓ to ½ cup Marsala wine

Preparation time/processor: 20 minutes
Preparation time/conventional: 20 to 25 minutes
Serves 4

1. Dredge the veal in mixture of flour, oregano, salt and pepper. Heat a little oil in a large skillet and sauté the veal until lightly browned. Add mushrooms and wine. Cover and cook for 5 to 10 minutes until tender.

Variation: Boneless chicken breasts, pounded thin, may be substituted for the veal.

Spanish Veal Stew

THE KOSHER KITCHEN SISTERHOOD OF TEMPLE SHAAREY ZEDEK AMHERST, NEW YORK

2 pounds boneless veal
¾ pound small white onions
  (or 16 oz. jar)
¼ cup flour
1 teaspoon salt
4 tablespoons oil
1 cup tomato sauce*
½ cup dry sherry
2 teaspoons chopped parsley
1½ teaspoons chopped
  thyme (or ½ tsp. dried)
2 cloves garlic, minced
½ pound mushrooms, sliced
1 jar (3 oz.) stuffed green
  olives, drained

Preparation time: 20 minutes
Pre-preparation: cook onions
Cooking time: 1 hour 15 minutes
Serves 4 to 6

1. Cut veal into 1-inch cubes. Cook fresh onions; drain (or drain jar) and reserve liquid.

2. Combine salt and flour on a plate. Dredge veal cubes, reserving any leftover flour. Brown meat in oil. Pour off drippings.

3. Add ½ cup onion liquid, tomato sauce, sherry, parsley, thyme, and garlic to the veal. Mix well. Cover pot tightly and simmer over low heat for 1 hour or until meat is tender. (If thicker sauce is desired dissolve remaining flour in onion liquid or water and stir into mixture.)

4. Add onions, mushrooms, and olives. Cook 15 minutes longer. Taste and adjust seasoning.

Turk's Turban Squash Stuffed with Veal and Red Peppers

ALL THIS AND KOSHER, TOO   BETH DAVID SISTERHOOD   MIAMI, FLORIDA

1 Turk's turban squash
1 pound mushrooms, sliced
¼ cup minced green onion
1 tablespoon oil
1 pound red (or green)
 peppers, sliced
1½ pounds ground veal
½ teaspoon paprika
1 tablespoon chopped
 marjoram (or 1 tsp. dried)
1 tablespoon chopped
 parsley
1 teaspoon salt
¾ teaspoon pepper
½ cup or more dry bread
 crumbs*

Preparation time/processor: 15 to 20 minutes
Pre-preparation: bake squash
Serves 6 to 8

1. Pierce squash in several places under turban. Loosely drape with plastic wrap and place on a glass pie plate. Bake in a microwave for about 15 minutes, turning from time to time. (In a conventional oven, cook uncovered at 350° for about 1 hour).

2. Sauté mushrooms and green onion in oil in a very large skillet over medium heat until lightly browned. Add peppers and cook until soft, 2 to 3 minutes. Transfer mixture to a large bowl.

3. Sauté meat in same skillet, adding a little more oil if necessary. Stir to crumble the meat. Add the cooked meat to the vegetables with the remaining ingredients. Add enough bread crumbs to keep the mixture together. Keep warm.

4. When the squash is soft to the touch, cut across just under the turban. Clean out all the seeds and stringy matter. Fill the cavity with the meat and vegetable mixture and top with the turban.

5. Serve on a warm platter, scooping out some meat and a little squash with each serving. This may be kept warm in a 300° oven until serving time.

Variation: Use 1½ pounds of mushrooms and 1 pound of veal. (If you have too much filling, serve in a bowl or casserole.)

Baked Veal Chops (Lo-Cal)

EAT, DARLING — AND ENJOY! BETH ISRAEL SISTERHOOD FLINT, MICHIGAN

6 veal chops, ½" thick
1 lemon, sliced
2 medium zucchini, sliced
Salt and pepper to taste
½ pound fresh mushrooms,
  sliced
1 large onion, sliced or
  chopped
1 large green pepper, sliced
1 tablespoon oil (optional)
1½ teaspoons chopped
  oregano or basil (or ½ tsp.
  dried)
1 clove garlic, minced
  (optional)
1 pound tomatoes (or 16 oz.
  can), peeled, seeded, and
  chopped
½ cup dry white wine
  (optional)

Preparation time/processor: 10 minutes
Preparation time/conventional: 20 + minutes
Baking time: 1 hour
Serves 6

1. Preheat oven to 350°.

2. Place chops in a large baking dish. Place lemon and zucchini slices over the chops. Sprinkle with salt and pepper.

3. Sauté mushrooms, onion, and green pepper in oil or in a non-stick frying pan. Arrange over the chops; sprinkle with oregano and garlic. Add tomatoes evenly over the chops. Bake for 1 hour.

4. Serve with wild or brown rice.

Variation: You can change the herbs to your liking.

Poultry

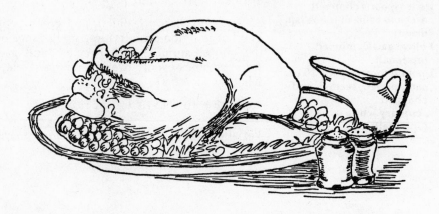

Chicken and Artichokes

HAPPY COOKER   WOMEN'S COMMITTEE OF TEMPLE SINAI   ATLANTA, GEORGIA

3 pounds chicken parts
1½ teaspoons salt
½ teaspoon paprika
¼ teaspoon pepper
4 tablespoons oil
1 can (14 oz.) artichoke
  hearts
¼ pound mushrooms
2 tablespoons flour
¾ cup beef stock*
3 tablespoons dry sherry

Preparation time: 15 to 20 minutes
Baking time: 45 to 55 minutes
Serves 4

1. Preheat oven to 375°.

2. Season chicken with salt, paprika, and pepper. Brown in oil. Arrange chicken and artichoke hearts in a 9 x 13 baking dish.

3. Cut mushrooms into quarters and sauté in remaining oil. Sprinkle with flour. Stir in stock and sherry. Simmer, stirring, for 5 minutes. Pour over chicken.

4. Cover and bake for 45 to 55 minutes. Transfer to a serving platter.

Chicken Mole

JEWISH-AMERICAN FAVORITES   SISTERHOOD OF SONS OF JACOB SYNAGOGUE   WATERLOO, IOWA

2 large onions, chopped
1 green pepper, chopped
3 cloves garlic, minced
2½ to 3 pounds chicken
  parts
1 tablespoon unsweetened
  cocoa powder
2½ cups tomato juice
2 tablespoons chili powder
¼ teaspoon ground
  coriander
⅛ teaspoon ground cloves
⅛ teaspoon cinnamon
⅓ cup chopped or slivered
  blanched almonds
1 tablespoon sesame seeds
  (optional)
2 tablespoons raisins
  (optional)
Salt and pepper to taste

Preparation time/processor: 5 to 10 minutes
Preparation time/conventional: 10 to 15 minutes
Baking time: 1¼ hours
Serves 4 to 6

1. Preheat oven to 350°.

2. Place onions, green pepper, and garlic in the bottom of a 9 x 13 baking dish. Arrange chicken on top.

3. Combine remaining ingredients and pour over chicken. Season with salt and pepper and bake for 1¼ hours, basting several times.

Cinnamon Curry Chicken

QUICK QUISINE   GREATER RED BANK SECTION NCJW   RED BANK, NEW JERSEY

½ cup dry sherry
2 teaspoons cinnamon
⅓ cup honey
2 tablespoons lemon juice
½ teaspoon curry powder
1 teaspoon minced garlic
1 teaspoon salt
3½ to 4 pounds chicken
  parts

Preparation time: 5 to 10 minutes
Marinating time: 8 hours
Baking time: 1 hour
Serves 6 to 8

1. Combine all ingredients (except chicken) and stir well. Pour over chicken in a shallow baking dish and marinate in the refrigerator for at least 8 hours or overnight.

2. Bake at 375° for 1 hour, basting from time to time.

Quick Ideas

● Roll skinned chicken in lots of minced garlic (3-6 cloves), roll in crumbs, drizzle with margarine or olive oil. Bake at 350° oven for 1 hour.

● Marinate chicken parts in oil. Sprinkle with garlic, grated orange rind, salt and pepper. Drizzle with ¼ cup honey if desired. Bake at 350° oven for 1 hour. Baste.

● Roll chicken parts in melted margarine and Dijon mustard (combine equal quantities). Pat fresh bread crumbs firmly into place. Bake at 350° for 1 hour. Baste.

● Pound boned chicken breasts flat. Sauté in hot oil until just tender. Remove. Add ¼ to ½ cup lemon juice to pan and deglaze. Return chicken to pan and sprinkle with parsley.

BAKED SWEET & SOUR CHICKEN. Place onion slices on bottom of baking pan. Cover with chicken pieces. Salt if desired. Cover with sauce. Cover and bake at 350° for 1½ hours, then uncover and bake for 45 minutes to 1 hour. (Sauce: Measure ⅓ cup ketchup in a glass measuring cup and add water to make ½ cup. Add a heaping tablespoon brown sugar and the juice of a large lemon. Mix well.)

BAKED CHICKEN. Sprinkle a 3 to 4 pound chicken with seasoned salt (inside and out). Wrap in foil and place on a rack in a shallow pan. Bake in a preheated 450° oven for 40 to 55 minutes, then unwrap and bake for about 20 minutes to brown.

DEVILED TURKEY. Dip slices of cooked turkey breast in a mixture of Dijon mustard, melted margarine, and a dash of ground red pepper. Pat with lots of fine dry bread crumbs. Broil until brown on both sides.

ROSEMARY'S CHICKEN. Place 4 chicken breasts rib side down in a baking dish. Add ½ inch of water. Brush with oil and sprinkle each piece with 1 teaspoon rosemary. Add salt and pepper to taste. Cover and bake at 350° for 1 hour. Serves 4.

Sherry-Orange Chicken

ONE MORE BITE THE SISTERHOOD OF TEMPLE BETH ISRAEL SAN DIEGO, CALIFORNIA

4 to 5 pounds chicken parts
½ cup flour
Salt and pepper to taste
4 tablespoons oil
1 medium onion, sliced
1 medium green pepper,
  sliced
1 tablespoon flour
½ cup orange marmalade
1 cup orange juice
¼ cup dry sherry
1 teaspoon salt
Pepper to taste
1 tablespoon grated orange
  peel (optional)*
Paprika, orange slices,
  parsley sprigs

*Preparation time/processor: 5 to 10 minutes
Preparation time/conventional: 10 to 15 minutes
Baking time: 1 hour
Serves 6*

1. Preheat oven to 350°.

2. Place flour seasoned with salt and pepper in a plastic bag; add chicken pieces and shake to coat. Arrange chicken, skin side up, on a shallow baking sheet (jelly roll pan).

3. Sauté onion and green pepper in oil for about 5 minutes. Add the flour and cook, stirring, for several seconds. Add orange juice, marmalade, sherry, and seasonings and stir well. Bring mixture to a boil and pour over chicken. Cook for 1 hour or until done, basting frequently.

4. To serve, sprinkle with paprika and garnish with orange slices and parsley sprigs.

Chicken Cashew

KOSHER GOURMET II   SISTERHOOD OF TEMPLE BETH-EL   NORTH BELLMORE, NEW YORK

1 pound boneless chicken
   breast
2 tablespoons dry sherry
2 tablespoons cornstarch
¼ pound mushrooms
1 medium onion
1 large clove garlic
1 piece gingerroot, 1" x 1"
   (or ¼ tsp. ground)
2 tablespoons water
2 tablespoons dry sherry
2 tablespoons soy sauce
1 teaspoon sugar
½ cup chicken bouillon or
   stock
1 teaspoon sesame oil
2 tablespoons vegetable oil
½ cup toasted, salted
   cashews
½ pound fresh snow peas or
   green peas

Preparation time: 15 to 20 minutes
Marinating time: 15 minutes
Serves 2 to 4

Food processor

1. Remove skin from chicken and cut into 1-inch cubes. Toss with sherry and cornstarch, and marinate for 15 to 30 minutes.

2. Insert slicing blade and slice mushrooms. Insert metal blade; drop onion (quartered), garlic, and gingerroot through the feed tube with the machine running. Scrape down sides of bowl and add water, dry sherry, soy sauce, sugar, and bouillon.

3. Heat the oils in a wok or large skillet. Stir-fry the chicken until the pink color disappears. Add the ginger-garlic sauce and bring to a boil, stirring constantly. Add cashews, mushrooms, and peas and lower heat. Simmer for 3 minutes. Do not overcook. Serve with rice.

Conventional

In step 2, slice mushrooms, mince garlic, and chop onion and gingerroot. Add other ingredients as indicated, and proceed with recipe.

Creole Oven Fried Chicken and Rice

JEWISH-AMERICAN FAVORITES   SISTERHOOD OF SONS OF JACOB SYNAGOGUE   WATERLOO, IOWA

½ cup flour
1½ teaspoons salt
¼ teaspoon poultry
  seasoning
⅛ teaspoon pepper
2½ to 3 pounds chicken
  parts
¼ cup oil
1 cup raw rice
½ cup chopped onion
1 cup chopped or sliced
  celery
¼ cup chopped green pepper
1 clove garlic, minced
2 tablespoons minced
  parsley (optional)
2½ cups chicken broth or
  stock
2 cups chopped, peeled
  tomatoes (or 16-oz. can)
Salt and pepper to taste

Preparation time/processor: 20 minutes
Preparation time/conventional: 20 to 30 minutes
Baking time: 40 to 45 minutes
Serves 4 to 6

1. Preheat oven to 400°.

2. Place flour and seasonings in a plastic bag and add chicken pieces, a few at a time. Shake well to coat.

3. Heat oil and brown the chicken on all sides.

4. Meanwhile, prepare the vegetables. Combine the rice, onion, celery, green pepper, garlic, and parsley in a 9 x 13 baking dish. Place chicken over mixture in a single layer. Pour stock and tomatoes over the chicken and season with salt and pepper. Bake 40 to 45 minutes.

5. Check after about 30 minutes and add more stock as necessary.

Baked Chicken and Cashew Stuffing

FLAVORED WITH LOVE   ADAT ARI EL SISTERHOOD   NORTH HOLLYWOOD, CALIFORNIA

14 slices thin white bread
¾ cup salted cashews,
  chopped
¾ cup chopped or sliced
  celery
½ cup chopped onion
  (optional)
¾ cup chicken stock or water
1 stick margarine (parve),
  melted
½ teaspoon poultry
  seasoning
4 chicken leg/thighs or
  wing/breasts
1 teaspoon salt
1 teaspoon pepper
Paprika

Preparation time/processor: 5 to 10 minutes
Preparation time/conventional: 10 to 15 minutes
Cooking time: 1½ hours
Serves 4

1. Preheat oven to 325°.

2. Toast bread and cut into cubes.

3. Combine bread cubes, nuts, celery, onion, stock, ¼ cup margarine, and poultry seasoning and place in a shallow 9 x 13 baking dish. Place the chicken pieces on top and sprinkle with salt, pepper, and paprika. Brush with the remaining melted margarine and bake for 1½ hours or until tender, brushing with margarine from time to time.

Almond Chicken

FIDDLER IN THE KITCHEN NATIONAL COUNCIL OF JEWISH WOMEN, GREATER DETROIT SECTION DETROIT, MI

1½ pounds boneless chicken breasts
1½ to 2 teaspoons minced gingerroot (or 1 tsp. ground)
1 tablespoon cornstarch
2 teaspoons sugar
3 tablespoons water
3 tablespoons soy sauce
3 tablespoons dry sherry
¼ cup peanut or vegetable oil
1 cup sliced blanched or slivered almonds
¾ pound snow peas (or 12 oz. frozen)

Preparation time/processor: 15 minutes
Preparation time/conventional: 20 minutes
Cooking time: 10 to 12 minutes
Serves 4

Conventional

1. Skin chicken and cut into ½-inch cubes.

2. Mix ginger, cornstarch, sugar, water, soy sauce, and dry sherry in a bowl.

3. Heat oil in a wok or large skillet. Add almonds; cook and stir for 3 minutes. Add chicken and cook only until meat turns white. Pour in cornstarch mixture. Cook until sauce thickens and turns glossy. Add snow peas (thawed and drained, if frozen) and cook until hot and glazed. Serve with rice.

Food processor

Drop gingerroot through feed tube with machine running (metal blade). Remove. Arrange partially frozen chicken breasts upright in feed tube and slice using the slicing blade. Proceed to step 2.

Chicken Teriyaki

EAT, DARLING — AND ENJOY! BETH ISRAEL SISTERHOOD FLINT, MICHIGAN

2½ to 3 pounds chicken
    parts
6 to 8 green onions, chopped
2 garlic cloves, minced
1" piece gingerroot, chopped
    (or 2 tsp. ground)
3 tablespoons white wine
¾ cup soy sauce
½ cup water
⅓ cup sugar

Preparation time/processor: 5 minutes
Preparation time/conventional: 5 to 15 minutes
Marinating time: 3 hours
Baking time: 1 hour
Serves 4

1. Place chicken in a large flat dish. Combine remaining ingredients and pour over chicken. Marinate at least 3 hours, or overnight if possible.

2. Preheat oven to 350°.

3. Transfer chicken and marinade to an ungreased baking dish; cover and bake for 45 minutes. Uncover and bake an additional 15 minutes to brown. (Or, if crispy skin is desired, bake uncovered for 1 hour.) Serve with hot rice and oriental vegetables.

Coconut Chicken

ESSEN 'N FRESSEN SISTERHOOD OF CONGREGATION BETH CHAIM HIGHTSTOWN, NEW JERSEY

1 large fryer
Vegetable oil
⅔ cup fine dry bread
    crumbs*
1 cup flaked coconut
    (unsweetened)
Curry powder to taste
Melted margarine (pareve)

Preparation time: 5 minutes
Cooking time: 1 hour
Serves 4

1. Preheat oven to 350°.

2. Cut chicken into 8 to 10 pieces, and rub with oil.

3. Combine bread crumbs, coconut, and curry powder. Dip the chicken in this mixture and pat to keep crumbs in place. Arrange in a shallow baking dish and sprinkle with any remaining crumbs. Drizzle with margarine and bake for about 1 hour.

Glazed Cornish Hens

TO STIR WITH LOVE   SISTERHOOD AHAVATH ISRAEL   KINGSTON, NEW YORK

3 Cornish game hens
Salt and pepper to taste
1 tablespoon paprika
½ teaspoon minced garlic
½ cup chicken fat (approx.)*
2 onions, sliced
½ cup dry sherry
½ cup orange marmalade
⅓ cup honey

Preparation time/processor: 5 minutes
Preparation time/conventional: 5 to 10 minutes
Baking time: 1 ½ hours
Pre-preparation: make stuffing (optional)
Serves 4 to 6

1. Preheat oven to 325°.

2. Combine salt, pepper, paprika, and garlic in a small dish. Rub hens with chicken fat, inside and out. Stuff with your favorite stuffing or wild rice stuffing (see recipes). Place onion slices in the bottom of a small baking dish. Set hens on onions and sprinkle with the garlic mixture.

3. Bake for 1 hour. Meanwhile heat sherry, marmalade, and honey and stir until smooth. Baste hens with this mixture and continue to bake for another ½ hour. Serve with basting sauce.

Chicken Fat and Cracklings (Schmaltz and Gribenes)

THE STUFFED BAGEL   HADASSAH CHAPTER   COLUMBIA, SOUTH CAROLINA

4 ounces raw chicken fat
1 medium onion, diced
Salt to taste

Preparation: 15 to 20 minutes
Makes about ½ cup

1. Place fat and onion in a small skillet and cook on medium heat until onions are browned.

2. Remove onions and drain on paper towels. Continue cooking chicken fat until the chicken fat solids (gribenes) are crisp and golden.

3. Strain through a fine sieve into a jar; store in refrigerator. Add the gribenes from the sieve to the fried onions and add salt.

Rock Cornish Hens with Cumberland Sauce

COOK UNTO OTHERS HILLEL JEWISH STUDENT CENTER, UNIVERSITY OF CINCINNATI CINCINNATI, OHIO

4 Cornish game hens
Oil
1 cup dry bread cubes
¼ cup chopped celery
1 tablespoon minced onion
¼ cup chopped pecans
Sprig of thyme (or pinch dried)
Salt to taste
Pinch poultry seasoning
Chicken stock, dry white wine, or sherry

Sauce
Grated peel of ½ orange*
¼ cup orange juice
1 tablespoon prepared horseradish*
1 teaspoon cornstarch
½ cup peach, plum, or currant jelly

Preparation time/processor: 10 to 15 minutes
Preparation time/conventional: 15 to 20 minutes
Baking time: 1 ¼ hours
Serves 4 to 8

1. Wash and dry hens; rub cavity with a little salt and rub skin with oil.

2. Combine bread cubes, celery, onion, pecans, seasonings and chicken stock to moisten. Loosely stuff the hens and place on a rack in a shallow pan, breast side up.

3. Place in cold oven and turn heat to 350°. Combine sauce ingredients and simmer until the jelly melts (5 minutes). Roast hens for 1¼ hours, basting with the sauce.

Duck à l'Orange

DO IT IN THE KITCHEN   WOMEN'S AMERICAN ORT, DISTRICT VI   HALLANDALE, FLORIDA

3½ to 4 pound duckling,
  quartered
⅓ cup orange marmalade
1 tablespoon soy sauce
1 teaspoon salt
1 tablespoon margarine
  (parve)
1 tablespoon flour
¾ cup dry white wine
1 tablespoon wine vinegar
¼ cup beef broth
¼ teaspoon pepper
1 orange, peeled and divided
  into sections

Preparation time: 15 to 20 minutes
Baking time: 45 minutes
Serves 4

1. Preheat oven to 450°.

2. Combine marmalade, soy sauce, and salt in a small bowl. Place duck on a rack in a shallow pan; brush with the sauce and bake for 15 minutes. Reduce heat to 400° and continue baking for another 30 minutes, basting from time to time with the sauce.

3. Meanwhile, heat margarine in a small pan. Add flour and cook until flour is lightly browned. Stir in wine, vinegar, and broth. Bring to a boil, stirring constantly. Cover and continue to simmer 10 minutes more.

4. When ready to serve, add any remaining marmalade mixture to the sauce and heat through. Add pepper; taste, and adjust seasoning. Arrange duckling and orange sections on platter and serve sauce in a bowl.

Fish, cheese & eggs

Fillet of Fish Corsica

KOSHER GOURMET II   TEMPLE BETH-EL OF BELLMORE   NORTH BELLMORE, NEW YORK

1 pound sole or flounder
   fillets
1 cup coarsely chopped
   onion
1 cup coarsely chopped
   green pepper
1 cup coarsely chopped
   mushrooms
1 cup coarsely chopped
   tomatoes
Salt and pepper to taste
3 tablespoons minced basil
   (or 1 Tbsp. dried)
¼ cup olive oil
½ pound mozzarella cheese,
   grated

Preparation time/processor: 5 to 10 minutes
Preparation time/conventional: 15 to 20 minutes
Cooking time: 45 to 50 minutes
Serves 4

Conventional
1. Preheat oven to 375°.
2. Wash fish fillets and pat dry. Arrange in a shallow baking dish. Cover with vegetables. Sprinkle with salt, pepper, and basil. Drizzle the oil over and bake for 30 minutes.
3. Remove from oven and sprinkle with the cheese. Bake for 15 to 20 minutes or until cheese is melted.

Food Processor
Grate partially frozen cheese and reserve. Insert the metal blade and chop the vegetables.

Note: This recipe is easily expanded to serve a crowd. If you want to brown the cheese, run under the broiler for a few moments.

Quick Ideas

- Rinse fish fillets in combined lemon juice and water. Dry and wrap before placing in refrigerator.

- Before cooking fish on the barbecue grill, always grease the grill.

- Wash hands in vinegar or lemon juice to remove fishy smell.

BROILED FISH. (1) Sprinkle fish with lemon juice and parsley, then broil or bake. (2) Spread fish with mayonnaise, then broil.

SAUTÉED FISH. Sprinkle fish with lemon juice, salt lightly, and dust lightly with flour. Sauté in medium-hot oil and butter. When crusty, turn over. Will cook in about 3 or 4 minutes per side.

BAKED FISH. Salt and pepper fish fillets and sprinkle with lemon juice. Place in shallow pan, pour a little wine or vinegar in bottom of pan, and bake at about 425° or 450° for 20 minutes. Don't turn over.

BAKED STUFFED FISH. Spread your favorite stuffing over fish fillets and roll up; place on end in greased muffin tins. Brush with margarine and bake.

CURRY TUNA SALAD. Combine cold cooked rice, toasted almonds or salted peanuts, curry powder, and lemon juice; add to your favorite tuna salad.

FISH AND PASTA SALAD: Flake cooked leftover fish and add to cold pasta; moisten with mayonnaise or a mayonnaise-based sauce.

FRESH-CAUGHT PAN-FRIED FISH. Dip 1 to 2 fillets per person in cornmeal and pan-fry in hot oil or margarine, about 4 to 5 minutes each side. Season and serve with lemon wedges.

MICRO-OMELET. Place two eggs in s small shallow microwave-proof dish, scramble lightly with fork, and season with salt and pepper. Heat in microwave about 2 minutes, check, loosen eggs with fork and turn dish; heat until desired doneness *almost* reached. Let stand 1 minute.

SCRAMBLED EGG AND OMELET VARIATIONS: add grated cheese, cheese cubes, croutons, chopped green pepper, chopped tomatoes, sliced mushrooms, chopped onion, leftover vegetables, curry powder.

Red Snapper Parmesan

MATZO MEALS BETH ISRAEL TEMPLE SISTERHOOD WARREN, OHIO

2 pounds red snapper
1 tablespoon lemon juice
½ teaspoon salt, or to taste
Pepper to taste
2 tablespoons butter
1 cup sour cream
¼ cup grated Parmesan
  cheese
1 tablespoon grated onion
Paprika

Preparation time: 5 to 10 minutes
Baking time: 25 to 35 minutes
Serves 6

1. Preheat oven to 350°.
2. Skin fillets; cut into 6 pieces. Place in a single layer in a buttered 7 x 11 baking dish. Sprinkle with lemon juice, salt and pepper. Dot with butter and cover dish with foil. Bake for 20 to 25 minutes or until nearly tender.
3. Combine sour cream, cheese, and onion. Spread over fish and sprinkle with paprika. Return to oven, uncovered, for 5 to 10 minutes or until fish is tender.

Sole Almondine

SECOND HELPINGS, PLEASE MT. SINAI CHAPTER, B'NAI B'RITH WOMEN MONTREAL, QUEBEC, CANADA

3 tablespoons butter or
  margarine
½ cup slivered blanched
  almonds
1 pound fillets of sole (or any
  firm-fleshed fish)
1 large clove garlic, minced
Salt and pepper to taste
1 teaspoon paprika
¼ cup dry bread crumbs*

Preparation time: 10 to 15 minutes
Baking time: 20 minutes
Serves 3 to 4

1. Preheat oven to 375°.
2. Put butter in a 9 x 13 baking dish, and place in oven for several minutes to melt. Watch carefully and do not brown. Add the almonds and stir to coat. Return pan to oven for about 2 minutes to brown the almonds. Remove almonds and most of the butter and reserve.
3. Place fish in the baking dish in one layer and turn to coat both sides with the butter. Sprinkle with garlic, seasonings, bread crumbs, and reserved almond-butter. Bake for about 20 minutes until just cooked through.

Fillet of Sole or Flounder

IN THE BEST OF TASTE   CONGREGATION BETH EL   SUDBURY, MASSACHUSETTS

2 pounds fillet of sole or
  flounder
1 tablespoon soy sauce
2 tablespoons peanut oil
½ pound mushrooms, sliced
6 shallots or green onions,
  minced
¼ cup orange juice
½ cup dry white wine
½ teaspoon salt
Dash white pepper
Orange wedges, paprika,
  minced parsley

Preparation time/processor: 5 to 10 minutes
Preparation time/conventional: 15 to 20 minutes
Cooking time: 40 minutes
Serves 6

1. Preheat oven to 350°.
2. Dry fish with paper towels and sprinkle with soy sauce.
3. Oil the bottom of 9 x 13 baking dish. Add mushrooms and shallots; arrange fish over mushrooms. Pour orange juice and wine over fish and season with salt and pepper. Bake for 40 minutes. Garnish before serving.

Salmon Loaf with Cottage Cheese

DO IT IN THE KITCHEN   WOMEN'S AMERICAN ORT, DISTRICT VI   HALLANDALE, FLORIDA

½ cup parsley leaves
4 slices good-textured bread
½ cup hot milk
1 egg
1 cup cottage cheese
1 can (16 oz.) salmon (do not
  drain)
Salt and pepper to taste
4 hard-cooked eggs

Preparation time/processor: 5 to 10 minutes
Preparation time/ conventional: 20 minutes
Cooking time: 1 hour
Serves 6 to 8

Food processor
1. Preheat oven to 350°.
2. Insert metal blade. Place parsley in work bowl and pulse to chop. Add bread, torn into quarters, and pulse to make fresh bread crumbs. Add the hot milk and allow to stand for a few minutes. Add egg, cottage cheese, salmon, and salt and pepper. Process until smooth.
3. Spoon one-third of mixture into a greased 8 x 4 loaf pan. Arrange cooked eggs in a row down the center. Top with salmon mixture and bake for 1 hour.
4. Serve hot, or cold with Tabasco Tartare Sauce (see recipe).

Conventional
May be made with a blender or mixer, but texture will not be as smooth.

Salmon Quiche

FIDDLER IN THE KITCHEN   NATIONAL COUNCIL OF JEWISH WOMEN, GREATER DETROIT SECTION   DETROIT, MI

Crust
1 cup whole wheat flour
⅔ cup coarsely grated sharp
  Cheddar cheese
¼ cup chopped almonds
½ teaspoon salt
¼ teaspoon paprika
6 tablespoons oil

Filling
1 can (16 oz.) salmon
3 eggs
1 cup sour cream
¼ cup mayonnaise*
½ cup coarsely grated sharp
  Cheddar cheese
1 tablespoon grated onion
¾ teaspoon snipped dill
  weed (or ¼ tsp. dried)
3 drops Tabasco sauce

Preparation time/processor: 10 to 15 minutes
Preparation time/conventional: 15 to 20 minutes
Baking time: 45 minutes
Serves 6

Conventional

1. Preheat oven to 400°.

2. Combine flour, cheese, almonds, salt, and paprika. Stir in oil with a fork. Set aside ½ cup of this mixture, and press the remainder into the bottom and up the sides of a 9-inch pie plate. Bake for 10 minutes. Remove from oven and reduce heat to 325°.

3. Drain salmon liquid into a measuring cup; add water to make ½ cup liquid. Flake salmon, removing bones and skin; set aside.

4. Beat eggs, sour cream, mayonnaise, and reserved salmon liquid. Stir in the salmon, grated cheese, onion, dill, and Tabasco sauce. Spoon filling into crust and sprinkle with the reserved crust mixture. Bake for 45 minutes or until firm in the center.

Food processor

In step 2, make crust using metal blade. In step 4, place ingredients in work bowl and pulse to combine. Work in batches if necessary.

Quick Ideas

- Grate cheese when it is cold and hard; soft cheese can be partially frozen. Leftover or dried out cheese can be grated and used in sauces and casseroles.

- Store sour cream upside down to prevent air from entering.

- Place leftover egg yolks in a strainer and simmer in water until cooked. Rub through sieve for garnishing vegetables and other dishes.

Crustless Zucchini Tuna Quiche

BEGINNING AGAIN   ROCKDALE TEMPLE SISTERHOOD   CINCINNATI, OHIO

2 cups shredded zucchini
½ teaspoon salt
2 tablespoons dry bread
  crumbs*
2 cans (6½ oz. each) tuna,
  drained
4 ounces Swiss cheese,
  grated
4 eggs, beaten
1¼ cups milk
½ cup finely chopped onion
1 tablespoon lemon juice
¼ teaspoon pepper
¾ teaspoon snipped dill
  weed (or ¼ tsp. dried)

Preparation time: 20 minutes
Cooking time: 40 minutes
Serves 6 to 8

1. Preheat oven to 350°.

2. Salt zucchini; let stand in a colander for 15 minutes. Squeeze to remove excess water.

3. Grease a 10-inch pie pan and sprinkle with bread crumbs. Set aside. Flake the tuna; combine tuna, cheese, and zucchini and spread evenly in the pan. Combine remaining ingredients and pour over zucchini mixture.

4. Bake for 40 minutes or until a knife comes out clean. Cool 5 to 10 minutes before cutting.

Beer and Cheese Quiche

SALT AND PEPPER TO TASTE   SISTERHOOD OF CONGREGATION ANSHEI ISRAEL   TUCSON, ARIZONA

1¼ cups cracker crumbs
6 tablespoons margarine,
  melted
2 tablespoons margarine
  or oil
3 medium onions, sliced thin
3 eggs
½ pound sharp Cheddar
  cheese, grated
¾ cup milk
½ cup beer
1 teaspoon salt
¼ teaspoon pepper

Preparation time/processor: 15 to 20 minutes
Preparation time/conventional: 20 minutes
Baking time: 45 minutes
Serves 6 to 8

1. Preheat oven to 325°.
2. Combine cracker crumbs and melted margarine. Press firmly into the sides and bottom of a 10-inch pie pan.
3. Heat 2 tablespoons margarine in a skillet; add onions and cook gently until transparent. Place evenly over the crust.
4. Beat the eggs and add remaining ingredients. Pour over onions and bake 45 minutes or until golden brown.

Crustless Asparagus Quiche

ESSEN 'N FRESSEN CONGREGATION BETH CHAIM HIGHTSTOWN, NEW JERSEY

½ pound asparagus (or
  10-oz. pkg. frozen)
5 eggs
1 cup milk
1 small onion
1½ teaspoons minced basil
  (or ½ tsp. dried)
1 teaspoon salt
⅛ teaspoon white pepper
½ pound Swiss cheese

Preparation time/processor: 10 to 15 minutes
Preparation time/conventional: 15 to 20 minutes
Baking time: 30 minutes
Serves 6 to 8

Food processor
1. Preheat oven to 325°.
2. Cook asparagus until crisp tender; drain well (dry thawed, frozen asparagus on paper towel). Arrange in a greased 9-inch pie plate.
3. Insert metal blade and beat the eggs with the milk. Add onion, basil, salt, and pepper and pulse several times to chop onion finely; remove. Insert grating blade and grate cheese. Add cheese to egg mixture, stirring with a rubber spatula, and pour carefully over the asparagus.
4. Bake for about 30 minutes or until a knife inserted 1 inch from edge comes out clean.

Conventional
Grate cheese and onion. Use blender, mixer, or wire whisk to combine ingredients.

Cheese Fondue

ARTISTRY IN THE KITCHEN TEMPLE WOMEN'S ASSOCIATION CLEVELAND, OHIO

1 large clove garlic
1½ cups dry white wine
1 pound Swiss cheese, grated
2 tablespoons cornstarch
Dash nutmeg
Dash pepper
¼ cup Kirsch or dry sherry
French bread, cubed

Preparation: 15 to 20 minutes
Serves 6 to 8

1. Insert a wooden toothpick in the garlic clove; place in a heavy pan, rubbing it around the pan to release some flavor. Add wine and place over moderate heat to warm. When wine is hot remove garlic.
2. Combine cheese and cornstarch. Gradually add to the heated wine, stirring constantly. Stir in nutmeg, pepper, and Kirsch. When bubbling, transfer to a fondue pot or chafing dish.
3. Serve with French bread cubes.

Variation: Serve with raw vegetable chunks, such as carrots, cauliflower, and zucchini, instead of bread.

No Crust Cheese and Spinach Pie

IN THE BEST OF TASTE   CONGREGATION BETH EL WOMEN'S GROUP   SUDBURY, MASSACHUSETTS

2 pounds fresh spinach (or
  10 oz. pkg. frozen chopped)
1 cup grated mozzarella
  cheese
3 large eggs
1 pound ricotta cheese
Small chunk onion
1 clove garlic
1 teaspoon salt
2 tablespoons oil

Preparation time/processor: 5 to 10 minutes
Preparation time/conventional: 15 to 20 minutes
Cooking time: 40 minutes
Serves 4 to 6

Food Processor
1. Preheat oven to 350°.
2 Cook spinach and squeeze dry. Chop if necessary.
3. While spinach is cooking, insert grating blade and grate mozzarella; remove. Insert metal blade. Place eggs, ricotta cheese, onion, and garlic in work bowl and process about 20 seconds to chop vegetables and mix. Add salt, oil, and spinach and pulse several times to blend. Add mozzarella and pulse to mix through.
4. Transfer to a greased 9-inch springform pan and bake for 40 minutes. Serve hot or cold.

Conventional
In step 3, mince garlic; chop onion; coarsely grate the mozzarella cheese. Combine with all the other ingredients. Proceed to step 4.

Sunday Night Scramble

SPECIALTY OF THE HOUSE   SISTERHOOD TEMPLE ISRAEL   BOSTON, MASSACHUSETTS

6 eggs
½ cup sour cream
½ cup coarsely grated
  Cheddar cheese
⅓ cup chopped green onions
2 tablespoons butter
½ teaspoon curry powder

Preparation time/processor: 10 minutes
Preparation time/conventional: 10 to 15 minutes
Serves 4

1. Beat eggs and sour cream until light and fluffy. Stir in cheese and onions.
2. Melt butter in a large skillet. Add curry powder and stir for a few seconds. Add eggs, lower heat, and stir gently until eggs are cooked to desired consistency.

Egg, Cheese, and Olive Casserole

COOK WITH TEMPLE BETH EMETH   TEMPLE BETH EMETH SISTERHOOD   ANN ARBOR, MICHIGAN

8 slices firm bread
½ pound Monterey Jack cheese
½ pound sharp Cheddar cheese
6 eggs
1 teaspoon dry mustard
1 quart milk
1 cup sliced ripe olives
8 green stuffed olives

Preparation time/processor: 5 to 10 minutes
Preparation time/conventional: 15 minutes
Chilling time: 1 hour
Cooking time: 1 hour
Serves 6 to 8

1. Remove crusts from bread. Coarsely grate cheese.
2. In a greased 9 x 13 baking dish, place alternate layers of bread, cheese, and sliced olives. Beat the eggs, milk, and dry mustard together and pour over the bread. Refrigerate at least 1 hour or overnight.
3. Preheat oven to 350°.
4. Bake the casserole for 1 hour. Garnish with stuffed olives and serve hot.

Variation: You may substitute Swiss cheese for the Monterey Jack or use all Cheddar.

Garlic Bread Supreme

EDITOR'S CHOICE

1 cup grated mozzarella cheese
1 cup grated Parmesan cheese
1 loaf Italian bread
½ stick butter or margarine
¼ cup olive oil
2 large garlic cloves, minced
6 tablespoons chopped oregano (or 2 Tbsp. dried)
Salt and pepper to taste

Preparation time/processor: 10 minutes
Preparation time/conventional: 10 to 15 minutes
Baking time: 10 to 15 minutes
Serves 6 to 8

1. Preheat oven to 350°.

2. Cut bread in half lengthwise and place on a baking sheet.

3. Melt butter; add oil and garlic and allow to stand for 5 minutes. Brush half this mixture evenly on the cut side of the bread. Spread generously with the cheeses, pour remaining butter on top, and sprinkle with oregano. Salt and pepper lightly.

4. Bake for 10 to 15 minutes or until cheese melts. Cut into individual slices and serve hot.

Hashed Brown Omelet

HISTORICALLY COOKING — 200 YEARS OF GOOD COOKING   K. K. BETH ELOHIM SISTERHOOD   CHARLESTON, SC

½ stick margarine
2 cups shredded cooked
  potatoes
¼ cup chopped onions
¼ cup chopped green pepper
4 eggs
¼ cup milk
½ teaspoon salt
Dash pepper
1 cup shredded Cheddar
  cheese

Preparation time/processor: 5 to 10 minutes
Preparation time/conventional: 10 to 15 minutes
Cooking time: 10 minutes
Serves 4 to 6

1. In a 10-inch skillet, heat margarine. Add the potatoes, onion, and green pepper and cook over low heat until underside is crisp and brown.

2. Beat the eggs, milk, salt and pepper together and add to the potatoes. Sprinkle with cheese. Cover and cook over low heat for about 10 minutes. Loosen omelet and serve in wedges.

Omelet for Two

LOVE, JEWISH STYLE   SHAREY TEFILO/ISRAEL   SOUTH ORANGE, NEW JERSEY

½ pound fresh spinach
  (or 4 oz. frozen chopped)
3 or 4 green onions
6 large mushrooms
4 ounces Swiss cheese
4 tablespoons butter
Dash nutmeg
5 eggs
⅓ cup milk or cream
Salt and pepper to taste

Preparation time/processor: 10 to 20 minutes
Preparation/conventional: 15 to 25 minutes
Serves 2 to 3

1. Cook spinach and drain well. As spinach is cooking, slice onions and mushrooms and grate the cheese. Set aside. Chop fresh spinach.

2. Sauté the onions in 2 tablespoons butter for a moment. Add mushrooms and cook until onions are translucent. Stir in spinach and nutmeg and remove from heat.

3. In a 10-inch skillet, melt the remaining butter. Whisk the eggs, milk, salt and pepper, and pour into skillet when the butter begins to bubble. Cook over medium heat until eggs are set.

4. Spread the spinach mixture over **eggs**. Sprinkle with cheese. With a spatula, carefully loosen and fold omelet in half. Cover with lid for 30 to 60 seconds to allow cheese to melt. Serve on warm plates.

Hoppel Poppel

EAT, DARLING — AND ENJOY! BETH ISRAEL SISTERHOOD FLINT, MICHIGAN

12 ounces beef salami
6 green onions
2 tomatoes
1 large green pepper
12 eggs
1 teaspoon salt
½ teaspoon pepper

Preparation time/processor: 5 to 10 minutes
Preparation time/conventional: 20 minutes
Cooking time: 30 minutes
Serves 12

Food processor
1. Preheat oven to 350°
2. Insert metal blade. Cut salami into 8 pieces and arrange evenly around the work bowl; pulse to chop. Remove and reserve. Place green onions (2-inch pieces), tomatoes (quartered), and green pepper (quartered) in work bowl and pulse to chop. Remove to bowl with salami. Place eggs, salt and pepper in work bowl and add any large-looking chunks of salami or vegetables. Pulse to chop, then add to salami-vegetable bowl; stir well.
3. Pour into a greased 9 x 13 baking dish and bake 30 minutes or until egg mixture is set.

Conventional
Chop salami, green onions, tomatoes, and green peppers. Beat eggs and seasonings. Combine with chopped meat and vegetables. Proceed to step 3.

Crisp Waffles

THE LEGACY OF GOOD COOKING TEMPLE BETH EL SISTERHOOD CORPUS CHRISTI, TEXAS

2½ cups flour
4 teaspoons baking powder
¾ teaspoon salt
1½ tablespoons sugar
2 eggs, beaten
2¼ cups milk
⅔ cup melted shortening
  or oil

Preparation time: 5 to 10 minutes
Makes 6 or 8 waffles

1. Sift dry ingredients.

2. Combine eggs, milk and shortening. Combine with dry ingredients and beat until smooth. Bake immediately in a hot waffle iron.

Baked Cheese Blintz

COOK UNTO OTHERS   HILLEL JEWISH STUDENT CENTER, UNIVERSITY OF CINCINNATI   CINCINNATI, OHIO

1 stick butter or margarine,
  melted
½ cup sugar
2 eggs
1¼ cups flour
1 teaspoon baking powder
½ teaspoon salt
¾ cup milk

Filling
1 pound ricotta cheese
1 egg
2 teaspoons melted butter or
  margarine
2 tablespoons sugar, or to
  taste
Cinnamon to taste

Preparation time/processor: 10 to 15 minutes
Preparation time/conventional: 15 to 20 minutes
Baking time: 1 hour
Serves 8 to 10

Food processor

1. Preheat oven to 350°.

2. Insert metal blade and process the butter and sugar until fluffy. Add eggs, flour, salt, milk, and baking powder; process until smooth, about 15 seconds. Pour into a 1-quart measuring cup. Do not wash work bowl.

3. Place filling ingredients in work bowl and process until smooth. Pour half the batter from the measuring cup into a greased 9 x 9 pan. Spread with the filling, and cover with the remaining batter. Bake 1 hour. Cut into squares.

Conventional

In step 2, use a blender or mixer to beat butter, sugar and eggs until smooth. Add flour, salt, milk, and baking powder and combine well. In step 3, beat filling ingredients with a mixer or whisk until very smooth. Continue with step 3.

═══ Quick Ideas ═══

● Freeze egg whites in individual ice cube molds. Transfer to a plastic bag for storage.

● Cold eggs separate easiest.

● Bring egg whites to room temperature for beating or baking. Place eggs into warm water for several minutes to bring to room temperature.

Healthy Pancakes
THE SPORT OF COOKING WOMEN'S AMERICAN ORT, DISTRICT VII CLEVELAND, OHIO

½ cup whole wheat flour
½ cup flour
½ cup wheat germ
½ cup non-fat dry milk
  powder
2 teaspoons baking powder
½ teaspoon salt
1½ cups milk
2 eggs
3 tablespoons safflower
  or corn oil
1 apple, grated (optional)

Preparation time: 15 to 20 minutes
Serves 3 to 4

1. Combine dry ingredients in a large bowl. Combine milk, eggs, and oil; beat into dry ingredients. Stir in apple.
2. Cook by ¼ cupfuls on a hot griddle or greased skillet.

Hootenanny Pancake
FOOD FOR SHOW/FOOD ON THE GO MOUNT SINAI HOSPITAL AUXILIARY MINNEAPOLIS, MINNESOTA

1 stick butter
6 eggs
1 cup milk
1 cup flour
½ teaspoon salt

Preparation time: 5 minutes
Baking time: 25 to 30 minutes
Serves 4 to 6

1. Preheat oven to 400°.
2. Melt butter in a 9 x 13 glass baking dish (place in oven). Beat eggs, milk, flour, and salt together. Add to baking dish without stirring. Bake for 25 to 30 minutes.
3. Cut in large squares and serve immediately. Top with jam or syrup.

Variation: Serve with sliced apples that have been sautéed in butter and sprinkled with cinnamon-sugar.

=====Quick Ideas=====

- Keep pancakes hot by covering with a colander, which lets out steam. Pancakes stay warm but don't get limp.

- When making a big batch of French toast, bake at 500° for 10-12 minutes on a well-greased cookie sheet.

- Freeze leftover waffles, individually wrapped in plastic sandwich bags. Toast frozen waffles in toaster.

French Toast Casserole

1 long loaf (10 oz.) French
  bread
8 large eggs
3 cups milk
4 teaspoons sugar
½ teaspoon salt, or to taste
1 tablespoon vanilla extract
2 tablespoons butter

Preparation time: 10 to 15 minutes
Chilling time: 4 hours
Baking time: 45 to 50 minutes
Serves 6 to 8

Food processor
1. Slice bread into 1-inch thick slices and arrange in a greased 9 x 13 baking dish.
2. Place eggs, milk, sugar, salt, and vanilla in work bowl and beat (work in batches). Pour over bread. Cover baking dish with foil and place in refrigerator for 4 hours or overnight.
3. Dot with butter and place in a cold oven set at 350°. Bake uncovered for 45 to 50 minutes. Let stand for 5 minutes. Serve with syrup, jam, honey, or sour cream.

Note: May be made ahead and kept in refrigerator up to 2 days.

Baked Orange French Toast
SALT AND PEPPER TO TASTE   CONGREGATION ANSHEI ISRAEL SISTERHOOD   TUCSON, ARIZONA

¼ cup dark brown sugar
½ teaspoon cinnamon
3 tablespoons melted butter
1 teaspoon grated orange
  peel*
3 eggs
2 teaspoons sugar
Dash salt
6 slices sour dough (or any
  coarse-textured) bread
2 oranges, sliced
Powdered sugar

Preparation time: 10 minutes
Baking time: 20 minutes
Serves 6

1. Preheat oven to 400°.
2. Sprinkle brown sugar and cinnamon evenly into a shallow baking pan. Drizzle with butter, then sprinkle with orange peel.
3. Beat eggs with sugar and salt. Dip bread in egg to coat both sides. Arrange in prepared pan and bake for 20 minutes. Serve immediately, sugar-side-up, on a heated platter. Dust with powdered sugar and garnish with orange slices.

Pasta & rice

Green Noodles with Tomatoes, Cheese, and Olives

NOSHES, NIBBLES AND GOURMET DELIGHTS   TEMPLE IN THE PINES SISTERHOOD   HOLLYWOOD, FLORIDA

1 pound green noodles (or ½ green and ½ egg noodles)
1 pound tomatoes (or 16 oz. can)
½ pound mozzarella cheese
1 stick butter
¼ cup olive oil
¾ cup chopped onions
1 clove garlic, minced (optional)
1½ teaspoons salt, or to taste
½ teaspoon black pepper
1 tablespoon chopped oregano (or 1 tsp. dried)
¼ cup grated Parmesan cheese
½ cup sliced black olives

Preparation time/processor: 15 minutes
Preparation time/conventional: 20 minutes
Baking time: 10 minutes
Serves 6 to 8

1. Preheat oven to 350°.

2. Cook the noodles according to package directions; drain.

3. While noodles are cooking, purée tomatoes in a food processor or blender; strain. Cut mozzarella into ¼-inch cubes.

4. Heat ½ stick butter and olive oil in a skillet. Sauté onions and garlic for 5 minutes. Add tomatoes, salt and pepper; bring to a boil and cook over high heat for 10 minutes. Add oregano.

5. Melt remaining butter in a 9 x 13 casserole. Add the noodles, 2 tablespoons Parmesan cheese, and the mozzarella. Toss well. Pour the sauce over, and sprinkle with the remaining Parmesan. Arrange the olives on top. Bake for about 10 minutes until mozzarella melts.

Spaghetti Casserole Nicoise

WITH LOVE AND SPICE   SHOSHANA CHAPTER, AMERICAN MIZRACHI WOMEN   WEST HEMPSTEAD, NEW YORK

1½ pounds spaghetti
½ cup chopped onion
1 tablespoon olive oil
1 cup ripe black olives
1 can (7½ oz.) tuna, drained
1 clove garlic, minced
1½ teaspoons salt, or to taste
1½ teaspoons chili powder
  (optional)
2 cups tomato sauce*
½ cup grated Swiss,
  Cheddar, or Parmesan
  cheese

Preparation time/processor: 15 minutes
Preparation time/conventional: 20 minutes
Baking time: 8 to 12 minutes
Serves 4

1. Preheat oven to 450°.

2. Cook spaghetti according to package directions; drain.

3. While spaghetti is cooking, sauté onion in oil until translucent. Cut olives in half. Flake the tuna.

4. Combine spaghetti with all ingredients except cheese and place in a 2-quart casserole; top with grated cheese. Bake for 8 to 12 minutes until piping hot and cheese is melted.

Noodles Creole

SPECIALTY OF THE HOUSE   SISTERHOOD OF TEMPLE ISRAEL   BOSTON, MASSACHUSETTS

1½ pounds wide noodles
½ pound mushrooms
2 Spanish onions
3 stalks celery
2 green peppers
1 clove garlic (optional)
1 stick butter or margarine
1 teaspoon lemon juice
1½ teaspoons snipped dill
  weed (or ½ tsp. dried)
1 jar (2 oz.) diced pimentos
1 teaspoon salt
Freshly ground black pepper
½ cup cornflake crumbs
2 tablespoons butter or
  margarine

Preparation time/processor: 10 to 15 minutes
Preparation time/conventional: 20 minutes
Baking time: 1 hour
Serves 12

1. Preheat oven to 350°.

2. Cook noodles according to package instructions; drain.

3. While noodles are cooking, slice the mushrooms, slice or chop the onions, celery, and peppers, and mince the garlic; sauté in butter until soft. Stir in the lemon juice, dill, pimento, salt and pepper.

4. Toss the vegetables with the noodles and transfer to a 9 x 13 baking dish. Sprinkle top with crumbs and dot with butter. Bake for 1 hour.

Ziti Casserole

EDITOR'S CHOICE

1 pound ziti
¼ pound mozzarella cheese
1 pound ricotta cheese
½ cup grated Parmesan
  cheese
1 egg
¾ teaspoon salt
¼ teaspoon pepper
6 cups spaghetti sauce or
  marinara sauce*

Preparation time: 10 to 15 minutes
Baking time: 40 minutes
Serves 4 to 6

1. Preheat oven to 350°.
2. Cook ziti; drain.
3. While ziti is cooking, dice mozzarella. Combine cheeses, egg, salt and pepper.
4. In a 9 x 13 baking dish, layer ziti, filling, and sauce, beginning and ending with the sauce. Bake for about 40 minutes until piping hot.

Italian Marinara Sauce

PORTAL TO GOOD COOKING, VOLUME IV   WOMEN'S AMERICAN ORT, VIII   CHICAGO, ILLINOIS

½ cup parsley sprigs
2 cloves garlic
4 medium onions
2 large green peppers
1 small stalk celery
½ cup olive oil
5 pounds tomatoes
2 teaspoons salt, or to taste
1 tablespoon each minced
  rosemary, thyme, and basil
  (or 1 tsp. dried)
1 teaspoon sugar
1½ teaspoons chopped
  oregano (or ½ tsp. dried)
¼ teaspoon nutmeg

Preparation time/processor: 10 to 15 minutes
Preparation time/conventional: 15 to 20 minutes
Cooking time: 2 hours
Makes about 5 pints

Food processor/blender

1. Place parsley in a food processor (metal blade) or blender and pulse until finely chopped. Remove and set aside. With the machine running, add garlic and onion (quartered) and pulse until chopped; remove. Chop green pepper (quartered) and add to onion.

2. Heat oil in a large Dutch oven or stock pot; add vegetables. Reduce heat and cook slowly. Peel tomatoes and remove seeds; process, several at a time, until finely chopped. Add tomatoes and remaining ingredients to the vegetables. Simmer uncovered for about 2 hours or until thickened.

To freeze: Pour into containers, leaving 1 inch headspace.

Baked Noodles with Cheese

RECIPES BY REQUEST B'NAI SHOLOM SISTERHOOD BLOUNTVILLE, TENNESSEE

1 package (8 oz.) wide
  noodles
1 cup cottage cheese
1 cup sour cream
1 teaspoon Worcestershire
  sauce
1 clove garlic, minced
Dash ground red pepper
1 teaspoon salt
¼ teaspoon pepper

Preparation time: 10 to 15 minutes
Baking time: 45 minutes
Serves 6 to 8

1. Preheat oven to 350°.

2. Cook noodles until tender; drain.

3. While noodles are cooking, combine cottage cheese, sour cream, and seasonings in a large bowl. Add noodles and toss gently to mix well. Transfer to a greased 2-quart casserole and bake for 45 minutes.

4. Serve hot with additional sour cream.

Salsa

FOOD FOR SHOW/FOOD ON THE GO MOUNT SINAI HOSPITAL AUXILIARY MINNEAPOLIS, MINNESOTA

1 cup fresh parsley leaves
1 clove garlic, or to taste
2 medium tomatoes
1 medium onion
1 medium green pepper
½ teaspoon salt
⅛ teaspoon pepper
⅛ teaspoon ground cumin
⅛ teaspoon chili powder, or
  to taste
Green chili peppers or other
  hot peppers (optional)

Preparation time/processor: 5 minutes
Preparation time/conventional: 10 to 15 minutes
Makes about 3 cups

Food processor/blender

1. Drop parsley and garlic through feed tube of a food processor (metal blade) or blender with the machine running. Cut tomatoes, onion, and green pepper in quarters; add with remaining ingredients and pulse until desired texture is reached (should be a little chunky). Serve with tortilla chips.

Conventional

Chop all vegetables. Add seasonings and stir well.

Variation: Can be served hot over pasta or rice, or chilled and mixed with yogurt, sour cream, or cottage cheese to make dips and spreads.

Pesto Sauce

THE COOK'S BOOK   TEMPLE ISRAEL SISTERHOOD   TULSA, OKLAHOMA

6 ounces Parmesan cheese
  (1½ cups grated)
2 cups fresh basil leaves,
  loosely packed
1 or 2 cloves garlic
½ cup pine nuts or walnuts
¼ teaspoon freshly ground
  black pepper
½ cup olive oil

Preparation time/processor: 5 to 10 minutes
Preparation time/conventional: 10 to 15 minutes
Makes about ¾ cup

Food processor

1. Insert metal blade and chop the Parmesan cheese. Add other ingredients (except oil) and process for 10 seconds. Slowly add oil with machine running. Serve over hot pasta or fresh tomato slices.

Conventional

Grate cheese. Chop basil and nuts. Combine all ingredients with a blender.

Winter version: Substitute 2 cups parsley for fresh basil and add 1 tablespoon dried basil.

Noodles Alfredo

THE SPORT OF COOKING   WOMEN'S AMERICAN ORT, DISTRICT VII   CLEVELAND, OHIO

1 package (8 to 10 oz.)
  medium noodles
1 stick butter, melted
2 cups sour cream
¼ cup milk or cream
1 cup freshly grated
  Parmesan cheese
¼ teaspoon salt
1 clove garlic, minced
1 tablespoon snipped dill
  weed (or 1 tsp. dried)
½ cup finely chopped
  parsley
Freshly ground black pepper

Preparation time: 10 to 15 minutes
Serves 4 to 6

1. Cook noodles according to package instructions; drain.
2. While noodles are cooking, combine the remaining ingredients except pepper in a large serving bowl or platter.
3. Add noodles to the sour cream mixture. Toss gently to mix well. Correct seasonings to taste. Grind black pepper over the top.

Noodles and Swiss Cheese

LOVE, JEWISH STYLE   SHAREY TEFILO/ISRAEL   SOUTH ORANGE, NEW JERSEY

1 pound medium noodles
½ pound Swiss cheese
1 clove garlic, minced
1 teaspoon Worcestershire
  sauce
¼ stick butter, melted
½ teaspoon salt
¼ teaspoon pepper
2 cups sour cream
½ cup buttered crumbs

Preparation time/processor: 15 minutes
Preparation time/conventional: 20 minutes
Baking time: 1 hour
Serves 6 to 8

1. Preheat oven to 350°.

2. Cook noodles according to package instructions; drain.

3. While the noodles are cooking, grate the cheese and combine with garlic, Worcestershire sauce, butter, salt, pepper, and sour cream.

4. Add noodles to the cheese mixture, mixing lightly. Place in a greased 9 x 13 baking dish. Top with crumbs and bake for 1 hour.

Macaroni and Cheese Deluxe

THE WAY TO A MAN'S HEART   BETH ISRAEL CONGREGATION   WASHINGTON, PENNSYLVANIA

1¾ cups uncooked macaroni
8 ounces sharp Cheddar
  cheese
2 cups ricotta cheese
1 cup sour cream
1 egg, slightly beaten
¾ teaspoon salt
Dash pepper
½ cup grated mozzarella
  cheese
Paprika

Preparation time/processor: 5 to 10 minutes
Preparation time/conventional: 10 to 15 minutes
Baking time: 40 minutes
Serves 4 to 6

1. Preheat oven to 350°.

2. Cook macaroni; drain well.

3. While macaroni is cooking, grate Cheddar cheese. Combine with ricotta, sour cream, egg, salt and pepper. Add macaroni and toss to mix well. Turn into a greased 9 x 9 baking dish. Sprinkle with paprika and bake for 40 minutes.

Noodles and Cabbage

GARDEN OF EATING SISTERHOOD OF TEMPLE BETH O'R CLARK, NEW JERSEY

1 large cabbage (about 2
  pounds)
1 medium onion
½ pound wide noodles
1½ tablespoons sugar
½ stick margarine (or ¼ cup
  chicken fat*)
¼ teaspoon pepper
Salt to taste
Caraway or poppy seeds

Preparation/processor + microwave: 20 minutes
Preparation time/conventional: 1 hour
Serves 6

Food processor/microwave

1. Shred cabbage finely with the slicing blade. Remove. Insert metal blade and chop onion.

2. Cook noodles according to package directions; drain.

3. Meanwhile, place cabbage, onion, sugar, margarine, and pepper in a large covered casserole. Cook in microwave, stirring from time to time, until cabbage is cooked, about 10 minutes. Add a little water if necessary. Stir in noodles and combine well. Adjust seasoning and sprinkle with seeds.

Conventional

In step 1, shred cabbage and chop onion. In step 3, cook cabbage, onion, sugar, margarine, salt and pepper until lightly browned, about 40 minutes. Stir in noodles, adjust seasoning, and sprinkle with seeds.

Fruited Noodle Pudding

QUICK AND EASY COOKBOOK   MAIN LINE REFORM TEMPLE SISTERHOOD   PHILADELPHIA, PENNSYLVANIA

1 pound wide noodles
4 eggs
½ teaspoon salt
1 cup light brown sugar
1 cup raisins
1 cup crushed pineapple,
drained
1 can (16 oz.) pitted apricots,
drained
3 apples, peeled, cut into
wedges
1 can orange juice
concentrate, thawed
½ cup melted butter or
margarine
½ cup light brown sugar
1 can (11 oz.) mandarin
oranges, drained

Preparation time: 15 to 20 minutes
Baking time: 40 minutes
Serves 8 to 10

1. Preheat oven to 350°.

2. Cook noodles according to package directions; drain.

3. While noodles are cooking, remove 2 tablespoons orange juice concentrate and set aside.

4. Beat the eggs until fluffy. Add salt, 1 cup sugar, raisins, pineapple, apricots, apples, orange juice, and 5 tablespoons melted butter. Stir in noodles and toss to mix well. Transfer to a greased 9 x 13 baking dish.

5. Combine ½ cup brown sugar, reserved orange juice concentrate, and mandarin orange segments, and spread over the noodle mixture. Drizzle with remaining melted butter and bake for 40 minutes. Cool to lukewarm before serving.

Quick Ideas

• When freezing a casserole (cooked or uncooked) for future use, line a freezer-safe baking dish with foil before filling. You can easily remove the contents from the dish after it is frozen and keep in freezer without the dish. Wrap well and label. To reheat, remove foil and place in same casserole dish.

• Do not use microwave for cooking rice. Fine for reheating cooked rice.

• Add 1 tablespoon oil to water for cooking pasta.

• Add garlic butter to any pasta.

• Add stock, sautéed onions, or mushrooms to grain dishes.

• Freeze cooked rice (preferably undercooked slightly) in 1 cup or 2 cup quantities.

Barley with Mushrooms

EAT, DARLING — AND ENJOY! BETH ISRAEL SISTERHOOD FLINT, MICHIGAN

4 tablespoons oil
½ pound mushrooms, sliced
1 large onion, chopped
1 cup pearl barley
2 cups chicken or beef stock
Salt and pepper to taste
Chopped parsley

Preparation time/processor: 5 minutes
Preparation time/conventional: 10 minutes
Baking time: 1 hour
Serves 6 to 7

1. Preheat oven to 350°.
2. Heat oil in skillet. Add mushrooms and onion; sauté until soft. Add barley and stock and bring to a boil. Transfer to a 1½-quart casserole. Cover and bake for 1 hour. Season with salt and pepper. Garnish with chopped parsley.

Note: If recipe is prepared ahead and refrigerated, increase baking time to 1¼ hours. If using quick barley, decrease cooking time by 15 minutes.

Green Rice

FAVORITE RECIPES FROM HADASSAH MID-MISSOURI DEBORAH CHAPTER COLUMBIA, MISSOURI

3 cups cold cooked rice
2 to 2½ ounces Cheddar cheese
Peel of 1 lemon, (zest)
1 large clove garlic
2 to 3 cups parsley sprigs
1 medium onion
1 small green pepper
2 eggs
1¼ cups half and half (or milk)
½ cup vegetable oil
Juice of 1 lemon
1 teaspoon salt, or to taste
½ teaspoon black pepper
Paprika

Preparation time/processor: 5 to 10 minutes
Preparation time/conventional: 15 to 20 minutes
Pre-preparation: cook rice
Baking time: 45 minutes
Serves 6 to 8

Food processor
1. Preheat oven to 350°.
2. Insert grating blade and grate the cheese. Add to rice in large mixing bowl. Insert metal blade and drop lemon peel and garlic through feed tube with the machine running. Process until lemon is chopped finely. Add parsley and pulse until minced. Add onion and green peppers (cut into quarters) and pulse to chop finely. Remove and add to rice mixture. Add eggs, half and half, oil, lemon juice, and seasonings to work bowl and process. Work in batches if necessary. Add egg mixture to rice mixture. Stir well.
3. Pour into a greased 2-quart baking dish and bake for about 45 minutes or until the consistency of a soft custard. Sprinkle with paprika.

Chinese Fried Rice I

CREATIVE COOKERY SISTERHOOD OF TEMPLE SHAARE TEFILAH NORWOOD, MASSACHUSETTS

2 cups coarsely chopped
  onion
2 tablespoons peanut oil
2 cups cooked rice (cold)
2 eggs, stirred slightly
½ tablespoon soy sauce

Preparation time/processor: 5 minutes
Preparation time/conventional: 10 minutes
Pre-preparation: cook rice
Serves 6 to 8

1. Sauté onions in oil until lightly browned. Add the rice and heat through. Make a well by pushing rice to edges of skillet; add eggs and soy sauce in the well. When eggs are just set, stir to incorporate into rice.

Chinese Fried Rice II

FROM OUR KITCHENS BRITH EMETH SISTERHOOD PEPPER PIKE, OHIO

1 cup raw rice
1 medium onion, chopped
¼ to ½ cup oil
1¾ cups chicken broth
2 tablespoons bead molasses
  (such as La Choy Brown
  Gravy Sauce)
1 pound bean sprouts (or
  16-oz. can)
1 can (8 oz.) water chestnuts,
  quartered

Preparation time: 10 minutes
Cooking time: 20 minutes
Serves 6 to 8

1. In a wok or large skillet, brown rice and onion in oil. Stir in the chicken broth and molasses. Cover and simmer until liquid has been absorbed and rice is tender, about 20 minutes.
2. While rice is cooking, blanch bean sprouts for 1 minute in boiling water
3. Combine rice, bean sprouts, and water chestnuts.

Almond Fried Rice

TO STIR WITH LOVE SISTERHOOD AHAVATH ISRAEL KINGSTON, NEW YORK

1 large onion, chopped
1 green pepper, chopped
½ stick margarine or butter
4 cups cooked rice
½ teaspoon salt
¼ cup soy sauce, or to taste
½ teaspoon pepper
1 cup toasted slivered
  almonds
1 tablespoon chopped
  pimento (optional)

Preparation time/processor: 15 minutes
Preparation time/conventional: 20 minutes
Pre-preparation: cook rice
Serves 6 to 8

1. Sauté onion and green pepper in margarine until tender. Add remaining ingredients and cook about 10 minutes or until hot.

Andalusian Rice

A BOOK FOR THE COOK BRANDEIS UNIVERSITY NATIONAL WOMEN'S COMMITTEE NEW YORK, NEW YORK

1½ cups raw rice (Italian
  type preferred)
½ cup grated Parmesan
  cheese
½ cup grated Cheddar
  cheese
¼ pound sliced mushrooms
½ cup chopped green pepper
⅓ cup chopped stuffed green
  olives
¼ cup chopped onion
¼ cup olive oil
Salt and pepper to taste
Parmesan cheese (topping)
Stuffed green olives
  (garnish)

Preparation time/processor: 10 to 15 minutes
Preparation time/conventional: 20 to 25 minutes
Baking time: 1 hour
Serves 6

1. Preheat oven to 350°.

2. Cook rice according to package directions.

3. While rice is cooking, prepare other ingredients. Combine with rice and transfer to a 1½-quart casserole. Bake for 1 hour.

4. Remove from oven and sprinkle with a little Parmesan cheese and garnish with additional olives. Return to oven for 5 minutes to brown.

Reis mit Pilze

INSPIRATIONS...FROM RENA HADASSAH   RENA GROUP HADASSAH, MOUNT VERNON CHAPTER   MOUNT VERNON, NY

1½ cups raw rice
1 large onion
1½ pounds mushrooms
3 tablespoons oil
¾ cup walnuts
Salt and pepper

Preparation time: 20 minutes
Serves 6

1. Cook rice according to package instructions.
2. While rice is cooking, slice onion and mushrooms. Sauté onion slices in oil until translucent. Add mushrooms and walnuts and cook until mushrooms are cooked but not browned.
3. Add salt, pepper, and rice. Stir well and correct seasonings.

Note: May also be used as stuffing for poultry or breast of veal

Brown Rice Almondine

WORLD OF OUR FLAVORS — CERTIFIED TA'AM   BETH HILLEL SISTERHOOD   WILMETTE, ILLINOIS

1 cup raw brown rice
2½ cups water
1 teaspoon salt
2 tablespoons butter or
  margarine
½ pound mushrooms, sliced
⅓ cup slivered almonds

Preparation time/processor: 5 to 10 minutes
Preparation time/conventional: 10 to 15 minutes
Baking time: 45 to 60 minutes
Serves 4 to 6

1. Preheat oven to 350°.
2. Place rice, water, salt, and 1 tablespoon butter in a 2-quart casserole. Cover and bake for 45 minutes to 1 hour or until water has been absorbed.
3. Sauté mushrooms and almonds in remaining butter until lightly browned. Stir into rice.

Granola

READING, WRITING, AND RECIPES   GATEWAY SCHOOL   ATLANTA, GEORGIA

4 cups uncooked rolled oats
1½ cups wheat germ
1 cup grated coconut
1 to 2 teaspoons cinnamon
½ cup honey
⅓ cup vegetable oil
1 to 2 teaspoons vanilla
   extract
½ cup sesame seeds
   (optional)
½ cup nuts, seeds, raisins,
   or dried fruit (optional)

Preparation time: 5 to 10 minutes
Baking time: 30 minutes
Makes about 6 cups

1. Preheat oven to 300°.

2. Combine oats, wheat germ, coconut, and cinnamon in a large mixing bowl. In a saucepan over low heat, combine honey, oil, and vanilla. Add to the dry ingredients and stir well until all particles are coated.

3. Spread on a large, shallow, greased baking sheet. Bake for about ½ hour. Cool. Place in an air-tight container with nuts, seeds, raisins, or dried fruit.

Vegetables

Israeli Skillet Eggplant

FOOD FOR SHOW/FOOD ON THE GO   MOUNT SINAI HOSPITAL AUXILIARY   MINNEAPOLIS, MINNESOTA

1 medium eggplant
   (unpeeled)
1 medium onion
1 medium green pepper
1 clove garlic (more to taste)
¼ cup oil
1 teaspoon salt, or to taste
½ teaspoon pepper
2 medium tomatoes
Grated Parmesan or
   mozzarella cheese
   (optional)

Preparation time: 20 minutes
Serves 6

1. Cut eggplant, onion, and green pepper into chunks. Mince garlic and heat in a large skillet with the oil. Add the vegetable chunks and salt and pepper. Cover and cook over medium heat, shaking pan from time to time, for about 10 minutes or until vegetables are tender.

2. Peel tomatoes and chop; add to pan and cook another 5 minutes. Top with cheese and serve immediately, or place in a covered casserole and keep warm in a 250° oven.

Squash Creole

FROM GENERATION TO GENERATION B'NAI AMOONA SISTERHOOD ST. LOUIS, MISSOURI

6 medium-sized zucchini or
  yellow squash
3 large tomatoes (or 2 cups
  canned)
1 small green pepper
1 small onion
3 tablespoons butter or
  margarine
3 tablespoons flour
1 teaspoon salt
1 tablespoon dark brown
  sugar
½ cup crumbs (bread,
  cracker, or cornflake)
2 tablespoons butter or
  margarine

Preparation time/processor: 5 to 10 minutes
Preparation time/conventional: 15 to 20 minutes
Baking time: 1 hour
Serves 4 to 6

Food processor

1. Preheat oven to 350°.

2. Insert slicing blade; slice squash and place into a shallow 1½-quart casserole. Insert metal blade and add tomatoes (peeled and quartered), green pepper (quartered) and onion (quartered) to the work bowl. Pulse once or twice to chop the vegetables.

3. In a saucepan, melt butter and add flour. Whisk until smooth. Add the tomato mixture, salt, and brown sugar. Cook, stirring, for 5 minutes. Spread over squash.

4. Sprinkle with crumbs and dot with butter. Bake for 1 hour.

Conventional

Slice the squash. Chop tomatoes, green pepper, and onion. Proceed to step 3.

Microwave: In step 3, melt the butter and add flour. Cook tomatoes, green pepper, and onion for approximately 1 minute in a small dish.

- Always rinse canned water chestnuts, bamboo shoots, or bean sprouts in cold water before using.

- Peel asparagus and broccoli stems with a loose-bladed vegetable peeler.

- Store mushrooms in a brown paper bag in the refrigerator.

MUSHROOMS MARSALA. In a large skillet, sauté 1 cup fresh mushrooms in 2 tablespoons butter, 2 tablespoons olive oil, and 1 clove mashed fresh garlic. Add 2 tablespoons Marsala and simmer 10 minutes. Serves 2.

SQUASH TOSS. Slice two large yellow squash into a baking dish. Add ½ sliced white onion and 1 large sliced tomato. Top with croutons and grated Cheddar cheese. Bake for 45 minutes. Serves 4.

CARROTS AND SOUR CREAM. Place 1 pound sliced carrots and 1 tablespoon sugar in a saucepan with water to cover. Bring to a boil and simmer until tender. Drain well and toss with 1 cup sour cream. Good with fish.

CURRY VEGETABLES. Combine 1 cup plain yogurt, 2 tablespoons chutney, and ½ to 1 tablespoon curry powder. Steam 2 cups sliced vegetables (cauliflower, zucchini, carrots, eggplant, or broccoli) until crisp-tender. Drain and spoon sauce over top.

RICE AND ONIONS. Cook 6 to 7 cups sliced onion in some margarine, adding 1 tablespoon sugar. When well-browned and caramelized combine with about 3 cups hot, cooked rice. Season with salt and pepper.

COLCANNON (an Irish dish). Combine leftover mashed potatoes with lots of cooked cabbage and onions (sliced). Reheat by tossing in a skillet with butter and chopped parsley.

QUICK SEASONINGS. Garlic butter, lemon juice, fresh herbs. Or drizzle Kennedy Center Mustard Salad Dressing (see recipe) over just about any vegetable while hot.

OVEN-FRIED POTATOES. Place unpeeled, quartered (the long way) potatoes in an open baking pan, brush with oil, sprinkle with seasoning, herbs, or seasoned salt and bake until brown (about 45 minutes) at 350°.

BAKED VEGETABLES. Marinate vegetables in Italian dressing or brush with oil. Shake in a plastic bag with seasoned crumbs and Parmesan cheese. Place on cookie sheet and bake at 350° for about 30 minutes.

Zucchini Spears

COOK'S DELIGHT   SISTERHOOD OF CONGREGATION OHEV SHALOM   ORLANDO, FLORIDA

1 medium zucchini per
 person
Salad oil
Seasoned bread crumbs*

Preparation time: 5 to 10 minutes
Baking time: 20 to 30 minutes

1. Preheat oven to 350°.

2. Cut zucchini into spears, dip into oil, then coat well with crumbs. Place on a lightly greased baking sheet, skin side down.

3. Bake for 20 to 30 minutes, until tender and lightly browned. Sprinkle with salt before serving.

Zucchini Casserole

ALL THAT SCHMALTZ   AUGUSTA CHAPTER OF HADASSAH   AUGUSTA, GEORGIA

4 large eggs
6 large zucchini
3 large carrots, peeled
1 large baking potato, peeled
1 large onion
¾ cup dry bread crumbs*
½ cup matzo meal
1 clove garlic
1 stick butter or margarine,
 melted
Salt and pepper to taste

Preparation time/processor: 10 to 15 minutes
Preparation time/conventional: 20 minutes
Baking time: 1 hour
Serves 8 to 10

Food processor

1. Preheat oven to 350°.

2. Beat eggs in a large bowl.

3. Insert grating blade; grate the zucchini, carrots, potato, and onion. You may have to work in batches. Add to eggs, along with remaining ingredients.

4. Transfer to a greased 7 x 11 baking dish and bake for 1 hour or until brown.

Conventional

Grate or chop the vegetables by hand or in a blender in step 3.

Zucchini Pancakes

COLLECTABLE DELECTABLES   RODEF SHOLOM TEMPLE SISTERHOOD   HAMPTON, VIRGINIA

½ cup finely chopped onion
2 cups shredded zucchini
1 cup shredded carrot
2 eggs
½ cup flour
1 teaspoon salt
¼ teaspoon pepper
Oil

Preparation time/processor: 5 to 10 minutes
Preparation time/conventional: 15 to 20 minutes
Cooking time: 10 to 15 minutes
Makes 12 to 14

1. Combine all ingredients except oil.

2. Heat oil in a large skillet to depth of ¼ inch. Drop mixture by tablespoons into skillet. Brown on both sides. Drain on paper towels.

3. Serve with sour cream or cottage cheese.

Variation:1¼ cups grated Parmesan cheese may be added to batter or sprinkled on pancakes.

Yellow Squash Casserole

ALL THIS AND KOSHER, TOO   BETH DAVID SISTERHOOD   MIAMI, FLORIDA

1 small onion
2 large eggs
1 pound yellow summer
  squash
½ cup flour
½ teaspoon baking powder
Salt and pepper to taste
1 tablespoon melted butter
  or margarine
¼ cup slivered almonds or
  chopped pecans
½ cup dry bread crumbs*
  or wheat germ
2 tablespoons maple syrup
2 tablespoons butter or
  margarine

Preparation time: 10 to 20 minutes
Baking time: 30 to 35 minutes
Serves 6 to 8

Food processor/blender

1. Preheat oven to 350°.

2. In a food processor (metal blade) or blender, place the onion (cut in half) and eggs and pulse twice. Working in batches, add squash (cut into chunks), flour, melted butter, baking powder, salt and pepper and pulse until mixture is very smooth and quite thin.

3. Pour into a greased shallow 1½-quart baking dish. Sprinkle with the nuts, then bread crumbs. Drizzle with maple syrup and dot with butter. Bake for 30 to 35 minutes until golden and set.

Acorn Squash

FROM GENERATION TO GENERATION B'NAI AMOONA SISTERHOOD ST. LOUIS,

3 acorn squash (about 4 lbs.)
Salt to taste
⅓ cup margarine
1½ cups pineapple chunks
1 apple, peeled and diced
2 tablespoons dark brown
  sugar
Pineapple juice

Preparation time: 5 to 10 ...
Cooking time: 30 to 40 minutes
Baking time: 30 minutes
Serves 6

1. Preheat oven to 350°.

2. Cut squash in half, leaving seeds and stem intact. Steam in a small quantity of water (30-40 min.) or cook in microwave (6-10 min.) until almost tender.

3. Remove seeds. Sprinkle cavity with salt and 1 tablespoon margarine. Combine pineapple, apple, and brown sugar. Place in squash cavities and dot with remaining margarine. Bake for about 30 minutes in oven, or microwave until done, basting with pineapple juice.

Stir-Fried Celery with Broccoli

EDITOR'S CHOICE

1 bunch celery (about 6
  stalks)
1 bunch (1 pound) broccoli
1 large onion
1 clove garlic, minced
¼ cup oil
3 tablespoons soy sauce
¾ teaspoon ground ginger
Black pepper

Preparation time: 15 to 20 minutes
Serves 6

1. Slice celery diagonally and measure 6 cups. Cut broccoli into flowerettes and slice stems thinly. Slice onion and separate into rings.

2. In a wok or large skillet heat the oil and sauté the garlic for 30 seconds over low heat. Increase heat and add the celery and broccoli. Stir-fry for 3 minutes. Add remaining ingredients and stir-fry until vegetables are crisp tender, about 2 to 3 minutes.

inach Oriental

UNTO OTHERS   HILLEL JEWISH STUDENT CENTER, UNIVERSITY OF CINCINNATI   CINCINNATI, OH

1 pound fresh spinach
8 large mushrooms, sliced
2 tablespoons oil
¼ cup chicken stock
1 can (8 oz.) bamboo shoots
Salt to taste

Preparation time: 15 to 20
Serves 2 to 3

1. Wash spinach and shake off excess water. Remove tough stems and tear into 2-inch pieces.

2. Heat oil in a large frying pan or wok. Add spinach and stir-fry for about 2 minutes. Add stock, bamboo shoots, mushrooms, and salt. Continue cooking several minutes to heat through. Serve immediately.

Spinach with Tomatoes

MADE TO ORTER   DAY, EVENING, JAMES RIVER CHAPTERS OF WOMEN'S AMERICAN ORT   RICHMOND, VIRGINIA

2 packages (10 oz. each)
  frozen chopped spinach
6 green onions
⅓ cup butter or margarine
¾ cup dry bread crumbs*
3 eggs, lightly beaten
1½ teaspoons minced thyme
  (or ½ tsp. dried)
½ teaspoon black pepper
½ teaspoon ground red
  pepper
Salt to taste
12 tomato slices
½ cup grated Parmesan
  cheese

Preparation time: 10 to 15 minutes
Baking time: 15 to 20 minutes
Serves 6 to 8

1. Preheat oven to 350°.

2. Cook spinach and drain, squeezing out excess liquid.

3. Chop green onions; sauté in the butter (can be done in microwave). Mix together all ingredients except tomato and cheese. Adjust seasoning.

4. Arrange tomato slices in a single layer in a buttered baking dish. Top with a mound of spinach and sprinkle with Parmesan cheese. Bake for 15 to 20 minutes.

Tangy Cauliflower

HISTORICALLY COOKING — 200 YEARS OF GOOD EATING   K.K. BETH ELOHIM SISTERHOOD   CHARLESTON, SC

1 large cauliflower (or 2
  10-oz. pkgs. frozen)
Salt to taste
½ cup mayonnaise*
2 teaspoons Dijon mustard
¾ cup grated sharp Cheddar
  cheese
2 tablespoons chopped
  chives (optional)

Preparation time: 5 to 10 minutes
Cooking time/conventional: 20 minutes
Serves 6

1. Preheat oven to 375°.

2. Cook cauliflower until just crisp; drain and arrange in a shallow baking dish. Sprinkle with salt.

3. Combine mayonnaise, mustard, and chives and spread over cauliflower. Sprinkle with grated cheese and bake for about 20 minutes until cheese melts.

Microwave

In step 2, place cauliflower in a shallow dish and cover with plastic wrap. Cook until just tender-crisp. Proceed to step 3.

Corn Custard

GARDEN OF EATING SISTERHOOD OF TEMPLE BETH O'R   CLARK, NEW JERSEY

4 large eggs
1 quart milk
2 tablespoons butter or
  margarine
2 cans (16 oz. each) creamed
  corn
Salt and pepper to taste

Preparation time: 5 minutes
Baking time: 2 hours
Serves 12 to 14

1. Preheat oven to 350°.

2. Beat eggs in a large bowl. Heat the milk and butter until hot but do not allow to boil. Slowly beat milk into eggs. Add corn and seasonings. Pour into a greased 9 x 13 baking dish and bake for 2 hours.

Asparagus Polanaise

QUICK QUISINE GREATER RED BANK SECTION NCJW RED BANK, NEW JERSEY

1½ to 2 pounds fresh
asparagus (or 2 10-oz pkg.
frozen)
¼ cup seasoned bread
crumbs*
6 tablespoons butter
1 hard-cooked egg, sieved

Preparation time: 20 minutes
Serves 6 to 8

1. Cook the asparagus (steam or microwave) until crisp-tender.

2. Meanwhile, sauté the bread crumbs in the butter until lightly browned. Sprinkle the crumbs over the hot asparagus and garnish with the egg.

Sweet and Sour Cabbage

MRS. COOPER'S ENCORE B'NAI JACOB SYNAGOGUE AUXILIARY CHARLESTON, WEST VIRGINIA

1 small onion
1 medium head cabbage
1 tart apple, peeled and
cored
2 tablespoons margarine
2 tablespoons lemon juice
¼ cup dark brown sugar
1 tablespoon ketchup*
Salt and pepper
2 teaspoons cornstarch
1 tablespoon cold water

Preparation time/processor: 10 to 15 minutes
Preparation time/conventional: 15 to 25 minutes
Cooking time: 15 minutes
Serves 4 to 6

Food processor

1. Insert metal blade; chop onion and remove. Insert slicing blade and slice the cabbage and apple.

2. Heat margarine in a skillet and sauté onion until browned lightly; add cabbage and apple and cook for about 1 minute. Add about ¾ cup water (to keep the cabbage from sticking), lemon juice, brown sugar, salt, pepper, and ketchup. Simmer until tender, about 15 minutes, stirring occasionally and adding more water if necessary.

3. Just before serving, dissolve cornstarch in the water and add, stirring until thick and shiny.

Note: Add a teaspoon of caraway seeds for extra zest. Reheats well in microwave.

Sweet and Sour Red Cabbage

THE FAIRMOUNT TEMPLE COOKBOOK   FAIRMOUNT TEMPLE   CLEVELAND, OHIO

1 large head red cabbage
½ cup boiling water
½ cup cider vinegar
½ stick butter or margarine
¾ cup red currant jelly
Salt and pepper to taste

Preparation time/processor: 5 to 10 minutes
Preparation time/conventional: 20 minutes
Cooking time: 45 to 60 minutes
Serves 8 to 10

1. Shred cabbage; place in a large saucepan or Dutch oven. Add boiling water, vinegar, and butter. Cover and cook slowly for 45 minutes.

2. Stir in the jelly, salt and pepper. Continue cooking until very little liquid is left and cabbage is tender.

3. Taste carefully and adjust seasoning.

Note: Freezes well.

Israeli Carrots

EDITOR'S CHOICE

1½ pounds young carrots
½ stick butter or margarine
⅓ cup dry white wine
½ teaspoon nutmeg
⅔ cup golden raisins
3 tablespoons light brown
  sugar

Preparation time: 20 minutes
Serves 6

1. Slice carrots. In a saucepan, place carrots, butter, wine, and nutmeg. Cover and cook over low heat until carrots are tender, about 15 minutes.

2. Stir in raisins and sugar and continue cooking a few minutes longer until raisins are plump and carrots are glazed.

Quick Ideas

● Leftover baked potatoes can be cooled, peeled, and used for hash browns, potato salads, and casseroles. Bake extra.

● Freeze odds and ends of leftover vegetables. When you have several cups, thaw, puree in a food processor or blender, and add broth or cream to make soup.

● Use leftover mousse, souffles, or vegetable casserole to fill crepes or omelets.

Carrot Casserole

CREATIVE COOKERY SISTERHOOD TEMPLE SHAARE TEFILAH NORWOOD, MASSACHUSETTS

4 to 6 carrots, peeled
3 large eggs
¼ teaspoon nutmeg
½ teaspoon salt
½ teaspoon white pepper
2 tablespoons melted butter
  or margarine
½ cup whipping cream or
  evaporated milk
½ small onion
¾ cup pecan halves

Preparation time/processor: 10 minutes
Preparation time/conventional: 15 to 20 minutes
Cooking time: 35 minutes
Serves 4 to 6

Food processor

1. Preheat oven to 325°.

2. Insert grating blade and grate carrots. Remove, measure out 2 cups, and reserve. Insert metal blade. Place eggs, nutmeg, salt, pepper, melted butter, and cream in the work bowl and process until well combined, about 15 seconds. Add the onion and pulse until finely chopped. Add pecans and pulse once to chop and mix. Add reserved carrots and fold in with a rubber spatula.

3. Transfer to a greased 1-quart casserole.

4. Set casserole in a pan of hot water and bake for about 35 minutes or until firm and set.

Note: This does not reheat well.

Conventional

Grate carrots and measure 2 cups. Chop onion and pecans. Beat together eggs, nutmeg, salt, pepper, melted butter, and cream. Add carrots, onions, and pecans and stir well. Proceed to step 3.

Quick Ideas

• Never store tomatoes beside cucumbers, or cucumbers will become mushy.

• Keep sweet potatoes from turning dark by placing in salted water (5 teaspoons salt to 1 quart water) immediately after peeling.

• To peel tomatoes, drop in boiling water for 10 seconds. Or, microwave for a minute or so.

Parmesan Potatoes
IN THE BEST OF TASTE CONGREGATION BETH EL SUDBURY, MASSACHUSETTS

4 to 6 medium white potatoes
  (or 6 to 8 red-skinned
  potatoes)
3 tablespoons margarine
3 tablespoons peanut oil
⅓ cup grated Parmesan
  cheese
Additional Parmesan cheese
Paprika

Preparation time: 15 to 20 minutes
Baking time: 30 to 45 minutes
Serves 4 to 6

1. Preheat oven to 350°.

2. Dice potatoes (do not peel) and pat dry.

3. Melt margarine and oil in a large skillet. Add potatoes, cover, and cook until tender, about 7 or 8 minutes. Stir frequently. Stir in cheese and transfer to a shallow 2-quart casserole. Sprinkle with more cheese and with paprika.

4. Bake for 30 to 45 minutes until golden and crispy.

Variation: Pre-cook potatoes in microwave with just a little margarine and oil to make a lower calorie version.

Oven Fried Potatoes
THE KOSHER KITCHEN SISTERHOOD TEMPLE SHAAREY ZEDEK AMHERST, NEW YORK

8 large baking potatoes
  (unpeeled)
½ cup oil
2 tablespoons grated
  Parmesan cheese (optional)
1 clove garlic, minced
1 teaspoon salt
½ teaspoon paprika
¼ teaspoon pepper

Preparation time: 10 minutes
Baking time: 45 minutes
Serves 8

1. Preheat oven to 375°.

2. Cut each potato into 8 wedges; arrange peel-side-down in a shallow baking pan. Combine remaining ingredients and brush over potatoes. Bake for about 45 minutes or until golden brown.

Sour Cream and Cheese Baked Potatoes

SALT AND PEPPER TO TASTE   SISTERHOOD OF CONGREGATION ANSHEI ISRAEL   TUCSON, ARIZONA

6 medium white potatoes
6 green onions
6 ounces sharp Cheddar
  cheese
½ stick butter or margarine
1½ cups sour cream
1 teaspoon salt
¼ teaspoon pepper
2 tablespoons butter or
  margarine

Preparation time/processor: 10 to 15 minutes
Preparation time/conventional: 20 to 25 minutes
Pre-preparation: bake potatoes
Baking time: 25 to 30 minutes
Serves 8 to 12

Food processor

1. Cook potatoes in their skins (bake, boil, or microwave), and allow to cool slightly. Meanwhile, proceed with recipe.

2. Preheat oven to 350°.

3. Insert metal blade and chop onions. Remove to a large mixing bowl and reserve. Insert the grating blade and grate the cheese; transfer to a medium saucepan.

4. Add the butter to the cheese and stir over low heat until almost melted (if it looks curdled add some sour cream and stir well). Remove from heat.

5. Peel the potatoes; grate using the grating blade. Combine potatoes with sour cream, onion, salt, pepper, and cheese mixture, folding thoroughly but gently. Turn into a greased 2-quart casserole. Dot with butter and bake for 25 to 30 minutes until bubbling.

Note: Can be prepared ahead and refrigerated — increase baking time to about 1 hour to allow for cold ingredients.

Food Processor-Freezer Potato Latkes

EDITOR'S CHOICE

2 pounds boiling potatoes
2 tablespoons vinegar
2 eggs
1 small onion
¼ cup matzo meal
Salt and pepper
Corn oil

Preparation time/processor: 15 to 20 minutes
Cooking time: 15 to 20 minutes
Makes about 24

Food processor

1. Peel potatoes. Grate with the grating blade, two at a time; place each batch in a large bowl of water with vinegar added. Allow to soak about 4 minutes.

2. Drain in a colander. Insert metal blade. Working in batches, place handfuls of the potatoes in the work bowl. Pulse twice only and remove to a second colander or bowl. Repeat until all potatoes have been processed.

3. Place eggs in work bowl and process 5 seconds. Add onion, cut in half, and pulse until finely chopped.

4. Squeeze the moisture out of the potatoes, using your hands. Place in a bowl; add the egg-onion mixture, matzo meal, and salt and pepper. Blend well with a spatula.

5. Cover bottom of skillet with oil; heat until a drop of water sizzles. Spoon potato mixture into skillet, using 2 tablespoons for each latke. Cook on each side until golden brown. Drain on paper towels and serve immediately.

To Freeze: Arrange cooked, cooled latkes in a single layer on a cookie sheet and place in the freezer. When frozen, stack in a freezer bag. To serve, preheat oven to 500° and bake frozen latkes on a cookie sheet for about 5 minutes or until piping hot.

Pecan Sweet Potato Puffs

NOT FOR NOSHERS ONLY   BETH ISRAEL SISTERHOOD   LEBANON, PENNSYLVANIA

½ cup grated Cheddar
  cheese
1 cup finely chopped pecans
3 cups mashed sweet
  potatoes
⅓ cup apricot preserves
1 large egg
½ teaspoon salt

Preparation time/processor: 5 minutes
Preparation time/conventional: 10 to 15 minutes
Baking time: 20 to 30 minutes
Makes about 15 puffs

1. Preheat oven to 350°.

2. Combine cheese and nuts and spread on a sheet of wax paper. Blend remaining ingredients and drop onto wax paper by the tablespoonful. Shape and roll until each mound is coated with the nut mixture.

3. Place in a greased shallow baking dish and bake for 20 to 30 minutes or until brown.

Food processor

Use grating blade to grate cheese. Change to metal blade to chop pecans. Use metal blade to mash sweet potatoes and combine with other ingredients.

Microwave: Sweet potatoes could be baked and scooped out, or peeled and cooked with some water in a dish covered with plastic wrap.

Oriental Vegetables

THE KOSHER KITCHEN   SISTERHOOD TEMPLE SHAAREY ZEDEK   AMHERST, NEW YORK

2 tablespoons oil
1 cup sliced carrots
1 cup diagonally sliced
  celery
1 cup sliced fresh
  mushrooms
½ cup sliced water chestnuts
½ cup green pepper strips
Chinese cabbage, sliced
Soy sauce, garlic, ginger to
  taste

Preparation time: 15 to 20 minutes
Serves 4 to 6

1. Heat oil in a wok or large skillet. Add vegetables and stir-fry until crisp but tender. Season to taste with soy sauce, garlic, or ginger.

Variation: Adjust quantities to reflect what you have on hand. Bean sprouts and chopped green onion are good additions.

Green Beans with Sour Cream

THE WAY TO A MAN'S HEART   BETH ISRAEL CONGREGATION   WASHINGTON, PENNSYLVANIA

1½ pounds green beans
1 medium onion, chopped
1 teaspoon sugar
2 tablespoons butter or
  margarine
1 tablespoon flour
1 teaspoon salt
½ teaspoon white pepper
1 cup sour cream
2 tablespoons grated cheese
  (Swiss, Cheddar, or
  mozzarella)
2 tablespoons chopped
  almonds

Preparation time: 15 to 20 minutes
Baking time: 15 to 20 minutes
Serves 6 to 8

1. Preheat oven to 400°.

2. Cut green beans into 2-inch pieces and cook until tender (or microwave). Drain. Combine beans, onion, and sugar in a greased 2-quart casserole.

3. In a saucepan, melt butter; remove from heat and stir in the flour. Return to heat and cook for 1 minute, stirring constantly. Stir in salt, pepper, and sour cream and heat, but do not boil.

4. Spoon sauce over vegetables and toss lightly until mixed through. Sprinkle with cheese and almonds. Bake for 15 to 20 minutes.

Microwave: Sprinkle a little paprika over the top to make the dish look as if it were browned in the oven.

Peas and Water Chestnuts

THE KOSHER KITCHEN   SISTERHOOD TEMPLE SHAAREY ZEDEK   AMHERST, NEW YORK

1¼ pounds green peas,
  shelled (or 2 pkg. frozen)
1 can (8 oz.) water chestnuts
6 tablespoons butter or
  margarine
1 teaspoon celery salt, or to
  taste

Preparation time: 10 to 15 minutes
Serves 6

1. Cook peas and drain.

2. Drain water chestnuts; slice.

3. Melt butter; mix in water chestnuts and celery salt. When hot, pour over peas.

Peas Oriental

THE PORTAL TO GOOD COOKING, VOL. 2   WOMEN'S AMERICAN ORT, VIII   CHICAGO, ILLINOIS

½ pound green peas, shelled
(or 10-oz. pkg. frozen)
2 tablespoons oil
½ cup diagonally sliced
celery
⅔ cup sliced fresh
mushrooms
2 tablespoons chopped
pimento
2 tablespoons finely chopped
onion
½ teaspoon salt
¾ teaspoon minced summer
savory (or ¼ tsp. dried)
Dash pepper

Preparation time/processor: 15 to 20 minutes
Preparation time/conventional: 20 to 25 minutes
Serves 4

1. Cook peas until tender. Drain.

2. Heat oil in a skillet. Add celery, mushrooms, pimento, onion, and seasonings. Stir-fry until celery is tender-crisp, about 5 to 7 minutes. Add peas and just heat through.

Snow Peas and Water Chestnuts

ALL THAT SCHMALTZ   AUGUSTA CHAPTER OF HADASSAH   AUGUSTA, GEORGIA

2 tablespoons vegetable oil
1 tablespoon chopped green
onion
½ clove garlic, minced
6 ounces snow peas
½ cup sliced water chestnuts
1 tablespoon soy sauce
¼ cup chicken stock
1 teaspoon cornstarch
1 tablespoon water

Preparation time: 10 to 15 minutes
Serves 3 to 4

1. Remove tips and strings from snow peas, if necessary.

2. Heat oil in a heavy skillet; sauté green onion and garlic; add snow peas, water chestnuts, and soy sauce. Cook 1 minute, stirring. Add chicken stock; cover and cook 2 minutes.

3. Combine cornstarch and water and add to the skillet. Cook, stirring, until sauce thickens and becomes glossy, about 1 minute.

Sweet and Sour Lentils

THE MJCC PRESENTS OUR FAVORITE RECIPES   MEMPHIS JEWISH COMMUNITY CENTER   MEMPHIS, TN

1 pound lentils
1 large onion, chopped
2 tablespoons oil
1 clove garlic, minced
4 cups water
3 tablespoons vinegar
1 tablespoon sugar
Salt to taste

Preparation time: 5 to 10 minutes
Pre-preparation: 2 hours
Cooking time: 30 to 45 minutes
Serves 6 to 8

1. Soak lentils in cold water for 2 hours; drain.

2. Sauté onion in oil until lightly browned. Place lentils, onions, and remaining ingredients in a saucepan and simmer for 30 to 45 minutes, until lentils are tender. If too dry, add a little more water.

Hungarian Mushroom Paprikas

EDITOR'S CHOICE

½ cup oil
1 small green pepper, chopped
3 cups chopped onion
2 large cloves garlic, minced
1 large tomato, chopped
1½ cups vegetable stock or water
1 pound mushrooms, thickly sliced
2 tablespoons Hungarian sweet paprika
1 teaspoon caraway seeds
Pinch sugar
Salt and pepper to taste

Preparation time/processor: 15 to 20 minutes
Preparation time/conventional: 20 to 25 minutes
Cooking time: 15 to 30 minutes
Serves 4

1. Heat oil in a large skillet. Add green pepper, onion, garlic, and tomato, and cook until onion is translucent.

2. Transfer to a food processor or blender and purée until smooth. Add stock gradually to make a smooth sauce. Return to skillet. Add mushrooms, paprika, caraway seeds, sugar, salt and pepper. Simmer briskly until desired consistency is reached (15 to 30 minutes), stirring from time to time.

3. Serve over noodles, topped with sour cream.

Onions Parmesan

FROM OUR KITCHEN   BRITH EMETH SISTERHOOD   PEPPER PIKE, OHIO

2 pounds medium onions
½ cup grated parmesan
  cheese
2 tablespoons flour
2 teaspoons salt
½ teaspoon seasoned salt
⅛ teaspoon pepper
¼ teaspoon Worcestershire
  sauce
1 cup light cream
Paprika

Preparation time: 10 to 15 minutes
Cooking time: 40 to 50 minutes
Serves 6

1. Slice onions and separate into rings. Place half the onions in a large greased skillet, top with half the cheese, then repeat the layers.

2. Combine flour, salt, pepper, seasoned salt, Worcestershire sauce, and cream. Beat until smooth. Pour over onions. Cover and simmer for 40 to 50 minutes or until tender-crisp. Check from time to time to see that onions do not stick to pan.

3. Dust with paprika and serve from skillet.

Roasted Onions

QUICK AND EASY COOKBOOK   MAIN LINE REFORM TEMPLE SISTERHOOD   PHILADELPHIA, PENNSYLVANIA

7 to 8 medium onions
½ stick margarine, melted
Salt and pepper to taste

Preparation time: 5 to 10 minutes
Baking time: 1 hour 15 minutes
Serves 4

1. Preheat oven to 350°.

2. Cut onions into quarters. Toss gently with margarine, salt and pepper.

3. Place in a shallow baking dish and bake for 1 hour 15 minutes. Turn 3 or 4 times during cooking.

quick breads & coffee cakes

illinois world of our flavors south bend indiana the cookery cedar rapids
wa specialties of the house alexandria louisiana kitchen treats cookboo
es to noshes lewiston maine sisterhood cookbook potomac maryland p
nelting pot lexington massa   thought cookbook newton
ok norwood massachus   ody massachusetts co
etts in the best of tast   e happy cooker of te
with temple beth   a used to make f
igan all the recip   o ask saint pau
iouri deborah c   o generation
rry hill new je   eating east
ion new jerse   with love s
le tinton fa   y the spice
poking? al   onderful
k cookie   york the
ng brook   osher ki
like it cli   east noi
new yo   great r
york th   it vern
na had   sher c
osher   nester
scars   what
ood ta   d nev
carol   d ohi
ount t   nd ol
iio in t   nia th
ania th   n per
ia peni   penr
n wynr   south
charles   rolina
e recipe   years
nnial co   oks fal
nchburg   n good
ie it parke   sin from
gham alab.   at and en
ste berkele   iills califor
california fr   hat's cookir
flavored with   iego californ
lectable collec   ease! rockvill
d connecticut for   passover made
earwater florida cle   a measures and tr
ght gainesville florid.   alabustas' more fave
it in the kitchen hollywo   s hollywood florida nit
ksonville florida what's coo.   ville florida try it you'll like
atellite beach florida our favorite recipes tallahassee florida knishes gefil
georgia golden soup atlanta georgia the happy cooker augusta georgi
ois portal to good cooking great lakes illinois the fort sheridan and great I

Quick breads

Carrot Corn Bread

FLAVORED WITH LOVE   ADAT ARI EL SISTERHOOD   NORTH HOLLYWOOD, CALIFORNIA

1 cup yellow cornmeal
½ teaspoon salt
½ teaspoon baking soda
½ teaspoon baking powder
2 carrots
1 egg
1 tablespoon vegetable oil
1 cup buttermilk

Preparation time/processor: 5 to 10 minutes
Preparation time/conventional: 15 to 20 minutes
Baking time: 20 to 25 minutes
Makes 16 squares

Food processor

1. Preheat oven to 450°.

2. Insert metal blade. Place cornmeal, salt, baking soda, and baking powder in the work bowl and pulse once to mix through. Remove and reserve. Insert the slicing blade and slice the carrots. Change to metal blade and process the carrot slices, egg, oil, and buttermilk until smooth, about 15 to 20 seconds. Add dry ingredients to work bowl and pulse once or twice to just mix.

3. Turn batter into a greased 8 x 8 pan and bake for 20 to 25 minutes. Cut into squares. May be split and toasted.

Conventional

In step 2, sift dry ingredients together and reserve. Slice carrots and place in blender with egg, oil, and buttermilk and blend until smooth. Add dry ingredients and mix. Proceed to step 3.

Quick Ideas

PARSLEY-CHIVE FRENCH BREAD. Split loaf of French bread lengthwise and spread with a mixture of ½ stick softened butter, 2 tablespoons sesame seeds, ¼ cup chopped parsley, and ¼ cup snipped chives. Bake until butter melts.

ORANGE CINNAMON BREAD. Cut loaf of French bread into 1 to 1½ inch slices. Spread with ⅓ to ½ cup soft butter and lots of orange marmalade. Sprinkle with cinnamon and broil until hot, 5 to 6 minutes. Cool slightly before serving.

HOMEMADE MELBA TOAST. Slice bread ⅛ inch thick. Trim crusts and place in a 250° oven until toast is golden and curls.

FRESH BREAD CRUMBS. Slice bread (white, whole wheat, or rye) or cut into small chunks. Place in a food processor (metal blade) or blender (in small batches); pulse until desired coarseness is reached. Store in air-tight container in freezer.

DRY BREAD CRUMBS. Place fresh bread crumbs on a paper plate in the microwave for about 3 to 6 minutes, stirring from time to time. Or place on a cookie sheet in a 300° oven until stale and dry (about 15 to 30 minutes); or place on a cookie sheet in a dry kitchen and allow to dry naturally.

SEASONED BREAD CRUMBS. Combine 1 cup dry bread crumbs, 1 tablespoon Italian herbs (see recipe), and 1 to 3 tablespoons freshly grated Parmesan cheese (optional).

CROUTONS. Cut good quality bread into cubes. Allow to get a little stale or place in oven for about 5 minutes. Place melted butter or olive oil in a skillet (use about 1 stick butter to 1 pound bread). Add minced garlic or herbs and bread cubes, and sauté on medium-high heat until lightly browned. Toss and stir as they cook. Drain on paper towels. Sprinkle with cheese if desired.

DIET CROUTONS. Place bread cubes on paper towel in microwave and sprinkle with herbs. Cook until crisp and dry, about 2 to 5 minutes. (Time will vary with quantity.)

BEER BREAD. Combine 3 cups self-rising flour, 2 tablespoons sugar, and a 12-ounce can beer (room temperature). Spoon into a 9 x 5 loaf pan and bake at 350° for 1 hour. Seasonings like herbs, cheese, or onion may be added.

INSTANT MUFFINS. Combine 1 cup sifted self-rising flour with 1 cup softened vanilla ice cream (do not overmix). Spoon into 12 greased miniature muffin cups and bake at 350° for 20 minutes.

Rye Muffins

½ cup rye flour
⅓ cup flour
¾ teaspoon baking powder
¼ teaspoon baking soda
¼ teaspoon salt
¼ teaspoon caraway seeds
¼ teaspoon poppy seeds
½ cup buttermilk
1 egg
1 tablespoon walnut or
  peanut oil
1 tablespoon honey
¼ cup walnuts or pecans

Preparation time/processor: 5 to 10 minutes
Preparation time/conventional: 10 to 15 minutes
Baking time: 15 minutes
Makes 12

Food processor

1. Preheat oven to 400°.

2. Insert metal blade. Place dry ingredients and seeds in work bowl and pulse once to mix; remove and reserve. Place buttermilk, egg, oil, and honey in work bowl and process to mix well, about 10 seconds. Add walnuts and pulse once to start chopping. Add dry ingredients and pulse once or twice to just mix through. Do not over process.

3. Spoon into 12 well-greased miniature muffin cups and bake for 15 minutes or until tests done.

Conventional

In step 2, sift dry ingredients and reserve. Beat buttermilk, egg, oil, and honey. Chop walnuts and add along with dry ingredients. Stir until just combined. Proceed with step 3.

French Muffin Puffs

A MATZO BALL IS NOT ANOTHER DRESS-UP DANCE!   B'NAI SHOLOM SISTERHOOD   HUNTINGTON, WEST VIRGINIA

1½ cups flour
1 teaspoon salt, or to taste
1½ teaspoons baking powder
½ cup sugar
⅓ cup oil
1 egg
½ cup milk
6 tablespoons melted butter
½ cup sugar, mixed with
1 teaspoon cinnamon

Preparation time: 10 minutes
Baking time: 20 to 25 minutes
Makes about 10

1. Preheat oven to 350°

2. Sift flour, salt, and baking powder together. Beat sugar, oil, and egg until smooth; add flour, alternating with milk, and beat until very smooth.

3. Fill greased muffin cups ⅔ full. Bake 20 to 25 minutes.

4. Dip top of muffin in melted butter then dip in cinnamon-sugar. Serve warm.

Zucchini Oatmeal Muffins

TASTE OF TRADITION SISTERHOOD OF TEMPLE ADATH ISRAEL LEXINGTON, KENTUCKY

4 eggs
1 medium zucchini
  (about 10 oz.), shredded
¾ cup oil
2½ cups flour
1½ cups sugar, or to taste
1 cup chopped pecans
½ cup quick oats
1 tablespoon baking powder
1 teaspoon salt, or to taste
1 teaspoon cinnamon

Preparation time/processor: 10 minutes
Preparation time/conventional: 15 to 20 minutes
Baking time: 25 minutes
Makes 8 to 10

1. Preheat oven to 400°.

2. In a medium bowl, beat the eggs with a fork. Stir in the zucchini and oil.

3. Place remaining ingredients in a large mixing bowl and stir to mix. Add egg mixture to the dry ingredients and stir to moisten. Batter will be lumpy.

4. Spoon batter into 8 to 10 greased muffin cups (or use paper liners) and bake about 25 minutes or until toothpick inserted in muffin comes out clean. Remove from pans and serve.

Continental Onion Popovers

UNDER THE CHEF'S H.A.T. HEBREW ACADEMY OF TOLEDO TOLEDO, OHIO

2 eggs
1 cup milk
1 cup flour
1 tablespoon oil
½ teaspoon salt
½ teaspoon onion powder

Preparation time: 5 to 10 minutes
Baking time: 35 to 45 minutes
Makes 6

Food processor

1. Preheat oven to 425°.

2. Insert metal blade. Combine all ingredients in work bowl and process for about 30 seconds, scraping down bowl once.

3. Pour into greased popover pans or custard cups until half full. Bake for 15 to 20 minutes until golden brown and puffed. Reduce heat to 350° and continue baking 20 to 25 minutes or until firm to the touch.

Conventional

In step 2, use blender or wire whisk.

Cranberry Muffins

FAVORITE RECIPES FROM OUR BEST COOKS   TEMPLE BETH SHOLOM SISTERHOOD   DANVILLE, VIRGINIA

2 cups flour
1 tablespoon baking powder
½ teaspoon salt
⅔ cup sugar
Peel (zest) of 1 orange
1 cup milk
3 tablespoons butter, melted
   and cooled
1 cup fresh cranberries

Preparation time/processor: 10 minutes
Preparation time/conventional: 20 minutes
Baking time: 25 minutes
Makes 12

Food processor

1. Preheat oven to 400°.

2. Insert metal blade. Place flour, baking powder, and salt in the work bowl and pulse once to stir. Remove. Add sugar and orange peel to work bowl and process 25 to 30 seconds or until the peel is finely chopped. Add the milk and butter and process about 10 seconds to combine.

3. Sprinkle flour mixture and cranberries evenly around the work bowl and pulse several times to just mix through. Do not overprocess.

4. Spoon into greased or paper-lined muffin cups, filling each about ⅔ full. Bake for 25 minutes or until golden and tests done.

Conventional

Sift flour, baking powder, salt, and sugar into a small bowl; chop cranberries and add. Grate orange peel and add to milk; stir in butter. Combine milk mixture with dry ingredients using a fork. Stir just enough to moisten flour. Proceed to step 4.

Mayonnaise Biscuits

A MATZO BALL IS NOT ANOTHER DRESS-UP DANCE!   B'NAI SHOLOM SISTERHOOD   HUNTINGTON, WEST VIRGINIA

2 cups self-rising flour
4 rounded tablespoons
   mayonnaise*
1 cup milk

Preparation time: 5 minutes
Baking time: 12 to 14 minutes
Makes 8

1. Preheat oven to 425°.

2. Mix ingredients together with a spoon or fork. Drop by tablespoon into 8 greased muffin tins. Bake for 12 to 14 minutes.

Coffee cakes

Cherry-Almond Coffee Cake

THE SPICE AND SPIRIT OF KOSHER JEWISH COOKING   LUBAVITCH WOMEN'S ORGANIZATION,
JUNIOR DIVISION   BROOKLYN, NY

1½ cups flour
½ teaspoon salt, or to taste
2½ teaspoons baking powder
¼ cup sugar
1 egg
¾ cup milk
¼ cup melted butter or
  margarine, cooled

Topping
¼ cup dark brown sugar
½ cup sliced or slivered
  almonds
2 tablespoons cinnamon
⅔ cup cherry (or other) jam

Preparation time/processor: 5 to 10 minutes
Preparation time/conventional: 10 to 15 minutes
Baking time: 25 to 30 minutes
Serves about 12

Food processor

1. Preheat oven to 375°.

2. Insert metal blade. Place flour, salt, and baking powder in the work bowl and pulse once to mix through. Remove. Process sugar and egg until fluffy, about 15 seconds. Add milk and melted butter and process to combine, about 10 seconds. Add flour mixture evenly around work bowl and pulse several times to mix.

3. Pour into a greased 9 x 9 square pan. Combine brown sugar, almonds, and cinnamon and sprinkle over the batter. Drizzle the jam over the topping and bake for 25 to 30 minutes.

Conventional

In step 2, place all cake ingredients in a large bowl and beat vigorously for 30 seconds. Proceed to step 3.

"Maali" — Romanian Corn Meal Cake

SHABBOS THE RABBI ATE LATE   MAAREV TEMPLE   ENCINO, CALIFORNIA

3 eggs
1 cup yellow corn meal
1 tablespoon flour
16 ounces cottage cheese
1 pint sour cream
Pinch salt
¾ tablespoon baking powder
½ stick butter or margarine,
  softened
4 to 6 tablespoons sugar

Preparation time: 5 to 10 minutes
Baking time: 1 hour
Makes 8 to 10 slices

1. Preheat oven to 350°.

2. Combine all ingredients with a food processor or mixer (may need to do in small batches). Pour into a greased 9 x 5 x 3 loaf pan and bake for 1 hour or until tests done. Serve topped with sour cream, sugar, cinnamon, jam, etc.

Coffee Cake A-La-Bama

THE MJCC PRESENTS OUR FAVORITE RECIPES   MEMPHIS JEWISH COMMUNITY CENTER   MEMPHIS, TENNESSEE

1 package (8 oz.) cream
  cheese, softened
1 stick margarine, softened
¾ cup sugar
¼ cup milk
2 eggs, well beaten
1 teaspoon vanilla extract
2 cups flour (unsifted)
1 teaspoon baking powder
½ teaspoon baking soda
¼ teaspoon salt
18 ounces apricot (or other)
  preserves
1 tablespoon lemon juice
½ cup chopped nuts
¼ cup light brown sugar

Preparation time/processor: 10 to 15 minutes
Preparation time/conventional: 15 to 20 minutes
Baking time: 30 to 40 minutes
Serves 10 to 12

1. Preheat oven to 350°.

2. Beat cream cheese, margarine, and sugar until fluffy. Stir in milk, eggs, and vanilla.

3. Sift together flour, baking powder, baking soda, and salt and add to cream cheese mixture. Mix until smooth (batter will be stiff). Spread half the batter in a greased 9 x 13 baking pan.

4. Combine the preserves, lemon juice, nuts, and brown sugar and spread over batter. Spread remaining batter evenly over the top (will not cover). Bake for 30 to 40 minutes until nicely brown on top and cake tests done.

Apple-Pear Coffee Cake

WORLD OF OUR FLAVORS — CERTIFIED TA'AM   BETH HILLEL SISTERHOOD   WILMETTE, ILLINOIS

2 cups flour
1 teaspoon baking soda
1 teaspoon baking powder
½ teaspoon salt
1 stick butter or margarine
1 cup sugar
2 large eggs
1 teaspoon vanilla extract
1 cup sour cream
2 large apples, peeled
1 large pear, peeled

Topping
1 cup brown sugar
½ cup chopped nuts
2 tablespoons butter or
  margarine, softened
1 teaspoon cinnamon

Preparation time/processor: 10 to 15 minutes
Preparation time/conventional: 15 to 20 minutes
Baking time: 45 to 55 minutes
Makes 16 squares

Food processor

1. Preheat oven to 350°.

2. Insert metal blade. Place flour, baking soda, baking powder, and salt in the work bowl and pulse once; remove and reserve. Process butter and sugar until fluffy. Add eggs and vanilla and mix well. Add sour cream and process until smooth. Add flour mixture and pulse once. (With a small work bowl, this recipe is easier if done in batches.)

3. Cut fruit into quarters; add to the batter in the work bowl. Pulse until fruit is finely chopped, about 4 or 5 times.

4. Spread the batter in a greased 9 x 13 baking pan. Combine topping ingredients and sprinkle evenly over batter. Bake for 45 to 55 minutes or until tests done.

Conventional

In step 2, sift dry ingredients together and reserve. Use a mixer to cream butter and sugar. Add eggs, vanilla, and sour cream and beat well. Stir in flour mixture. In step 3, chop apples and pears into small pieces and fold into batter. Proceed to step 4.

Chocolate Chip Coffee Cake

EDITOR'S CHOICE

1 cup semi-sweet chocolate
chips
½ cup dark brown sugar
2 tablespoons instant coffee
powder
3 cups flour
1 tablespoon baking powder
1 teaspoon baking soda
½ teaspoon salt
1 cup sugar
3 large eggs
2 sticks butter or margarine
1 cup sour cream

Preparation time/processor: 10 to 15 minutes
Preparation time/conventional: 15 to 20 minutes
Baking time: 35 to 45 minutes
Serves 10 to 12

Food processor

1. Preheat oven to 350°.

2. Combine chocolate chips, brown sugar, and coffee powder in a small dish and reserve.

3. Insert metal blade. Place flour, baking powder, baking soda, and salt in work bowl and pulse once to mix. Remove and reserve. Place sugar and eggs in work bowl and process 1 minute. Cut butter into 8 pieces and add; process 1 minute. Add sour cream and process 5 seconds, scrape bowl, and process another 5 seconds. Sprinkle with dry ingredients and pulse twice to just combine.

4. Spread half the batter in a greased 9 x 13 baking pan. Sprinkle with the chocolate chip mixture.

5. Thin the remaining batter in the work bowl with 2 to 3 tablespoons of milk for easier spreading. Spread over the chocolate layer. Bake for 35 to 45 minutes until cake tests done.

Conventional

In step 3, sift dry ingredients together into a small bowl. With a mixer, cream butter and sugar until fluffy. Add eggs and sour cream and beat until smooth. Add flour and beat well. Proceed to step 4.

Orange Streusel Coffee Cake

THE WONDERFUL WORLD OF COOKING   BALDWIN HADASSAH   BALDWIN HARBOR, NEW YORK

2 cups flour
1 tablespoon baking powder
Pinch salt
1 cup light brown sugar
1 teaspoon grated orange
  peel*
2 eggs
1 stick butter, melted and
  cooled
½ cup milk
½ cup orange juice
2 teaspoons vanilla extract
  (or 1 tsp. vanilla + 1 tsp.
  orange extract)

Streusel Topping
⅓ cup dark brown sugar
⅓ cup flour
3 tablespoons melted butter
1 teaspoon grated orange
  peel*

Preparation time/processor: 10 minutes
Preparation time/conventional: 15 to 20 minutes
Baking time: 45 minutes
Serves 9 to 12

Food processor

1. Preheat oven to 350°.

2. Insert metal blade. Place flour, baking powder, and salt in work bowl and pulse twice to stir. Remove and reserve.

3. Add light brown sugar, orange peel, and eggs to work bowl and process until smooth and fluffy, about 20 seconds. Add melted butter, milk, and orange juice and process about 10 seconds, scraping down sides of bowl. Add vanilla and pulse to mix. Add flour mixture and pulse until just combined.

4. Pour batter into a greased 9 x 9 pan. Combine streusel ingredients; mix until crumbly and sprinkle over cake. Bake for 45 minutes or until golden.

Conventional

In step 2, sift dry ingredients together, reserve. In step 3, cream butter and light brown sugar until fluffy; add eggs and beat well. Add dry ingredients and beat until well-mixed. Add orange juice, milk, vanilla, and grated orange peel and blend well. Proceed to step 4.

Quick Ideas

• Keep powdered buttermilk (available in most grocery stores) on hand for baking. Or substitute 1 tablespoon vinegar or lemon juice added to fresh milk to equal 1 cup; let stand a few minutes before using.

• Remove whole pecans from shell by pouring boiling water over the nuts, allowing to cool, then hitting the small end of the nuts with a hammer.

Cinnamon Bread

COOK UNTO OTHERS HILLEL JEWISH STUDENT CENTER, UNIVERSITY OF CINCINNATI CINCINNATI, OHIO

2 cups flour
1 teaspoon baking powder
½ teaspoon baking soda
½ teaspoon salt
1 cup sugar
2 large eggs
½ stick melted butter or
  margarine
1 cup buttermilk
1 teaspoon vanilla extract
2 tablespoons sugar mixed
  with 1 teaspoon cinnamon

Preparation/processor: 10 to 15 minutes
Preparation/conventional: 15 to 20 minutes
Baking time: 50 minutes
Makes 1 loaf

Food processor

1. Preheat oven to 350°.

2. Insert metal blade. Place flour, baking powder, baking soda, and salt in the work bowl and pulse once to mix. Remove. Place sugar and eggs in work bowl and process until fluffy, about 60 seconds. Add melted butter and buttermilk and process to combine well, about 10 seconds. Add vanilla and pulse to mix. Add flour and pulse to just combine.

3. Pour half the batter into a greased 9 x 5 x 3 loaf pan. Sprinkle with 1 tablespoon cinnamon-sugar. Carefully pour remaining batter into pan. Sprinkle with remaining cinnamon-sugar. Bake about 50 minutes or until it tests done.

Conventional

In step 2, sift flour, baking powder, soda, and salt into a small bowl. Beat butter in medium bowl until smooth; gradually add sugar and continue to beat until light and fluffy. Beat eggs and buttermilk together and add to batter alternately with the flour mixture (beginning and ending with flour). Stir in vanilla. Proceed to step 3.

═══ Quick Ideas ═══

• Line baking pan with foil so you can lift out coffee cake.

• Keep bread in your freezer. Defrost in refrigerator, wrapped, or at room temperature, unwrapped.

• Dust fruits like cranberries and raisins with flour before using and they won't sink into the batter or dough.

Sour Cream Pecan Coffee Cake

ALL THAT SCMALTZ   AUGUSTA CHAPTER OF HADASSAH   AUGUSTA, GEORGIA

1½ cups unbleached flour
½ teaspoon salt
1 teaspoon baking powder
½ teaspoon baking soda
¾ cup light brown sugar
1 tablespoon flour
1 teaspoon cinnamon
½ stick butter or margarine
1 heaping cup pecans or
  walnuts
2 eggs
1 teaspoon vanilla extract
¼ cup maple syrup
⅔ cup sour cream
¼ cup milk

Preparation time/processor: 5 to 10 minutes
Preparation time/conventional: 15 to 20 minutes
Baking time: 30 minutes
Makes 8 to 10 squares

Food processor

1. Preheat oven to 375°.

2. Insert metal blade. Place flour, salt, baking powder, and baking soda in work bowl and pulse twice to mix; remove. Place brown sugar, 1 tablespoon flour, and cinnamon in the work bowl and pulse once. Cut butter into 4 pieces and place evenly around the work bowl and pulse until it is almost incorporated. Add nuts and pulse several times to chop. Remove and reserve for topping.

3. Wipe work bowl with a paper towel. Add eggs and process until light, about 25 seconds. Place vanilla, maple syrup, sour cream, and milk in work bowl and process to blend well. (Work in batches if necessary.)

4. Spoon flour and 1 cup of reserved topping mixture into work bowl and pulse once or twice to just mix through. Do not overmix.

5. Transfer batter to a greased 8 x 8 baking pan. Sprinkle with remaining topping. Bake for 30 minutes or until center springs when lightly pressed with fingertip. Cool slightly on wire rack. Serve warm from pan.

Conventional

In step 2, sift the dry ingredients together and reserve. Cut in the butter with a pastry blender. Add nuts and set aside. In step 3, beat the eggs until thick and light colored. Add vanilla, maple syrup, sour cream and milk. Beat until well blended. Gently stir flour mixture into egg mixture. Stir in 1 cup of reserved brown sugar-nut mixture. Proceed to step 5.

Glazed Lemon Nut Loaf

CREATIVE COOKERY SISTERHOOD OF TEMPLE SHAARE TEFILAH NORWOOD, MASSACHUSETTS

¾ cup walnuts
1 cup sugar
3 pieces lemon peel
  (½" x 2" each)
1 stick butter or margarine
2 large eggs
½ cup milk
1¼ cups flour
1 teaspoon baking powder
½ teaspoon salt

Glaze
3 tablespoons lemon juice
¼ cup sugar

Preparation time/processor: 10 minutes
Preparation time/conventional: 20 minutes
Cooking time: 1 hour
Makes 1 loaf

Food Processor

1. Preheat oven to 350°.

2. Insert metal blade. Place walnuts in work bowl and pulse once or twice to chop. Set aside. Process the sugar and lemon peel until peel is finely chopped. Add butter and process until fluffy. Add eggs and milk and process until mixture is smooth.

3. Sift the flour, baking powder, and salt onto a paper plate. Sprinkle evenly around the work bowl. Pulse once or twice. Add nuts and pulse once to mix.

4. Transfer batter to a greased 9 x 5 loaf pan and bake for 1 hour or until bread tests done.

5. For the glaze, blend juice and sugar together and pour over warm bread. Allow bread to soak in glaze before removing from pan.

Conventional

Soften butter. In step 2, chop walnuts and grate lemon peel; set aside. Cream butter and sugar until fluffy. Beat in eggs. In step 3, add sifted flour alternately with milk. Beat until smooth Stir in nuts and lemon peel. Proceed to step 4.

Quick Coffee Cake

IN THE BEST OF TASTE   CONGREGATION BETH EL   SUDBURY, MASSACHUSETTS

1½ cups flour
2 teaspoons baking powder
½ teaspoon salt
¾ cup sugar
1 egg
½ stick butter or margarine
½ cup milk
1 teaspoon grated orange or
lemon peel (optional)

Topping
2 tablespoons melted butter
½ cup brown sugar
2 teaspoons cinnamon
2 tablespoons flour
½ cup nuts (or uncooked
rolled oats)

Preparation time/processor: 10 to 15 minutes
Preparation time/conventional: 15 to 20 minutes
Baking time: 25 to 30 minutes
Makes 9 to 12 squares

Food processor

1. Preheat oven to 350°.

2. Insert metal blade. Place flour, baking powder, and salt in work bowl and pulse once. Remove. Add sugar and egg and process for 1 minute. Add butter (cut into 4 pieces) and process 1 minute. Scrape down bowl and add milk; process 5 seconds. Add flour mixture and orange peel; pulse several times to combine.

3. Place half of batter in a greased 9 x 9 baking pan. Combine topping ingredients and sprinkle half over batter in pan. Top with remaining batter and then the rest of the topping. Bake for 25 to 30 minutes.

Conventional

In step 2, beat sugar and butter until fluffy. Add egg and milk and mix well. Add flour, baking soda, and salt and combine. Proceed to step 3.

desserts

llinois world of our flavors south bend indiana the cookery cedar rapids
wa specialties of the house alexandria louisiana kitchen treats cookboo
es to noshes lewiston maine sisterhood cookbook potomac maryland p
nelting pot lexington massa   hought cookbook newton
ok norwood massachus   ody massachusetts cc
etts in the best of tast   e happy cooker of te
i with temple beth   a used to make f
igan all the recip   o ask saint pau
iouri deborah d   o generation l
rry hill new je   eating east
ion new jerse   with love s
le tinton fa   y the spice
ooking? al   onderful
k cookie   york the
ig brook   osher ki
like it cli   ast no
new yo   great r
york th   it vern
na had   sher c
osher   nestei
scarso   what
ood ta   d nev
carol   d ohi
ount t   nd ol
iio in t   nia th
ania th   n per
ia penr   penr
n wynr   south
charles   rolina
e recipe   ) years
nnial co   oks fall
nchburg   n good
te it parke   sin from
gham alab   at and en
ste berkele   iills califor
california fr   hat's cookir
flavored with   iego californ
lectable collec   iease! rockvill
d connecticut foc   passover made
earwater florida cle   a measures and tr
ght gainesville florida   alabustas' more fav
it in the kitchen hollywe s hollywood florida nik
ksonville florida what's coo. .ville florida try it you'll like
atellite beach florida our favorite recipes tallahassee florida knishes gefil
i georgia golden soup atlanta georgia the happy cooker augusta georgi
ois portal to good cooking great lakes illinois the fort sheridan and great

Cakes

Poppy Seed Cake

FROM THE BALABUSTA'S TABLE SISTERHOOD OF TEMPLE ISRAEL NATICK, MASSACHUSETTS

1 cup sugar
3 eggs
1 stick butter or margarine
1 teaspoon vanilla extract
1¼ cups flour
1 teaspoon baking powder
3 ounces small poppy seeds
¼ cup chopped nuts
1 teaspoon cinnamon

Preparation time/processor: 10 to 15 minutes
Preparation time/conventional: 20 minutes
Baking time: 35 minutes
Serves 9

Food processor

1. Preheat oven to 350°.

2. Insert metal blade. Place sugar and eggs in the work bowl and process for 1 minute. Add butter (cut into 8 pieces) and vanilla and process for 1 minute. Combine flour, baking powder, and poppy seeds; sprinkle around work bowl. Pulse 2 to 3 times to combine.

3. Pour batter into a greased 8 x 8 pan. Combine nuts and cinnamon and sprinkle over top. Bake for about 35 minutes until golden.

Conventional

Melt butter. Beat eggs; add sugar, melted butter and vanilla and beat well. Add flour, baking powder, and poppy seeds and beat well. Proceed to step 3.

- When making chocolate cake, sprinkle greased cake pan with cocoa instead of flour.

- Baked crusts should be cooled before adding filling.

- Make crumbs from stale cookies; sprinkle on baked fruit.

- Chill bowl and beaters when whipping cream.

- When chopping dates in a food processor, grease metal blade and add a little granulated sugar.

- Nuts: Drop nuts into boiling water for 3 to 5 minutes to loosen skins. Store nuts in freezer; they get rancid quickly. Add nuts last to a recipe using the food processor; pulse 1 to 2 times to mix and chop.

- To make powdered sugar with food processor, process 1 cup granulated with 1 tablespoon cornstarch for 2 minutes.

"CREME FRAICHE." Add 1 tablespoon plain yogurt to 1 cup heavy cream. Let stand at room temperature until thick.

CRUMB CRUST. Substitute crushed granola or zweiback in crusts calling for graham cracker crumbs.

FRUIT CUP. Mix sliced bananas, canteloupe, blueberries and/or other fresh fruit with sour cream and brown sugar.

FROZEN BANANAS. Cut large bananas into 3 pieces, sprinkle with lemon juice, roll in sour cream and then coconut. Freeze. Serve partially frozen.

BAKED FRUIT. Slice fruit (apples, peaches, pears, etc.) Add sugar, lemon juice, cinnamon. Cook in microwave.

ICE CREAM VARIATIONS. (1) Cover with 2 tablespoons liqueur. (2) Top vanilla ice cream with dark sweet cherries that have been marinated in cherry wine or liqueur. (3) Serve in cream puff shells, topped with sauce or sweetened fruit and whipped cream.

PARFAIT. Soften 1 quart ice cream and mix in ¼ to ⅓ cup liqueur. Freeze in mold or parfait glasses.

ICE CREAM PIE. Pack softened ice cream into graham cracker crust, and freeze. Top with a sauce or sweetened fruit and whipped cream.

LOVE POTION. Combine in blender or food processor, 2 scoops vanilla ice cream, ½ ounce Drambuie, ½ ounce Grand Marnier or Cointreau, and a dash of grenadine if desired. Serve in a stemmed glass with a spoon. Serves 2.

CHOCOLATE MOUSSE. Combine in a blender or food processor: 6 ounces chocolate bits, ¾ cup scalded milk, 2 eggs, 3 tablespoons strong hot coffee (espresso best), 1 to 2 tablespoons orange flavored liqueur or dark rum. Process for 1½ minutes. Pour into serving dishes and chill, overnight if possible.

Strawberry Parfait Cake

PORTAL TO GOOD COOKING, VOL. 2   WOMEN'S AMERICAN ORT, VIII   CHICAGO, ILLINOIS

½ pound vanilla wafer
  crumbs
1½ cups confectioners' sugar
1 stick butter
2 eggs
2 cups heavy cream
1 pint fresh strawberries (or
  16 oz. pkg. frozen)
½ cup chopped walnuts

Preparation time/processor: 10 minutes
Preparation time/conventional: 15 to 20 minutes
Chilling time: 24 hours
Serves 12

Food processor

1. If using frozen strawberries, thaw and drain.

2. Butter a 7 x 11 baking dish. Spread bottom evenly with half the wafer crumbs.

3. Insert metal blade. Process butter and sugar until light and fluffy. Add eggs and process until smooth; pour over crumbs. Wash and dry work bowl.

4. Pour cream into work bowl and process until whipped. Add strawberries and nuts and pulse once or twice to mix.

5. Spread over the butter layer. Top with remaining crumbs, pressing down lightly with fingertips. Refrigerate at least 24 hours.

Conventional

Soften butter. In step 3, cream the sugar and butter until light and fluffy. Beat in the eggs thoroughly and pour the mixture over the crumbs in the pan. Whip the cream until stiff and fold in the berries and nuts. Proceed to step 4.

Marjorie's Honey Cake
EDITOR'S CHOICE

3½ cups flour
¼ teaspoon salt
1½ teaspoons baking powder
1 teaspoon baking soda
½ teaspoon cinnamon
½ teaspoon nutmeg
½ teaspoon ginger
⅛ teaspoon ground cloves
4 eggs
¼ cup oil
1½ cups honey
½ cup strong brewed coffee

Preparation time/processor: 5 to 10 minutes
Preparation time/conventional: 10 to 15 minutes
Baking time: 50 minutes
Serves 24

Food processor

1. Preheat oven to 325°.

2. Line two 9 x 9 cake pans with aluminum foil and set aside.

3. Insert metal blade. Place all dry ingredients in work bowl and pulse once or twice to mix. Remove and reserve. Add eggs to work bowl and process until light and fluffy, about 1 minute. Add oil, honey, and coffee to the eggs (work in batches if necessary) and process until well combined. Sprinkle flour mixture evenly around work bowl and pulse several times to mix through.

4. Divide evenly between the two pans and bake for 50 minutes or until a toothpick inserted in the center of cakes comes out clean. Remove cakes from pans and from foil and cool on a wire rack.

Conventional

In step 3, sift dry ingredients together and reserve. Beat eggs in a large mixing bowl until light and fluffy. Add oil, honey, and coffee and beat to combine. Stir in flour mixture and beat thoroughly. Proceed to step 4.

Pumpkin Cake

WORLD OF OUR FLAVORS — CERTIFIED TA'AM   BETH HILLEL SISTERHOOD   WILMETTE, IL

3 cups flour
1 teaspoon salt, or to taste
2 teaspoons baking soda
2 teaspoons baking powder
2 teaspoons pumpkin pie
  spice
4 large eggs, well-beaten
1¼ cups vegetable oil
2 cups pumpkin (fresh or
  canned)
2 cups sugar
½ cup chopped nuts
Cream cheese frosting
  (optional)*

Preparation time: 10 to 15 minutes
Baking time: 1 hour
Serves 12 to 15

1. Preheat oven to 350°.

2. Combine dry ingredients in a large bowl. Add eggs, oil, pumpkin, and sugar and beat well (use an electric mixer). Fold in nuts.

3. Pour batter into a greased, floured 9 x 13 baking pan, Bundt pan, or 2 loaf pans. Bake for about 1 hour or until done. Cool on a rack. Frost if desired.

Cream Cheese Frosting

NOSHES, NIBBLES, AND GOURMET DELIGHTS   TEMPLE IN THE PINES SISTERHOOD   HOLLYWOOD, FLORIDA

1 package (8 oz.) cream
  cheese
1 stick butter or margarine
1 box (1 lb.) confectioners'
  sugar, or to taste
1 teaspoon vanilla extract
½ cup nuts (optional)

Preparation time/processor: 5 minutes
Preparation time/conventional: 10 minutes
Frosts one layer cake or one 9 x 13 cake.

Food processor

1. Insert metal blade and place the cream cheese and butter in the work bowl; process until smooth. Add sugar and vanilla and process until well mixed. Add nuts and pulse once or twice to chop and mix in.

Conventional

Soften cream cheese and butter; add sugar and vanilla and beat with a mixer or whisk. When very smooth, fold in nuts.

Variation: Add ¼ cup unsweetened cocoa powder to make a chocolate frosting.

Lemon Pudding Cake

UNDER THE CHEF'S H.A.T.   HEBREW ACADEMY OF TOLEDO   TOLEDO, OHIO

½ cup flour
½ teaspoon baking powder
¼ teaspoon salt
1½ cups sugar
1 piece lemon peel (2" x ½")
4 eggs
⅓ cup fresh lemon juice
1 tablespoon melted butter
  or margarine
1½ cups milk
Confectioners' sugar

Preparation time/processor: 10 minutes
Preparation time/conventional: 15 minutes
Baking time: 50 minutes
Serves 8 to 10

Food processor

1. Preheat oven to 350°.

2. Insert metal blade. Place flour, baking powder, and salt in work bowl and pulse twice; remove and reserve. Place sugar and lemon peel in work bowl and process until peel is finely grated. Add eggs and process until thick, about 1 minute. Add lemon juice and butter and process to combine. Sprinkle flour mixture evenly around work bowl and pulse twice. Scrape sides of bowl. Add milk and pulse twice to just mix through.

3. Pour into greased 2-quart casserole or 8-inch square baking dish. Place dish in a shallow pan containing an inch of hot water. Bake for about 50 minutes or until lightly browned and center springs back when touched. Cool slightly.

4. Sprinkle with confectioners' sugar and serve warm; may be spooned out of pan or cut into squares. Serve with whipped cream.

Conventional

In step 2, sift dry ingredients together and reserve. Grate lemon peel. With an electric mixer, beat eggs and sugar at high speed until very thick, about 5 minutes. At low speed beat in lemon juice, butter, and lemon peel. Stir in flour until just mixed. Add milk and stir to just mix in. Proceed to step 3.

Oma's Foolproof Sponge Cake

COOKING WITH CHUTZPAH JEWISH WOMEN'S COUNCIL OF CARLISLE CARLISLE, PENNSYLVANIA

6 large eggs (or 7 medium)
1 cup plus 1 tablespoon
  sugar
2 tablespoons whiskey or
  liqueur
1 cup flour
1 tablespoon baking powder
1 teaspoon vanilla extract or
  other flavoring (optional)

Preparation time/processor: 15 minutes
Preparation time/conventional: 20 to 25 minutes
Baking time: 30 to 35 minutes
Serves 10 to 12

Food processor (large capacity bowl only)

1. Preheat oven to 375°.

2. Insert metal blade. Place eggs and sugar in work bowl and process for exactly 7 minutes. Meanwhile, combine flour and baking powder.

3. Add whiskey with machine running. Stop and add flour mixture. Pulse several times to incorporate.

4. Transfer batter to an ungreased 10-inch angel food cake pan and bake for 30 to 35 minutes. Turn upside down and let cool before removing from pan.

5. Serve with sliced fruit and whipped cream.

Conventional

Beat eggs and sugar with mixer on highest speed for about 13 to 14 minutes. Add whiskey while beating. Lower speed and add flour mixed with baking powder. Beat until blended. Proceed to step 4.

Carrot Cake

MRS. COOPER'S ENCORE   B'NAI JACOB SYNAGOGUE AUXILIARY   CHARLESTON, WEST VIRGINIA

2½ cups flour
1½ teaspoons baking soda
1½ teaspoons cinnamon
½ teaspoon salt
¼ teaspoon nutmeg
4 to 6 carrots
¼ cup buttermilk
4 large eggs
2 cups sugar
2 sticks butter
1 teaspoon vanilla extract
1⅓ cups pecans
Confectioners' sugar

Preparation time/processor: 10 to 15 minutes
Preparation time/conventional: 20 minutes
Baking time: 1¼ hours
Serves 16 to 20

Food processor

1. Preheat oven to 350°.

2. Insert metal blade. Combine dry ingredients in work bowl and pulse twice. Remove and reserve. Insert grating blade and grate enough carrots to measure 1½ cups. Remove carrots and combine with buttermilk.

3. Insert metal blade and add eggs and sugar. Process until fluffy, about 1 minute. Add butter (cut into 16 pieces) and vanilla and process to blend well, about 30 to 50 seconds. Scrape bowl once or twice. Add flour mixture and pulse once or twice to just combine. Add carrot mixture and nuts and run spatula around work bowl to combine gently. (Work in batches in a small size processor.)

4. Transfer to a greased and floured 10-inch tube pan and bake for 60 to 65 minutes or until it tests done. Cool on rack for 15 minutes. Sprinkle with confectioners' sugar before serving.

Conventional

Soften butter. In step 2, sift dry ingredients together. Grate carrots and mix with buttermilk. In step 3, cream the butter and sugar until fluffy. Add eggs and vanilla and beat until well mixed. Add flour and beat until smooth. Add carrot/buttermilk mixture and nuts and blend well. Proceed to step 4.

Sour Cream Apple Squares

EAT, DARLING — AND ENJOY! BETH ISRAEL SISTERHOOD FLINT, MICHIGAN

2 cups flour
1¼ cups dark brown sugar
1 stick butter or margarine
1 cup nuts
1 egg
1 cup sour cream
1 teaspoon cinnamon
1 teaspoon baking soda
½ teaspoon salt
1 teaspoon vanilla extract
3 to 4 tart apples, peeled

Preparation time/processor: 10 to 15 minutes
Preparation time/conventional: 15 to 20 minutes
Cooking time: 25 to 35 minutes
Makes 12 to 15 squares

Food processor

1. Preheat oven to 350°.

2. Insert metal blade. Place flour, sugar, and butter in the work bowl and pulse twice. Add nuts and pulse once to chop. Remove 2½ cups of this mixture and press into the bottom of an ungreased 9 x 13 baking pan.

3. To the remaining mixture in the work bowl add the egg, sour cream, cinnamon, soda, salt, and vanilla. Pulse once, then scrape down sides of bowl. Pulse again to mix thoroughly. Quarter the apples and add to the work bowl; pulse several times to chop finely.

4. Spoon the apple mixture evenly over the crumb crust and bake for 25 to 35 minutes.

Conventional

In step 2, combine flour and sugar in a mixing bowl. Using a pastry blender or fork, cut in the butter until it resembles crumbs. Stir in chopped nuts. Pat 2½ cups of this mixture into baking pan. In step 3, add egg, sour cream, cinnamon, soda, salt, and vanilla to the remaining mixture and beat well. Slice apples and stir in. Proceed to step 4.

Banana Cake

POT OF GOLD   SISTERHOOD CONGREGATION HAR SHALOM   POTOMAC, MARYLAND

2 cups flour
2 teaspoons baking powder
1 teaspoon baking soda
2 cups sugar
3 eggs
1 stick butter
3 large ripe bananas
1 cup sour cream

Preparation time/processor: 10 to 15 minutes
Preparation time/conventional: 20 minutes
Baking time: 1 hour
Serves 9 to 12

Food processor

1. Preheat oven to 350°.

2. Insert metal blade. Place flour, baking powder, and baking soda in the work bowl and pulse once to combine. Remove. Process sugar and eggs for 1 minute. Add butter (cut into 8 pieces) and process 1 minute. Add bananas and sour cream and process until smooth and blended, 20 seconds or so. Add flour and pulse several times to incorporate. (Work in batches in a small size processor.)

3. Transfer to a greased 9 x 9 pan and bake for about 1 hour or until golden and tests done.

Conventional

Soften butter. In step 2, sift dry ingredients together. Cream butter and sugar until fluffy; add eggs, mashed bananas, and sour cream and beat until well blended. Add dry ingredients and beat well. Proceed to step 3.

Jody's Applesauce-Spice Squares

TO STIR WITH LOVE SISTERHOOD AHAVATH ISRAEL KINGSTON, NEW YORK

2 cups flour
2 teaspoons baking soda
¾ teaspoon cinnamon
¼ teaspoon ground cloves
¼ teaspoon nutmeg
1 cup sugar
1 egg
1 stick margarine or butter
1½ cups applesauce
1 teaspoon vanilla extract
1 cup walnuts
1 cup raisins
Confectioners' sugar
  (optional)

Preparation time/processor: 10 minutes
Preparation time/conventional: 15 to 20 minutes
Baking time: 25 minutes
Serves 12 to 15

Food processor

1. Preheat oven to 350°.

2. Insert metal blade. Place flour, baking soda, cinnamon, cloves, and nutmeg in the work bowl. Pulse twice; remove to a bowl. Place sugar and egg in work bowl and process for 1 minute. Add margarine (cut into pieces) and process 1 minute. Add applesauce and vanilla and pulse to mix well, scraping down sides of bowl if necessary. Return flour mixture to work bowl and pulse to mix through. Add walnuts and pulse once or twice to chop and mix in.

3. Add raisins and fold in with a spatula as you transfer the batter to a greased 9 x 13 baking pan. Bake about 25 minutes or until cake tests done. Cool and sprinkle with confectioners' sugar.

Conventional

Soften margarine and chop walnuts. In step 2, sift dry ingredients together. In a large mixing bowl, cream margarine and sugar together until fluffy. Add egg and beat to combine. Stir in vanilla and applesauce and beat until smooth. Add flour mixture and beat until well-combined. Fold in walnuts and raisins. Proceed with step 3.

Cheesecake

Praline Cheesecake

SUPER CHEF BETH ISRAEL TEMPLE SISTERHOOD WARREN, OHIO

Crust
1 cup graham cracker
   crumbs
3 tablespoons sugar
3 tablespoons melted
   margarine

Filling
3 packages (8 oz. each) cream
   cheese
1¼ cups dark brown sugar
2 tablespoons flour
3 eggs
1½ teaspoons vanilla extract
½ cup pecan halves

Maple syrup
Pecan halves

Preparation time: 10 to 15 minutes
Baking time/crust: 10 minutes
Baking time/filling: 50 to 55 minutes
Chilling time: 2 hours
Serves 10 to 12

Food processor

1. Preheat oven to 350°.

2. Combine crumbs, sugar, and margarine; press into bottom of a 9-inch springform pan and bake for 10 minutes.

3. Insert metal blade. Place cream cheese in work bowl and process until fluffy. Add sugar and flour and process until combined. Add eggs and vanilla and process for 20 seconds, scraping down sides of bowl as necessary. Add pecans and pulse once or twice to chop. (Make in batches if your processor has a small capacity bowl.)

4. Pour into springform pan and bake for 50 to 55 minutes. Cool on rack. Chill thoroughly before removing rim. Brush with maple syrup and decorate with pecan halves before serving.

Conventional

Soften cream cheese. In step 3, beat cream cheese with sugar until fluffy. Add flour and eggs and beat until very smooth. Stir in vanilla and chopped pecans. Proceed to step 4.

Super Cheesecake

UNDER THE CHEF'S H.A.T.   HEBREW ACADEMY OF TOLEDO   TOLEDO, OHIO

Crust
1⅓ cups graham cracker
  crumbs
1 stick melted butter
⅓ cup sugar
½ teaspoon cinnamon

Filling
¼ cup sugar
Peel of ½ lemon
1 package (8 oz.) cream
  cheese
2 large eggs
¼ teaspoon vanilla extract

Topping
1 cup sour cream
2 tablespoons sugar
1 teaspoon vanilla extract

Preparation time/processor: 10 to 15 minutes
Preparation time/conventional: 15 to 20 minutes
Baking time: 30 minutes
Serves 10 to 12

Food processor

1. Combine crust ingredients and press firmly into the bottom and sides of a 9-inch pie pan. Chill until ready to use.

2. Preheat oven to 325°.

3. Filling: Insert metal blade and process sugar and peel until the peel is very finely chopped and the sugar is damp. Add cream cheese and process until fluffy. Add eggs and vanilla. Process until well combined, about 20 seconds.

4. Pour into crust (mixture will be fairly thin and will not fill crust). Bake for 30 minutes or until set.

5. Combine topping ingredients. Spread over cheesecake, bringing out to touch crust. Bake 5 minutes longer. Remove from oven and cool on rack. Serve plain or topped with sweetened crushed strawberries or raspberries.

Conventional

Soften cream cheese. In step 3, grate lemon peel. Beat cream cheese and sugar until fluffy. Add eggs, vanilla, and lemon peel and beat well. Proceed to step 4.

E-Z Marble Cheesecake with Chocolate Cinnamon Crust

QUICK QUISINE   GREATER RED BANK SECTION NCJW   RED BANK, NEW JERSEY

Crust
1¼ cups chocolate wafer
  crumbs
¼ to ½ teaspoon ground
  cinnamon
½ stick butter or margarine,
  melted

Filling
½ cup sugar
2 strips lemon peel (½" x 2"
  each)
4 packages (3 oz. each) cream
  cheese
2 large eggs
1½ cups sour cream
1 package (8 oz.) semi-sweet
  chocolate chips, melted and
  cooled

Preparation time/processor: 10 to 15 minutes
Preparation time/conventional: 20 minutes
Baking time: 35 to 40 minutes
Chilling time: 2 hours
Serves 10

Food processor

1. Preheat oven to 350⁻.

2. Combine crust ingredients and mix well. With damp fingers press into bottom and sides of a 9-inch springform pan. Chill.

3. Insert metal blade and process sugar and lemon peel until peel is very fine. Add cream cheese and process until fluffy. Add eggs and sour cream and process until smooth, about 10 seconds.

4. Drizzle the chocolate evenly around the work bowl; use a rubber spatula to make a marble pattern, and transfer to the crust. Bake for 35 to 40 minutes or until set. Chill at least 2 hours before serving.

Conventional

Soften cream cheese. In step 3, grate the lemon peel and reserve. Beat cream cheese with the sugar until fluffy. Add eggs, sour cream, and lemon peel and beat until smooth. Proceed to step 4.

No-Crust Cream Cheese Pie

JEWISH AMERICAN FAVORITE RECIPES   SISTERHOOD OF SONS OF JACOB SYNAGOGUE   WATERLOO, IOWA

2 packages (8 oz. each) cream cheese
⅔ cup sugar
3 eggs
½ teaspoon almond extract

Topping
2 cups sour cream
3 tablespoons sugar
1 teaspoon vanilla

Preparation time/processor: 5 to 10 minutes
Preparation time/conventional: 15 minutes
Baking time: 35 minutes
Chilling time: 20 minutes
Serves 8

Food processor

1. Preheat oven to 350°.

2. Insert metal blade and process the cream cheese and sugar until light and fluffy, about 45 to 60 seconds. Scrape down sides of bowl as necessary. Add eggs and almond extract and process until well combined, about 20 seconds.

3. Pour into a well-buttered 9-inch pie pan and bake about 25 minutes; remove from oven when the center of the pie has risen to be level with the edge. Cool on a rack for 20 minutes (the center will shrink as it cools).

4. Combine topping ingredients. Spread evenly over the cooled pie.

5. Return pie to oven and bake another 10 minutes. Chill before serving.

Conventional

Soften cream cheese. In step 2, beat cream cheese and sugar until fluffy. Add eggs and almond extract and beat well. Proceed to step 3.

Judy's Special Chocolate Cheese Pie

SEASONED WITH LOVE   WHITE MEADOW TEMPLE SISTERHOOD   ROCKAWAY, NEW JERSEY

1 cup sugar
3 packages (8 oz. each) cream
  cheese
5 eggs
1 tablespoon vanilla extract
1 package (4 oz.) German's
  sweet chocolate, melted
  and cooled
1 tablespoon lemon juice

Preparation time/processor: 5 to 10 minutes
Preparation time/conventional: 15 to 20 minutes
Baking time: 40 to 45 minutes
Serves 12

Food processor

1. Preheat oven to 350°.

2. Insert metal blade. Place sugar and cream cheese in work bowl and process until fluffy. Add eggs and vanilla and process 10 seconds; scrape down bowl, then process another 10 seconds or until smooth. (Make in batches in small capacity processor.)

3. Remove 2 cups of this mixture, and swirl in the chocolate (cover with cheese mixture; don't completely mix in).

4. Add lemon juice to remaining mixture in work bowl and process 5 seconds to blend. Pour into a well-buttered 10-inch pie plate or springform pan. Top with the chocolate mixture. Bake for 40 to 45 minutes; cool, then chill.

Conventional

Soften cream cheese. In step 2, beat cream cheese and sugar together until fluffy. Add eggs and vanilla and beat until well-mixed. Proceed to step 3.

Frozen Yogurt Pie

PASSOVER MADE EASY   EMANUEL SYNAGOGUE   WEST HARTFORD, CONNECTICUT

9-inch baked pie crust,
  crumb crust, or Passover
  pie crust*
2 packages (8 oz. each) cream
  cheese
1 pint plain yogurt
½ cup honey

Preparation time/processor: 5 minutes
Preparation time/conventional: 10 minutes
Pre-preparation: make pie crust
Freezing time: 4 hours
Serves 8 to 10

Food processor

1. Insert metal blade and process the cream cheese, yogurt, and honey until smooth, about 25 to 30 seconds.

2. Pour into crust, cover with plastic wrap, and freeze 4 to 5 hours or until firm.

3. Let stand about 20 minutes before serving. Garnish with sliced peaches, strawberries, or crushed raspberries.

Conventional

Soften cream cheese; beat together with yogurt and honey until smooth. Proceed to step 2.

Ricotta Cake

EDITOR'S CHOICE

¾ cup sugar
1 slice lemon peel (2" x ½")
1 pound whole milk ricotta
  cheese
2 large eggs
½ teaspoon vanilla extract
Lemon slices
Fresh fruit or fruit sauce (see
  recipes)

Preparation time/processor: 5 to 10 minutes
Preparation time/conventional: 10 to 15 minutes
Baking time: 1 hour
Serves 6

Food processor

1. Preheat oven to 350°.

2. Insert metal blade. Place lemon peel and sugar in work bowl and process until peel is very finely chopped. Add ricotta, eggs, and vanilla and process until thoroughly blended, about 25 seconds. (Make in batches if necessary.)

3. Pour into a well-greased 6-cup ring mold or Bundt pan and cover with foil. Place in a pan of hot water and bake for 1 hour.

4. Cool, unmold, and garnish with lemon slices. Serve with fresh fruit or fruit sauce.

Conventional

Grate lemon peel and reserve. With a mixer or whisk, beat ricotta, sugar, eggs, and vanilla until well combined. Proceed to step 3.

Pies

Apple Cream Pie
TO SERVE WITH LOVE   SISTERHOOD OF TEMPLE AVODA   FAIR LAWN, NEW JERSEY

Crust
1½ cups graham cracker
  crumbs
⅓ cup melted butter or
  margarine

Filling
1 egg
1 cup sour cream
¾ cup sugar
¼ teaspoon salt
2 tablespoons flour
1 teaspoon vanilla extract
3 large tart apples, peeled
Graham cracker crumbs

Preparation time/processor: 5 to 10 minutes
Preparation time/conventional: 10 to 15 minutes
Baking time: 45 minutes
Serves 8

Food processor

1. Preheat oven to 375°.

2. Mix crumbs and melted butter; press firmly into bottom and sides of an 8-inch pie plate.

3. Insert metal blade; place egg, sour cream, sugar, salt, flour, and vanilla in work bowl. Process until smooth, about 15 to 20 seconds. Quarter apples and place pieces evenly around the work bowl; pulse several times to chop coarsely. Pour mixture into crust.

4. Bake for about 25 minutes, remove pie from oven, sprinkle with graham cracker crumbs, and return to oven. Bake another 20 minutes.

Conventional

In step 3, beat together egg, sour cream, sugar, salt, flour, and vanilla. Dice apples, stir into mixture, and pour into crust. Proceed to step 4.

Sour Cream Raisin Pie

MADE TO ORTER DAY, EVENING, JAMES RIVER CHAPTERS, WOMEN'S AMERICAN ORT   RICHMOND, VIRGINIA

9-inch pie crust, baked or
    crumb
¾ cup sugar, or to taste
1½ tablespoons flour
⅛ teaspoon salt
1 teaspoon cinnamon
2 egg yolks
1 cup sour cream
1 cup raisins
2 egg whites
½ teaspoon cream of tartar

Preparation time: 15 to 20 minutes
Pre-preparation: make pie crust
Baking time: 12 minutes
Serves 6 to 8

1. Preheat oven to 350°.

2. Combine ½ cup sugar, flour, salt, and cinnamon. Place egg yolks in a saucepan and beat well. Add sugar mixture, sour cream, and raisins and place over medium heat. Cook, stirring constantly, until mixture thickens. Pour into pie crust.

3. Beat egg whites until foamy; add cream of tartar and continue beating. Slowly add remaining ¼ cup sugar while beating to form a meringue.

4. Spread meringue on pie. Bake for about 12 minutes until meringue is golden brown. Filling becomes thicker as it cools.

Note: This is a very sweet pie; you may wish to decrease the sugar.

Blueberry Pie

THE MJCC PRESENTS OUR FAVORITE RECIPES MEMPHIS JEWISH COMMUNITY CENTER MEMPHIS, TN

9-inch graham cracker crust*
⅓ cup cold water
1 envelope unflavored
    gelatin
1 can (14 oz.) sweetened
    condensed milk*
¼ cup lemon juice
1 cup sour cream
2½ cups Jiffy Blueberry
    Sauce*

Preparation time: 20 minutes
Pre-preparation: make crust, blueberry sauce
Chilling time: 3 hours
Serves 8

1. Add gelatin to water in a small saucepan and allow to soften for 10 minutes. Place over medium heat and stir until dissolved.

2. Combine milk and lemon juice. Stir in gelatin. Fold in sour cream. Mix in 1¼ cups of the blueberry sauce. Pour into crust and chill well, about 3 hours. Spread remaining blueberry sauce over pie just before serving.

No-Roll Apple Pie

QUICK AND EASY COOKBOOK   MAIN LINE REFORM TEMPLE SISTERHOOD   WYNNEWOOD, PENNSYLVANIA

Crust
1 stick butter
½ cup sugar
1½ cups flour
Pinch salt

Filling
5 apples, peeled (approx.)
½ cup sugar
2 tablespoons cornstarch
¾ teaspoon cinnamon

Preparation time/processor: 10 to 15 minutes
Preparation time/conventional: 15 to 20 minutes
Baking time: 40 to 50 minutes
Serves 6 to 8

1. Preheat oven to 425°.

2. Insert metal blade. Place butter (cut into 4 pieces), sugar, flour, and salt in work bowl and pulse several times until mixture resembles coarse crumbs. Set aside ¾ cup of mixture and press the remainder into a 9-inch pie plate. Crumbs should not extend onto rim.

3. Slice apples; you will need about 5 cups. Combine sugar, cornstarch, and cinnamon and sprinkle over the apple slices. Place in pie shell and bake for 20 minutes. Sprinkle with the remaining ¾ cup crumbs. Bake another 20 to 30 minutes until apples are tender. Be careful not to burn.

Conventional

Soften butter. In step 2, use a pastry blender.

Vanilla Wafer or Chocolate Wafer Crust
EDITOR'S CHOICE

1⅓ cups vanilla or chocolate
  wafer crumbs
½ stick butter or margarine,
  melted
¼ cup chopped walnuts
  (optional)

Preparation time: 5 minutes
Baking time: 8 minutes
Makes one 9-inch crust

1. Combine all ingredients and press into a 9-inch pie plate.

2. Chill well before filling. Or bake in a preheated 350° oven for 8 minutes.

Chocolate Chip Pecan Pie

FOOD FOR SHOW/FOOD ON THE GO   MOUNT SINAI HOSPITAL AUXILIARY   MINNEAPOLIS, MINNESOTA

10-inch pie shell, regular or
  graham cracker, unbaked*
4 eggs
1 cup sugar
1 cup light corn syrup
1 teaspoon vanilla extract
1 stick butter, melted and
  cooled
1 heaping cup pecans
1 package (6 oz.) semi-sweet
  chocolate chips

Preparation time/processor: 5 to 10 minutes
Preparation time/conventional: 10 to 15 minutes
Pre-preparation: make pie shell
Baking time: 50 minutes
Serves 6 to 8

Food processor

1. Preheat oven to 350°.

2. Insert metal blade. Combine eggs, sugar, corn syrup, vanilla, and butter in work bowl and process until smooth. Add pecans and chocolate chips and pulse once to just mix.

3. Pour into pie shell and bake for 50 minutes or until set.

Conventional

Use a mixer or whisk to combine eggs, sugar, corn syrup, vanilla, and butter. Fold in chopped pecans and chocolate chips. Proceed to step 3.

Pecan Crust

EDITOR'S CHOICE

2½ cups pecans
⅔ cup light brown sugar
½ teaspoon instant coffee
  powder
½ teaspoon cinnamon
½ stick butter, melted

Preparation: 5 to 10 minutes
Baking time: 10 to 12 minutes
Makes one 9-inch crust

1. Preheat oven to 350°.

2. Place all ingredients in a food processor or blender and process until fine and crumbly. (Do not overprocess.) Press into bottom and sides of a 9-inch pie plate and bake for 10 to 12 minutes. Cool.

Pumpkin Ice Cream Pie

EDITOR'S CHOICE

9-inch crumb crust*
1 quart vanilla ice cream,
  softened
¾ cup cooked or canned
  pumpkin
¼ cup honey
½ teaspoon cinnamon
¼ teaspoon ground ginger
¼ teaspoon salt, or to taste
⅛ teaspoon nutmeg
⅛ teaspoon ground cloves
⅓ cup chopped pecans
Whipped cream
Pecan halves

Preparation time: 10 minutes
Pre-preparation: make crust
Freezing time: 2 hours
Serves 6 to 8

1. Combine ice cream, pumpkin, honey, cinnamon, ginger, salt, nutmeg, cloves, and pecans. Spoon into pie crust and freeze until serving time. Top with whipped cream and pecan halves just before serving.

Key Lime Pie

DO IT IN THE KITCHEN   WOMEN'S AMERICAN ORT, DISTRICT VI   HALLANDALE, FLORIDA

9-inch graham cracker crust*
1 can (14 oz.) sweetened
  condensed milk*
1 cup sour cream
⅓ cup fresh lime juice
1 cup heavy cream, whipped

Preparation time: 10 minutes
Pre-preparation: make crust
Chilling time: 1 hour or more
Serves 8

1. Combine condensed milk and sour cream. Beat until smooth. Add lime juice and stir well. Pour into prepared crust and chill at least one hour before serving. Top with whipped cream.

Cookies

Pecan Bars

FAMILY FAVORITES   TEMPLE SOLEL SISTERHOOD   HOLLYWOOD, FLORIDA

1 stick butter or margarine
⅓ cup dark brown sugar
⅓ cup dark corn syrup
1 large egg
¾ cup flour
½ teaspoon baking soda
1 cup pecans
Confectioners' sugar

Preparation time/processor: 10 to 15 minutes
Preparation time/conventional: 15 to 20 minutes
Baking time: 25 to 30 minutes
Makes about 4 dozen

Food processor

1. Preheat oven to 350°.

2. Insert metal blade; process the butter and brown sugar until fluffy, about 15 seconds. Add syrup and egg and process about 10 seconds, scraping down bowl once or twice. Mix flour and baking soda with a fork and sprinkle evenly around the work bowl. Pulse several times to mix well. Add pecans and pulse once or twice to mix and chop.

3. Transfer to a greased 9 x 9 pan and bake 25 to 30 minutes. Cool and cut into bars. Sprinkle with confectioners' sugar.

Conventional

Soften butter. Cream butter and sugar together until fluffy. Add syrup and egg and beat well. Mix flour and baking soda with a fork and add to the egg mixture. Beat well. Add chopped pecans and stir to combine. Proceed to step 3.

Oatmeal Bars

THE WAY TO A MAN'S HEART   BETH ISRAEL CONGREGATION   WASHINGTON, PENNSYLVANIA

2 sticks butter or margarine
1 cup dark brown sugar
2¼ cups flour
¼ teaspoon baking soda
2 cups quick rolled oats
1 cup preserves (apricot,
   pineapple, or strawberry)

Preparation time/processor: 5 to 10 minutes
Preparation time/conventional: 15 to 20 minutes
Baking time: 40 minutes
Makes about 24

Food processor

1. Preheat oven to 350°.

2. Insert metal blade. Place butter and sugar in work bowl and process till fluffy. Combine flour and baking soda; add to work bowl and pulse until mixed (will be crumbly). Add oats and pulse once or twice to just mix.

3. Transfer two-thirds of this mixture to a greased 9 x 13 baking pan. Pat down. Spread evenly with the preserves. Sprinkle with the remaining dough and spread evenly. Bake for 40 minutes.

4. When cool, cut into squares. These will keep well in the refrigerator.

Conventional

Soften butter, then cream with sugar until fluffy. In step 2, add oats, flour, and soda, using a mixer or pastry blender to make a crumbly mixture. Proceed to step 3.

Bourbon Balls

INTERFAITH TEA COOKIE BOOK   TEMPLE ISRAEL SISTERHOOD   BINGHAMTON, NEW YORK

1 cup vanilla wafer crumbs
1 cup confectioners' sugar
1 heaping cup pecans
2 tablespoons white corn
   syrup
2 tablespoons cocoa powder
¼ cup bourbon or rum
Granulated sugar

Preparation time/processor: 5 minutes
Preparation time/conventional: 10 to 15 minutes
Makes about 2 dozen

1. Place all ingredients (except granulated sugar) in a food processor or blender and pulse several times to mix and chop nuts.

2. Roll into balls about the size of a walnut and roll in granulated sugar. These can be made in advance and stored in an airtight container.

Chocolate Dream Bars

COOK WITH TEMPLE BETH EMETH   TEMPLE BETH EMETH SISTERHOOD   ANN ARBOR, MICHIGAN

1 cup flour
½ cup dark brown sugar
1 stick butter or margarine

Topping
1 cup dark brown sugar
2 tablespoons flour
½ teaspoon baking powder
1 teaspoon vanilla extract
¼ teaspoon salt (optional)
2 large eggs
1 package (12 oz.) semi-sweet
  chocolate chips

Preparation time/processor: 5 to 10 minutes
Preparation time/conventional: 10 to 15 minutes
Baking time: 35 to 40 minutes
Makes 3½ dozen

Food processor

1. Preheat oven to 350.

2. Insert metal blade. Place flour and brown sugar in work bowl and pulse twice to stir. Add butter (cut into 8 pieces) and pulse until crumbly.

3. Pat firmly into a greased 9 x 13 pan. Bake for about 15 minutes until slightly brown. Remove from oven and place on rack.

4. Combine topping ingredients (except chocolate chips) in work bowl and process until well mixed, about 10 seconds. Add chocolate chips and pulse once to mix in.

5. Pour carefully over warm baked crust and spread to edges. Bake for 20 to 25 minutes or until set and golden. When cool, cut into small bars.

Conventional

Soften butter. In step 2, add butter to flour and brown sugar and mix until crumbly. Proceed to step 3. In step 4, beat all topping ingredients except chocolate chips until well mixed. Fold in chocolate chips. Proceed to step 5.

Date-Nut Bars

FROM OUR KITCHENS BRITH EMETH SISTERHOOD PEPPER PIKE, OHIO

½ cup flour
¼ teaspoon salt
½ teaspoon baking powder
2 large eggs
¾ cup dark brown sugar
2 tablespoons melted butter
  or margarine
1 teaspoon vanilla extract
1¼ cups walnuts
1½ cups pitted dates

Preparation time/processor: 10 to 15 minutes
Preparation time/conventional: 15 to 20 minutes
Baking time: 25 to 30 minutes
Makes 18 large or 36 small bars

Food processor

1. Preheat oven to 325°.

2. Insert metal blade. Place flour, salt, and baking powder in work bowl and pulse once to mix. Remove and reserve. Place eggs and brown sugar in work bowl and process until fluffy, about 15 seconds. Add butter and vanilla; process 5 seconds.

3. Sprinkle flour mixture over egg-sugar mixture and pulse once or twice to blend. Arrange walnuts and dates evenly around work bowl and pulse 2 or 3 times to chop coarsely and combine.

4. Transfer to a greased 9 x 9 pan and bake 25 to 30 minutes until golden and set.

Conventional

Chop dates and nuts. In step 2, sift flour, salt, and baking powder. In step 3, beat eggs and brown sugar until fluffy. Add butter and vanilla and beat until smooth. Add flour mixture and blend well. Stir in the dates and nuts. Proceed to step 4.

Pineapple Bars

TO SERVE WITH LOVE SISTERHOOD OF TEMPLE AVODA FAIR LAWN, NEW JERSEY

1 cup crushed pineapple,
  partially drained
¾ cup sugar, or to taste
3 tablespoons cornstarch
Pinch salt

Crust
1 cup quick rolled oats
1 cup light brown sugar
1 cup flour
¼ teaspoon salt
1 teaspoon baking powder
1 stick butter, softened

Preparation time/processor: 5 to 10 minutes
Preparation time/conventional: 10 to 15 minutes
Baking time: 30 minutes
Makes about 16

1. Preheat oven to 350°.

2. Combine pineapple, sugar, cornstarch, and salt in a small saucepan and cook, stirring constantly, until thick and clear. (Or use microwave.) Set aside to cool

3. Combine crust ingredients with a fork or in a food processor pulsing once or twice. Pat half into a greased 8 x 8 pan. Spread with pineapple mixture. Cover with remaining crust mixture Bake for about 30 minutes.

Note: This is very sweet, so you may wish to reduce sugar in pineapple filling.

Kahlua Balls

THE COOKIE COOKERY BRITH SHALOM SISTERHOOD BELLAIRE, TEXAS

1 cup vanilla wafer crumbs
¾ cup pecans
¼ cup coffee liqueur
½ cup powdered sugar
2 tablespoons melted butter
1 tablespoon instant coffee
  powder
1½ tablespoons light corn
  syrup
Powdered sugar

Preparation time: 5 to 10 minutes
Makes about 60

1. Place all ingredients (except powdered sugar) in a food processor or blender and pulse several times to mix and chop nuts.

2. Shape into small balls and roll in powdered sugar. Store in an airtight container or freeze.

Butter Crunch Squares

FROM OUR KITCHENS BRITH EMETH SISTERHOOD PEPPER PIKE, OHIO

1 cup sugar
2 cups flour
½ to 1 teaspoon cinnamon
1 egg yolk
2 sticks butter

Topping
½ cup sugar
1 teaspoon cinnamon
1 egg white
1¼ cup nuts

Preparation time/processor: 10 to 15 minutes
Preparation time/conventional: 20 minutes
Baking time: 35 minutes
Makes 48 small bars

Food processor

1. Preheat oven to 350°.

2. Insert metal blade. Place sugar, flour, cinnamon, and egg yolk in the work bowl and pulse once to mix. Add butter (cut into 8 pieces) and pulse several times until the mixture resembles cornmeal. (Should be done in batches in a small size processor.)

3. Pat firmly into a greased 9 x 13 pan.

4. To make topping, place sugar, cinnamon, and egg white in (unwashed) work bowl and process 10 seconds. Add nuts and pulse once or twice to chop.

5. Sprinkle over dough and bake for about 35 minutes.

Conventional

Soften butter. In step 2, combine sugar, flour, cinnamon, and egg yolk in a medium bowl. Add butter and use a pastry cutter or mixer to make a crumbly mixture. In step 4, chop nuts. Combine topping ingredients with a mixer. Fold in nuts. Proceed to step 5.

Boozie Nickerson's Apricot Squares

IN THE BEST OF TASTE   CONGREGATION BETH EL   SUDBURY, MASSACHUSETTS

1 cup sugar
1½ sticks butter or
  margarine
1 large egg
1 teaspoon vanilla extract
¼ teaspoon salt
2 cups plus 2 tablespoons
  flour
1⅓ cups coconut
½ cup chopped nuts
1 jar (12 oz.) apricot
  preserves

Preparation time/processor: 10 minutes
Preparation time/conventional: 15 to 20 minutes
Baking time: 35 minutes
Makes 16 to 20

Food processor

1. Preheat oven to 350°.

2. Insert metal blade. Place sugar, butter, egg, and vanilla extract in work bowl and process until fluffy, about 30 to 45 seconds. Combine flour and salt and add to work bowl; pulse several times to blend. Add coconut and nuts and pulse to just combine. (You may need to work in batches in a small-size processor.)

3. Spread half this mixture in a greased 9 x 9 pan and press down well. Spread with apricot preserves, then cover with remaining dough. Bake for 35 minutes. Cool on rack before cutting.

Conventional

Soften butter. In step 2, beat with mixer until fluffy. Combine flour and salt, then add to the butter mixture along with the coconut and nuts. Beat to combine. Proceed to step 3.

Portuguese Walnut Squares

FROM GENERATION TO GENERATION   B'NAI AMOONA SISTERHOOD   ST. LOUIS, MISSOURI

2 cups walnuts
6 tablespoons flour
½ teaspoon baking powder
1 stick butter or margarine
¾ cup light brown sugar
1 egg
½ teaspoon vanilla extract
2 tablespoons milk
5 tablespoons tawny or ruby
  Port

Glaze
1 cup confectioners' sugar
1 tablespoon butter, softened
1 tablespoon Port
1 drop red food coloring

Preparation time/processor: 10 to 15 minutes
Preparation time/conventional: 20 minutes
Baking time: 15 to 20 minutes
Makes 16

Food processor

1. Preheat oven to 350°.

2. Insert metal blade. Place 1 cup walnuts in work bowl and pulse to chop coarsely. Remove. Place remaining walnuts in the work bowl and pulse to chop very finely (they will look ground). Add flour and baking powder and pulse once or twice to just mix through; remove to a bowl.

3. Place butter, sugar, egg, vanilla, milk, and 2 tablespoons Port in the work bowl, and process until fluffy. Return dry ingredients to work bowl and pulse to just mix through; do not overbeat.

4. Place in a lightly greased 9 x 9 baking pan and bake 15 to 20 minutes until set. Remove from oven and immediately brush with 2 to 3 tablespoons Port. Cool to room temperature.

5. To make glaze, place all ingredients in food processor or blender and mix until smooth (or mix by hand). Spread over cake and sprinkle with the chopped walnuts.

Conventional

In step 2, chop 1 cup walnuts coarsely and reserve. Grind other cup walnuts finely and combine with flour and baking powder. In step 3, beat butter, sugar, egg, vanilla, milk, and 2 tablespoons Port until fluffy. Add dry ingredients and stir well to combine. Proceed to step 4.

Double Chocolate Brownies

A MATZO BALL IS NOT ANOTHER DRESS-UP DANCE! B'NAI SHOLOM SISTERHOOD HUNTINGTON, WEST VIRGINIA

¾ cup flour
¼ teaspoon baking soda
¼ teaspoon salt
⅓ cup margarine
¾ cup sugar
2 tablespoons water
1 teaspoon vanilla extract
1 package (12 oz.) semi-sweet chocolate chips
2 eggs
½ cup chopped nuts

Preparation time/conventional: 15 minutes
Baking time: 30 to 35 minutes
Makes 16 squares

1. Preheat oven to 325°.

2. Combine flour, baking soda, and salt; set aside.

3. In a small saucepan, combine margarine, sugar, and water. Bring to a boil, then remove from heat. Stir in vanilla and half the chocolate chips. Stir until chips melt and mixture is smooth. Transfer to a large bowl.

4. Add eggs, one at a time, beating well after each addition. Gradually blend in flour mixture. Stir in remaining chocolate chips and nuts. Spread in a greased 9 x 9 baking pan and bake 30 to 35 minutes. Cool completely. Cut into 16 squares.

Microwave

In step 3, heat butter, sugar, and water in a 1 quart measuring cup. Add vanilla and half the chocolate chips and stir well. Proceed to step 3; use measuring cup as a bowl and mix the brownies directly in it. To bake, check manufacturer's manual for cooking time for bar cookies or use conventional oven.

Fudge Meltaways (No-Bake Cookies)
A BOOK FOR THE COOK   BRANDEIS UNIVERSITY NATIONAL WOMEN'S COMMITTEE   NEW ROCHELLE, NEW YORK

Crust
1 stick butter
**1 square (1 oz.) unsweetened
  chocolate**
**2 cups graham cracker
  crumbs**
¼ cup sugar
1 teaspoon vanilla extract
1 egg
1 heaping cup nuts

Filling
½ stick butter
2 tablespoons milk
2 cup confectioners' sugar
1 teaspoon vanilla extract

Glaze
**1½ squares (1½ oz.)
  unsweetened chocolate**

Preparation time/processor: 8 minutes
Preparation time/conventional: 15 to 20 minutes
Chilling time: see recipe
Makes 36 to 48

Food processor

1. Melt butter with chocolate.

2. Insert metal blade. Place crumbs, sugar, vanilla, and egg in the work bowl and pulse to mix well. Add chocolate mixture and nuts and pulse to combine and chop nuts.

3. Pat into an ungreased 9 x 9 baking pan lined with foil. Refrigerate until firm.

4. Place all filling ingredients in work bowl (metal blade) and process until smooth. Spread over crust and chill until firm.

5. Melt remaining chocolate and spread over filling (work fast, since chocolate hardens quickly). Chill again. Before completely firm, cut into squares.

Conventional

Soften butter for filling. Use electric mixer for steps 2 and 4.

Crisp Toffee Bars

DELECTABLE COLLECTABLES SISTERHOOD OF TEMPLE JUDEA TARZANA, CALIFORNIA

2 sticks butter or margarine
1 cup dark brown sugar, packed
1 teaspoon vanilla extract
2 cups sifted flour
1 heaping cup walnuts
1 package (6 oz.) semi-sweet chocolate chips

Preparation time/processor: 10 minutes
Preparation time/conventional: 15 minutes
Baking time: 20 to 25 minutes
Makes about 60

Food Processor

1. Preheat oven to 350°.

2. Insert metal blade; process the butter, brown sugar, and vanilla until fluffy, about 15 seconds. Add flour to work bowl and pulse until mixed. Add walnuts and pulse once or twice to mix and chop. Mix in chocolate chips with a rubber spatula.

3. Transfer to an ungreased 15½ x 10 baking sheet (jelly roll pan) and bake for 20 to 25 minutes. Cut into bars while still warm. Cool before removing from pan.

Conventional

Soften butter. Cream butter, sugar, and vanilla together until fluffy. Add flour and beat well. Add chopped walnuts and chocolate chips; stir to combine. Proceed to step 3.

Puddings, fruit & desserts

Cranberry Crunch

SUPER CHEF   BETH ISRAEL TEMPLE SISTERHOOD   WARREN, OHIO

1 cup rolled oats (uncooked)
½ cup flour
1 cup brown sugar
1 stick butter or margarine
1 can (16 oz.) cranberry
sauce (jellied or whole
berry)

Preparation time/processor: 10 minutes
Preparation time/conventional: 20 minutes
Baking time: 45 minutes
Makes 8 to 12

Food processor

1. Preheat oven to 350°.

2. Insert metal blade. Place oats, flour, and sugar in work bowl and pulse once to stir. Place butter (cut into 8 pieces) around work bowl and pulse until mixture is crumbly.

3. Pat half of mixture into a greased 8 x 8 baking pan. Spread with the cranberry sauce. Lightly spread or pat the remaining oatmeal mixture over the sauce. Bake for 45 minutes, or until golden and crisp.

4. Cut into squares. Serve plain or with vanilla ice cream or whipped cream.

Conventional

Soften butter. Combine butter, oats, flour, and sugar and use a pastry cutter or mixer to work into a crumbly mixture. Proceed to step 3.

Baked Fresh Fruit Compote

THE NEW PORTAL TO GOOD COOKING, VOL. II   WOMEN'S AMERICAN ORT, VIII   CHICAGO, ILLINOIS

8 small peaches, apples, or
  pears (or combination)
⅔ cup red wine
⅔ cup sugar
½ stick cinnamon
4 whole cloves
⅛ teaspoon salt
½ lemon, thinly sliced

Preparation time: 10 to 15 minutes
Baking time: 20 to 40 minutes
Serves 4 to 6

1. Preheat oven to 325°.

2. Peel fruit and place in a baking dish (whole or sliced).

3. Combine remaining ingredients in a saucepan. Bring to a simmer (do not boil) and pour over fruit. Bake (covered or uncovered) until tender. If uncovered, baste with the syrup every 10 minutes. Serve hot.

Baked Bananas and Blueberries

COLLECTABLE DELECTABLES   RODEF SHOLOM TEMPLE SISTERHOOD   HAMPTON, VIRGINIA

6 bananas
1 cup fresh blueberries
½ cup dark or light brown
  sugar
1 cup orange juice
2 tablespoons butter
Sour cream

Preparation time: 10 minutes
Cooking time: 20 minutes
Serves 6

1. Preheat oven to 350°.

2. Slice bananas lengthwise and place in a greased 9 x 13 casserole. Sprinkle with blueberries, then sugar. Pour orange juice over and dot with butter.

3. Bake for 20 minutes (or cook in microwave until hot and sauce is slightly caramelized). Serve hot, topped with sour cream.

Apricot Brandy Pears

THE WAY TO A MAN'S HEART   BETH ISRAEL CONGREGATION   WASHINGTON, PENNSYLVANIA

4 fresh Bartlett pears
¾ cups sugar
1¼ cups water
Dash salt
½ cup apricot jam
¼ cup apricot brandy or
  orange juice
⅓ cup slivered toasted
  almonds
Chocolate shavings

Preparation time: 10 to 15 minutes
Chilling time: 1 hour
Serves 4 to 6

1. Peel pears and cut in half. Combine sugar, water, and salt in a saucepan; heat to boiling and add pears. Simmer uncovered for 8 minutes, turning twice. Chill fruit in syrup.

2. Warm jam and force through sieve. Mix with brandy.

3. Serve pears with brandy sauce, slivered almonds, and chocolate shavings.

Applesauce Sherbet

EDITOR'S CHOICE

2 cups buttermilk
2 cups applesauce
1 cup sugar
2 tablespoons lemon juice
1 tablespoon lime juice
Grated lemon peel

Preparation time: 5 to 10 minutes
Freezing time: 2 hours
Serves 6

Food processor
1. Combine all ingredients (except lemon peel), stirring well. Pour into ice cube trays with cube dividers. Freeze 2 to 3 hours or until firm.

2. Insert metal blade. Pop cubes into work bowl and process until fluffy and white. Work in batches. Garnish with grated lemon peel and serve immediately.

Pears Sicily
QUICK QUISINE GREATER RED BANK SECTION NCJW RED BANK, NEW JERSEY

4 large pears, peeled
¼ cup chopped almonds
1 tablespoon butter, melted
2 drops almond extract
¾ cup dry sherry

Preparation time/processor: 5 minutes
Preparation time/conventional: 10 minutes
Baking time: 30 minutes
Serves 4

1. Preheat oven to 350°.

2. Cut pears in half; place in a small baking dish. Combine almonds, butter, and almond extract; place in the pear cavities. Pour the sherry over and bake for 30 minutes. Serve hot or cold.

Strawberries Romanoff à la Lila
SPECIALTY OF THE HOUSE SISTERHOOD TEMPLE ISRAEL BOSTON, MASSACHUSSETTS

1 quart fresh strawberries
1 cup heavy cream
1 pint vanilla ice cream, softened
1 to 2 tablespoons Kirsch or Cointreau

Preparation time: 10 minutes
Chilling time: 1 hour
Serves 4 to 6

1. Place strawberries in a large serving bowl.

2. Whip cream. Fold together ice cream, whipped cream, and liqueur. Pour over the strawberries and refrigerate until serving time, at least 1 hour.

Honeydew Crème de Menthe
TO SERVE WITH LOVE SISTERHOOD OF TEMPLE AVODA FAIR LAWN, NEW JERSEY

4 cups honeydew melon balls
¼ cup fresh lime juice
¼ cup sugar
3 tablespoons crème de menthe
Sprigs of fresh mint

Preparation time: 5 to 10 minutes
Chilling time: 3 hours
Serves 4

1 Combine melon balls, lime juice, sugar and liqueur. Chill 3 to 4 hours or overnight.

2. Serve in sherbet glasses garnished with mint sprigs.

Hot Peach Dessert

FAMILY FAVORITES TEMPLE SOLEL SISTERHOOD HOLLYWOOD, FLORIDA

1½ to 2 pounds fresh ripe
  peaches (or nectarines,
  plums, apricots)
1 to 2 tablespoons lemon
  juice
½ cup flour
1 cup rolled oats
¾ cup light brown sugar
½ teaspoon salt, or to taste
1 stick butter or margarine,
  melted

Preparation time: 20 minutes
Baking time: 25 minutes
Serves 6

1. Preheat oven to 350°.

2. Peel and slice fruit; arrange in the bottom of a greased 9-inch pie plate or 9 x 9 baking dish. Sprinkle with lemon juice and bake for about 15 minutes until soft.

3. Meanwhile, combine the remaining ingredients with a fork. Crumble over the partially cooked fruit. Return to oven and bake for 25 minutes. Serve warm with vanilla ice cream or whipped cream.

Peach Cobbler

EDITOR'S CHOICE

1 stick margarine
1 cup sugar
1 cup flour
2 teaspoons baking powder
1 cup milk
4 to 6 fresh peaches, sliced (6
  to 7 cups)

Preparation time/processor: 10 minutes
Preparation time/conventional: 15 minutes
Baking time: 30 to 40 minutes
Serves 6 to 8

1. Preheat oven to 375°

2. Place margarine in a 9 x 13 baking dish and place in hot oven for 3 minutes or until melted.

3. Combine sugar, flour, and baking powder. Add milk and stir until smooth. Pour mixture over margarine. Arrange peach slices on top. Bake for 30 to 40 minutes until brown. Crust will rise to top and cover peaches.

Summer Peach Melba

THE JOY OF FRESSING   BETH ISRAEL SISTERHOOD   LANSDALE, PENNSYLVANIA

1 package (10 oz.) frozen
  raspberries
1 tablespoon cornstarch
2 tablespoons cold water
4 to 6 fresh peaches
2 tablespoons lemon juice
  (approx.)
1 quart vanilla ice cream

Preparation time: 20 minutes
Serves 6

1. Place raspberries in a small saucepan. Combine cornstarch and water to make a paste and stir into the raspberries. Place over moderate heat and stir constantly until thickened and clear. Let cool.

2. Peel and slice the peaches. Sprinkle with lemon juice to keep from discoloring.

3. To serve, place 1 scoop of ice cream in 6 sherbet cups or stemmed glasses. Arrange peach slices around the ice cream and top with the raspberry sauce.

Danish Red Pudding

SALT AND PEPPER TO TASTE   SISTERHOOD CONGREGATION ANSHEI ISRAEL   TUCSON, ARIZONA

2 packages (10 oz. each)
  frozen raspberries
2 packages (10 oz. each)
  frozen strawberries
⅓ cup cornstarch
½ cup water
1 tablespoon lemon juice
Sugar to taste

Preparation time: 15 to 20 minutes
Cooling time: 2 hours
Serves 8

Food processor/blender

1. Thaw raspberries and strawberries; place in a food processor (metal blade) or blender and process until puréed, about 20 seconds. Rub through a sieve into a mediun saucepan. Bring to a simmer.

2. Combine cornstarch and water and add to saucepan. Simmer, stirring constantly, until mixture is transparent, about 3 minutes. Remove from heat and stir in lemon juice.

3. Allow mixture to cool for several minutes, then pour into a glass serving dish or individual glasses. Sprinkle with a little sugar. Cool completely. Cover and chill for at least 2 hours or overnight. Served with whipped cream, sour cream and/or almonds.

Rhubarb Crunch

FROM GENERATION TO GENERATION   B'NAI AMOONA SISTERHOOD   ST. LOUIS, MISSOURI

5 cups diced fresh rhubarb
(or 20 oz. pkg. frozen)
1 cup sugar
3 tablespoons flour (4 Tbsp.
if using frozen fruit)
1 cup brown sugar
1 cup rolled oats (quick or
regular)
1½ cups flour
1½ sticks butter or
margarine

Preparation time/processor: 5 to 10 minutes
Preparation time/conventional: 15 minutes
Baking time: 40 to 50 minutes
Serves 9 to 12

Food processor

1. Preheat oven to 350°. Thaw frozen rhubarb.

2. Combine rhubarb, sugar and 3 (or 4) table-spoons flour. Spread evenly on bottom of a 9 x 13 baking pan.

3. Insert metal blade. Place brown sugar, oats, 1½ cups flour, butter (cut into 8 pieces) in the work bowl; pulse once or twice until mixture is coarse and crumbly.

4. Sprinkle over the rhubarb and bake for 40 to 50 minutes until golden. Serve warm or chilled with whipped cream or vanilla ice cream.

Conventional

Soften butter. In step 3, use a pastry cutter to make a streusel by cutting butter into sugar, oats, and flour. Proceed to step 4.

Grapes Juanita

FROM CHARLESTON, WITH LOVE   SYNAGOGUE EMANU-EL SISTERHOOD   CHARLESTON, SOUTH CAROLINA

2 pounds seedless grapes
1 cup sour cream
½ cup light brown sugar
Grated orange peel*

Preparation time: 10 minutes
Chilling time: 2 hours
Serves 6 to 8

1. Combine grapes and sour cream. Sprinkle with brown sugar. Chill for at least 2 hours. Garnish with grated orange peel.

Variation: Combine grapes with blueberries, cut-up nectarines, and/or sliced melon.

Mocha Custard

12 ounces semi-sweet
  chocolate
2 tablespoons butter
1½ cups milk
2 large eggs
3 tablespoons
  coffee-flavored liqueur
Whipped cream (optional)

Preparation time/processor: 15 minutes
Preparation time/conventional: 20 minutes
Chilling time: 2 hours
Serves 5

Food processor

1. Insert metal blade. Break chocolate into pieces and process until fine. Transfer to a small saucepan; add butter and ½ cup milk. Melt over low heat, stirring from time to time.

2. Place remaining 1 cup milk in the work bowl. Add eggs and liqueur and process until well mixed, about 30 seconds. Add the melted chocolate mixture and process about 1 minute. The result will be quite runny.

3. Transfer to 6 ramekins or custard cups and chill until set, about 2 hours. Garnish with whipped cream.

Conventional

In step 1, place chocolate pieces in saucepan with butter and milk. In step 2, use a blender or mixer.

Grated Orange Peel

1. Peel the orange part from the fruit using a loose-bladed vegetable peeler. Be careful to remove only the colored part.

2. Spread out to dry. This can be done on paper towels in a dry kitchen, in a microwave, a very slow oven, or in the sun.

3. When dry, grind to a fine powder in the food processor or blender. Use in baked goods, as a topping for ice cream, or in any tomato sauce dish.

Honey Custard

ALL THIS AND KOSHER, TOO   BETH DAVID SISTERHOOD   MIAMI, FLORIDA

4 eggs
½ cup honey
¼ teaspoon salt
2 cups milk
½ teaspoon vanilla extract
Extra honey
Toasted coconut

Preparation time: 5 to 10 minutes
Baking time: 50 minutes
Chilling time: 1 hour
Serves 6

Food processor

1. Preheat oven to 325°.

2. Insert metal blade. Place eggs, honey, and salt in work bowl and process for 5 seconds. Add milk and vanilla with the machine running. It may be necessary to do this in batches.

3. Pour into 6 buttered custard cups and place cups in a pan of hot water. Bake for about 50 minutes or until knife inserted in center comes out clean. Cool. Serve chilled with a drizzle of honey and a little toasted coconut.

Conventional

In step 2, use a blender, mixer, or whisk. Proceed to step 3.

Sweet Nuts

A MATZO BALL IS NOT ANOTHER DRESS-UP DANCE!   B'NAI SHOLOM SISTERHOOD   HUNTINGTON, WEST VIRGINIA

2 egg whites
1 tablespoon water
1 cup sugar
1 teaspoon cinnamon
1 teaspoon salt
1 pound pecan halves

Preparation time: 10 minutes
Cooking time: 30 to 45 minutes
Makes about 3 cups

1. Preheat oven to 300°.

2. Beat egg whites and water until frothy, not stiff. Place sugar, cinnamon, and salt in a plastic bag and shake to mix.

3. Add pecans to egg whites and stir to mix. Transfer to plastic bag and shake to coat. Spread on a cookie sheet and bake for 30 to 45 minutes, stirring often. (Or use microwave.)

Cheese Roulade

WITH LOVE AND SPICE SHOSHONA CHAPTER, AMERICAN MIZRACHI WOMEN WEST HEMPSTEAD, NEW YORK

1 pound farmer's cheese
½ pound cream cheese
½ cup sugar
1 teaspoon vanilla extract
3 eggs
Cornflakes or cornflake
   crumbs

Preparation time/processor: 5 minutes
Preparation time/conventional: 15 to 20 minutes
Baking time: 10 minutes
Serves 6 to 8

Food processor

1. Preheat oven to 350°.

2. Insert metal blade and process the farmer's cheese, cream cheese, sugar, and vanilla until smooth. Add eggs and process to blend well.

3. Place cornflakes on a sheet of wax paper. Drop large spoonfuls of cheese mixture onto cornflakes and roll into small cylinders or mounds. Arrange on a greased baking sheet. Bake for 10 minutes. Serve immediately with strawberries and sour cream.

Conventional

Use a mixer in step 2.

Note: May be made in advance and refrigerated or frozen. Defrost before baking.

Mascarpone

ONE MORE BITE TEMPLE BETH ISRAEL SISTERHOOD SAN DIEGO, CALIFORNIA

1 package (8 oz.) cream
   cheese
¼ cup confectioners' sugar
2 tablespoons heavy cream
2 tablespoons Amaretto
   liqueur
2 tablespoons toasted sliced
   almonds

Preparation time/processor: 5 minutes
Preparation time/conventional: 10 minutes
Chilling time: several hours
Serves 4 to 6

1. Combine all ingredients (except almonds) in work bowl of food processor or bowl of mixer (soften cream cheese) and beat until smooth. Chill for several hours.

2. Mound on a serving plate, swirling into a tall cone. Sprinkle with almonds. Serve surrounded by fresh fruit.

Jiffy Blueberry Sauce

INSPIRATIONS ... FROM RENA HADASSAH   RENA GROUP HADASSAH   MOUNT VERNON, NEW YORK

1 cup fresh blueberries (or
  other berries)
¼ cup fresh lemon juice
¼ cup sugar
¼ teaspoon vanilla extract

Preparation time: 10 to 15 minutes
Makes 1 ½ cups

1. Place all ingredients in a saucepan over medium heat. Cook until hot, stirring and crushing blueberries with a spoon. Serve hot with pancakes or pudding, or chill and serve on ice cream, or use as a jam.

Note: Sweetness can be adjusted by varying amount of sugar and lemon juice.

Fast Hot Fudge Sauce

PALATE TREATS   MOUNT ZION TEMPLE SISTERHOOD   ST. PAUL, MINNESOTA

6 ounces semi-sweet
  chocolate chips
1 teaspoon butter
½ to ⅔ cup whole milk, half
  and half, or heavy cream
1 drop vanilla extract

Preparation time: 10 to 15 minutes
Makes about ¾ cup.

1. Combine all ingredients in a small saucepan over low heat, stirring frequently.

2. Serve over ice cream or cake, or use as a dip for fresh fruits or berries.

Variation: Add coffee, orange, or mint liqueur.

Sweetened Condensed Milk

EDITOR'S CHOICE

1 cup instant nonfat dry milk
  powder
⅔ cup sugar
⅓ cup boiling water
3 tablespoons melted
  margarine

Preparation time: 5 minutes
Makes about 1 ¼ cups

Food processor/blender

1. Combine all ingredients and process until smooth. Store in refrigerator until ready to use.

Grapenuts Pudding

FLAVORED WITH LOVE   ADAT ARI EL SISTERHOOD   NORTH HOLLYWOOD, CALIFORNIA

1 quart milk
1 cup Grapenuts cereal
3 eggs
1 cup sugar
1 tablespoon melted butter
1 teaspoon vanilla extract
½ teaspoon cinnamon
Pinch salt
Pinch nutmeg

Preparation time: 10 minutes
Baking time: 1½ hours
Serves 6 to 8

1. Preheat oven to 350°.

2. Scald milk; pour 2 cups milk over Grapenuts. Let stand while beating the eggs in a large bowl. Add remaining ingredients and the Grapenuts mixture to the eggs, and stir well to combine.

3. Pour into a greased 2-quart baking dish. Bake for 1½ hours, stirring after 45 minutes. Pudding will be quite solid.

Brownie Pudding

THE SPORT OF COOKING   WOMEN'S AMERICAN ORT, DISTRICT VII   CLEVELAND, OHIO

1 cup flour
2 teaspoons baking powder
¼ teaspoon salt
¾ cup sugar
¼ cup cocoa (unsweetened)
2 tablespoons melted butter
½ cup milk
¾ cup chopped nuts
1 teaspoon vanilla extract
1¾ cups hot water
¾ cup dark brown sugar
2 tablespoons cocoa
  (unsweetened)

Preparation time: 10 to 15 minutes
Baking time: 35 to 40 minutes
Serves 6

1. Preheat oven to 350°.

2. In a large bowl, combine flour, baking powder, salt, sugar, ¼ cup cocoa, melted butter, milk, chopped nuts, and vanilla, and stir well. Spread batter evenly in an ungreased 7 x 11 or 8 x 8 baking pan.

3. Combine hot water, brown sugar, and remaining 2 tablespoons cocoa and stir well. Pour over the batter and bake for 35 to 40 minutes. Serve warm with whipped cream or ice cream.

Out-of-This-World Bread Pudding

5000 YEARS IN THE KITCHEN   SISTERHOOD OF TEMPLE EMANU-EL   DALLAS, TEXAS

6 slices white or whole wheat
  bread
3 eggs
¾ cup milk
¼ cup sugar
1 teaspoon vanilla extract
½ teaspoon cinnamon
½ teaspoon nutmeg
½ cup nuts
¼ cup raisins

Sauce (Optional)
2 tablespoons butter
½ cup sugar
1 cup scalded milk
1 tablespoon flour
¼ cup cold water
1 teaspoon vanilla extract

Preparation time: 10 to 15 minutes
Standing time: 15 minutes
Baking time: 30 to 40 minutes
Preparation time/sauce: 10 minutes
Serves 6

1. Preheat oven to 350°.

2. Cut bread into small squares and place in a buttered 8 x 8 baking dish. Place eggs, milk, sugar, vanilla, cinnamon, and nutmeg in a food processor or blender and process until well combined. Add nuts and raisins and pulse to just mix.

3. Pour over bread and let stand for 15 minutes. Bake for 30 to 40 minutes.

4. To make sauce, melt butter and sugar together in a saucepan. When slightly brown, remove from heat and slowly add milk. Blend flour and cold water together in a small jar. Add slowly to the milk mixture and cook until smooth and slightly thickened. Stir in vanilla. Serve hot or cold on pudding.

Parfait Crunch

FROM THE BALABUSTA'S TABLE   SISTERHOOD OF TEMPLE ISRAEL   NATICK, MASSACHUSETTS

Ice cream
Chocolate or coffee syrup (or
  orange or chocolate
  liqueur)
100% natural cereal
Maraschino cherries

Preparation time: 5 minutes
Serves any number

1. In a parfait glass, alternate ice cream, syrup, and cereal. Top with a cherry.

2. Serve immediately or keep in freezer. If frozen solid, let stand at room temperature for a few minutes before serving.

Coffee Ice Cream Dessert

COLLECTABLE DELECTABLES   RODEF SHOLOM TEMPLE SISTERHOOD   HAMPTON, VIRGINIA

1 package (8½ oz.) chocolate
  wafers or chocolate chip
  cookies
1 stick butter or margarine,
  melted
½ gallon coffee ice cream,
  softened
1 can (5½ oz.) chocolate
  syrup
1 cup heavy cream, whipped
Slivered almonds or pecan
  halves

Preparation time: 10 minutes
Freezing time: 2½ hours
Serves 12 to 15

1. Crush cookies. Add butter and combine. Press this mixture firmly into a 9 x 13 pan. Freeze for 30 minutes.

2. Spoon ice cream over the cookie crust. Freeze 2 to 3 hours. Dribble with chocolate syrup and freeze.

3. To serve, cover with whipped cream and garnish with nuts.

Note: Line pan with foil or plastic wrap if you want to remove from pan to serve. If making ahead, whip the cream just before serving.

Tia Maria Torte

FOOD FOR SHOW/FOOD ON THE GO   MOUNT SINAI HOSPITAL AUXILIARY   MINNEAPOLIS, MINNESOTA

2 pounds crisp chocolate
  chip cookies
1 cup milk
¾ cup coffee liqueur
2 cups whipping cream
3 tablespoons confectioners'
  sugar
1 teaspoon vanilla extract
Shaved chocolate
Sliced almonds

Preparation time: 10 to 15 minutes
Chilling time: 2 hours
Serves 12 to 15

1. Dip cookies in milk and then in liqueur. Arrange on bottom and sides of an 8-inch springform pan.

2. Whip cream with sugar and vanilla. Alternate layers of whipped cream and cookies in the pan, ending with whipped cream.

3. Garnish with shaved chocolate and sliced almonds. Refrigerate until serving time.

llinois world of our flavors south bend indiana the cookery cedar rapids
wa specialties of the house alexandria louisiana kitchen treats cookboo
es to noshes lewiston maine sisterhood cookbook potomac maryland p
melting pot lexington massa   thought cookbook newton
ok norwood massachus   ody massachusetts cc
etts in the best of tast   e happy cooker of te
i with temple beth   a used to make f
igan all the recip   to ask saint pau
souri deborah c   o generation l
rry hill new je   eating east
ion new jerse   with love so
le tinton fa   y the spice
poking? al   onderful
k cookie   york the

passover

ng brook   osher ki
like it cli   ast nor
new yo   great r
york th   it vern
na had   sher c
osher   nester
scarsc   what
ood ta   d nev
i carol   d ohi
ount t   nd oh
io in t   nia th
ania th   n per
ia pen   penr
n wynr   south
charles   rolina
e recipe   years
nnial co   oks fal
nchburg   n good
ke it parke   sin from
gham alab   at and en
ste berkele   ills califor
california fr   hat's cookir
flavored with   iego californ
lectable collec   ease! rockvill
d connecticut fo   passover made
earwater florida cle   measures and tr
ght gainesville floria   alabustas' more favo
it in the kitchen hollywo   s hollywood florida nit
ksonville florida what's coo.   ville florida try it you'll like
atellite beach florida our favorite recipes tallahassee florida knishes gefil
a georgia golden soup atlanta georgia the happy cooker augusta georgia
is portal to good cooking great lakes illinois the fort sheridan and great l

Passover

Potato Mushroom Kugel

RECIPE FAVOR BOOKLET (PASSOVER) B'NAI ISRAEL SISTERHOOD TOLEDO, OHIO

½ pound fresh mushrooms
3 or 4 stalks celery
1 large onion
1 clove garlic, minced
½ stick margarine
2 large potatoes, peeled
4 large eggs
¼ cup water
1 teaspoon salt, or to taste
Dash pepper
½ cup matzo meal

Preparation time/processor: 10 to 15 minutes
Preparation time/conventional: 20 minutes
Baking time/conventional: 50 to 60 minutes
Serves 6 to 8

Food processor

1. Preheat oven to 350°.

2. Insert slicing blade and slice mushrooms, celery, and onion. Sauté with garlic in the margarine until onion is translucent. Transfer to a large mixing bowl. Slice potatoes and add.

3. Insert metal blade and process eggs, water, salt, pepper, and matzo meal. Combine with vegetables.

4. Transfer to a well-greased 8 x 8 baking dish. Bake for 50 to 60 minutes or until puffed and golden.

Microwave: Place mushrooms, garlic, celery, onion, and margarine in an 8 x 8 baking dish. Cook uncovered, stirring frequently, until onions become translucent. Add potatoes and egg mixture and toss to mix well. Proceed to step 4.

Passover Farfel Kugel with Ground Beef

THE HAPPY COOKER TEMPLE SINAI ATLANTA, GEORGIA

1 pound ground beef
1 large onion, chopped
¼ pound mushrooms, sliced
3 hard-cooked eggs, chopped
  fine
1 large clove garlic, minced
Oil
Salt and pepper to taste
3 cups matzo farfel
3 raw eggs, well beaten

Preparation time/processor: 10 to 15 minutes
Preparation time/conventional: 15 to 20 minutes
Baking time: 30 minutes
Serves 4

1. Preheat oven to 350°.

2. Sauté ground beef, onion, mushrooms, and garlic in oil until meat loses pink color. Season with salt and pepper.

3. Soak farfel in water, drain, and squeeze out excess water.

4. Combine all ingredients and mix well. Transfer to a greased 8 x 8 baking dish and bake for about 30 minutes or until top is golden.

Matzo Vegetable Farfel Ring (Passover)

NOSHES, NIBBLES AND GOURMET DELIGHTS TEMPLE IN THE PINES SISTERHOOD HOLLYWOOD, FLORIDA

½ pound fresh mushrooms,
  sliced
½ cup diced green pepper
1 cup minced onion
1 cup diced celery
¼ cup peanut oil
3 cups matzo farfel
2 eggs
1 cup chicken broth
1½ cups boiling water
2 teaspoons paprika
1 teaspoon salt
¼ teaspoon pepper

Preparation time/processor: 10 to 15 minutes
Preparation time/conventional: 15 to 20 minutes
Baking time: 30 minutes
Serves 6 to 8

1. Preheat oven to 375°.

2. Sauté mushrooms, green pepper, onion, and celery in oil. Do not brown. Add the farfel and mix.

3. Beat eggs with broth and water. Add to farfel mixture. Stir in seasonings and allow to stand for 5 minutes or until some liquid has been absorbed.

4. Transfer to a greased 6-cup ring mold and bake for 30 minutes.

Matzo Balls

EDITOR'S CHOICE

3 eggs, lightly beaten
¾ cup matzo meal
½ teaspoon salt

Preparation time: 5 minutes
Standing time: 20 minutes
Cooking time: 45 minutes
Makes 12 large balls

1. Combine ingredients, adding more matzo meal to stiffen mixture if you prefer a firmer matzo ball. Cover and refrigerate 20 minutes.

2. Form balls with two spoons. Drop into boiling salted water or soup stock. Cover and cook gently for 45 minutes, or until completely cooked (test one by cutting in half).

Charoseth

KOSHER COOKING FOR EVERYONE   SISTERHOOD PLAINVIEW JEWISH CENTER   PLAINVIEW, NEW YORK

2 apples
6 walnuts
2 tablespoons sweet red wine
½ teaspoon cinnamon
½ teaspoon ground ginger

Preparation time/processor: 5 to 10 minutes
Makes about 1 cup

Food processor

1. Peel and quarter apples. Insert metal blade. Place with other ingredients in work bowl and pulse to chop to desired consistency.

Conventional

1. Peel and chop apples. Chop nuts. Or chop together in a chopping bowl. Mix apples and nuts with remaining ingredients and chill until ready to use.

Note: Do not chop too finely — should resemble mortar.

Passover Sour Cream Pancakes

FAVORITE RECIPES FROM HADASSAH   MID-MISSOURI DEBORAH CHAPTER OF HADASSAH   COLUMBIA, MISSOURI

3 eggs
1 cup sour cream
6 tablespoons matzo meal
½ teaspoon salt, or to taste
¼ teaspoon pepper
  (optional)

Preparation time: 20 minutes
Makes about 11

1. Beat eggs and sour cream together until smooth. Add remaining ingredients and mix well. Drop by spoonfuls onto a greased skillet. Brown on both sides.

Matzo Brie (Fried Matzos)

EDITOR'S CHOICE

4 matzos
3 eggs, lightly beaten
2 tablespoons butter

Preparation time: 10 minutes
Serves 4

1. Break up matzos and place in a colander. Pour boiling water over. Mix into beaten eggs, stirring until egg is slightly absorbed. Heat butter in a skillet, pour in matzos, and cook until golden. Turn and cook other side. May cook as a single layer or break up as desired.

Cheese Latkes (A Pesach Treat)

WITH LOVE AND SPICE   SHOSHANA CHAPTER, AMERICAN MIZRACHI WOMEN   WEST HEMPSTEAD, NEW YORK

4 eggs, lightly beaten
1 package (8 oz.) farmer's
  cheese
3 tablespoons sugar
3 tablespoons oil
¼ cup matzo meal

Preparation time/processor: 20 minutes
Preparation time/conventional: 20 to 25 minutes
Makes 12

1. Combine eggs, cheese, sugar, and oil. Mix until smooth. Add matzo meal and mix well. Add more matzo meal if mixture becomes too watery.

2. Fry by ¼ cupfuls in a greased hot skillet until brown on both sides.

Carrot and Sweet Potato Tzimmes

1 bunch carrots, scraped
6 large sweet potatoes,
   peeled
½ cup pitted prunes
¼ to ½ cup beef stock or
   orange juice
¼ to ½ cup honey
¼ teaspoon cinnamon
⅛ to ¼ cup chicken fat or
   margarine

Preparation time: 20 minutes
Baking time: 40 minutes
Serves 8

1. Preheat oven to 350°.

2. Cut carrots into 1-inch slices; cut sweet potatoes into pieces about the same size as the carrots. Boil in salted water to cover until tender but still firm; drain. Place in a casserole with remaining ingredients. Stir gently to combine.

3. Cover and bake for 30 minutes. Stir gently and bake, uncovered, for another 10 minutes.

Passover Derma

WHY IS THIS COOKBOOK DIFFERENT... BECAUSE IT'S FOR PASSOVER   BETH ISRAEL SISTERHOOD   LANSDALE, PA

½ cup chopped celery
¾ cup chopped onion
½ cup grated carrot
3 cups crushed matzos
2 cloves garlic, minced
2 eggs
2 sticks margarine, melted
1 teaspoon salt
¼ teaspoon pepper
¼ teaspoon poultry
   seasoning

Preparation time/processor: 5 to 10 minutes
Preparation time/conventional: 10 to 15 minutes
Baking time: 45 minutes
Serves 12 to 16

1. Preheat oven to 350°.

2. Combine vegetables and crushed matzos. Add all remaining ingredients and mix well.

3. Place a 20-inch sheet of aluminum foil on a cookie sheet. Shape the matzo mixture into a roll 16 inches long. Bring the long sides of foil up over the roll; fold loosely in a series of locked folds, to allow for heat circulation and expansion. Fold short ends up and over; crimp and seal.

4. Bake for 45 minutes. Cut while hot into ½-inch slices.

Note: Mixture could be used to stuff a turkey or capon.

Matzo Farfel Pudding

OUR COOKBOOK   BETH SHOLOM CONGREGATION   ELKINS PARK, PENNSYLVANIA

2 cups matzo farfel
Peel of 1 orange (zest)
¼ cup sugar
2 sticks melted butter or
  margarine
2 eggs
¼ cup water
½ teaspoon cinnamon
¼ teaspoon nutmeg
¼ cup apricot preserves
1 large apple, peeled
¼ cup raisins

Preparation time/processor: 10 to 15 minutes
Preparation time/conventional: 15 to 20 minutes
Baking time: 1 hour
Serves 9 to 12

Food processor

1. Preheat oven to 350°.

2. Place farfel in a colander and pour about 1 quart of boiling water over it.

3. Insert metal blade. Place orange peel and sugar in work bowl and process until the peel is finely chopped, about 25 seconds. Add butter, eggs, water, cinnamon, nutmeg, and preserves. Process until well mixed, about 10 seconds. Cut the apple in quarters; place in work bowl and pulse 3 or 4 times to chop. Add the raisins and farfel and pulse once or twice to just combine.

4. Transfer to a greased 8 x 8 baking dish and bake for 1 hour. Serve warm.

Conventional

In step 3, grate orange peel. Beat sugar, butter, eggs, water, and seasonings until well combined. Chop apples into small pieces and add. Add raisins and farfel and stir well. Proceed to step 4.

Passover Pie Crust

PASSOVER MADE EASY   EMANUEL SYNAGOGUE   WEST HARTFORD, CONNECTICUT

1 cup matzo meal
¼ cup peanut oil
2 tablespoons sugar
¼ teaspoon cinnamon
⅛ teaspoon salt

Preparation time: 5 to 10 minutes
Baking time: 15 to 20 minutes
Makes one 9-inch crust

1. Preheat oven to 375°.

2. Blend ingredients together in a mixing bowl. Press mixture into a 9-inch pie plate. Bake for 15 to 20 minutes until light brown. Cool and fill.

Lemon Sponge Pudding
RECIPE FAVOR BOOKLET (PASSOVER)   B'NAI ISRAEL SISTERHOOD   TOLDEO, OHIO

1 cup sugar
¼ cup matzo cake meal
½ tablespoon potato starch
⅛ teaspoon salt
2 tablespoons peanut oil
4 to 5 tablespoons lemon
  juice
1 teaspoon grated lemon
  peel
2 egg yolks, well beaten
1 cup water
2 egg whites

Preparation time: 10 to 15 minutes
Baking time: 40 to 50 minutes
Serves 6 to 8

1. Preheat oven to 350°.

2. Combine dry ingredients in mixing bowl. Add oil, lemon, juice, and lemon peel. Combine egg yolks and water and add. Stir well.

3. Beat the egg whites until stiff and fold in gently. Pour into an 8 x 8 baking dish. Place in a pan of hot water and bake for 40 to 50 minutes.

Passover Granola
PASSOVER MADE EASY   EMANUEL SYNAGOGUE   WEST HARTFORD, CONNECTICUT

4 cups matzo farfel
1 cup coarsely chopped nuts
¼ cup peanut oil
¼ cup honey
¼ cup raisins

Preparation time: 5 to 10 minutes
Baking time: 20 to 30 minutes
Makes about 5 ½ cups

1. Preheat oven to 350°.

2. Combine farfel, nuts, oil, and honey. Spread out on a cookie sheet and bake for 20 to 30 minutes, stirring from time to time.

3. When cool, add raisins and store in an airtight container.

Note: Can be eaten as a snack or with milk as a cereal.

Matzo-Apple Charlotte

JEWISH CREATIVE COOKING   JEWISH COMMUNITY CENTER OF GREATER WASHINGTON   ROCKVILLE, MD

3 matzos
¾ cup dark brown sugar
Peel of 1 lemon
6 eggs
½ stick butter or margarine,
  melted and cooled
2 teaspoons cinnamon
3 large apples, peeled
⅔ cup currants (or substitute
  raisins)
½ cup raisins
¾ cup walnuts or pecans
  (optional)

Preparation time/processor: 10 to 15 minutes
Preparation time/conventional: 15 to 20 minutes
Baking time: 35 to 40 minutes
Serves 9

Food processor

1. Preheat oven to 350°

2. Crumble matzos and place in a colander. Pour about 1 quart of hot water over the matzos. Let drain.

3. Insert metal blade. Place brown sugar and lemon peel in work bowl and process for 25 seconds or until peel is finely chopped. Add eggs, butter, and cinnamon and process 15 seconds to mix well. (Work in batches in small size processor.)

4. Quarter the apples and add them evenly around the work bowl. Pulse 3 to 4 times to chop. Add the currants, raisins, nuts, and reserved matzos. Pulse once or twice to just combine.

5. Transfer to a greased 9 x 9 pan and bake for 35 to 45 minutes or until apples are tender and Charlotte is golden.

Conventional

In step 3, grate lemon peel. Beat eggs and sugar until fluffy, then add butter, cinnamon, and lemon peel and mix well. In step 4, chop apples finely and add to egg mixture along with the currants, raisins, nuts, and reserved matzos. Proceed to step 5.

Lorna's Passover Fudge Squares

½ cup matzo cake meal
½ cup potato starch
½ teaspoon salt
4 tablespoons or more cocoa
  (unsweetened)
4 eggs
2 cups sugar
1 cup oil
2 cups pecans or walnuts,
  chopped

Preparation time/processor: 5 to 10 minutes
Preparation time/conventional: 10 to 15 minutes
Baking time: 35 minutes
Makes about 25 squares

Conventional

1. Mix dry ingredients together and reserve. Beat eggs and sugar until thick and fluffy. Add oil and mix well.

2. Add dry ingredients and blend well. Stir in chopped nuts and spread in an oiled 8 x 8 or 9 x 9 pan. Bake for 35 minutes. Cool slightly and cut into 1½-inch squares.

Food processor

Place dry ingredients in work bowl (metal blade) and pulse several times to mix; remove. Add eggs and sugar to work bowl and process 1 minute. Add oil and process several seconds to mix well. In step 2, add dry ingredients and pulse until combined. Add whole nuts and pulse to chop and mix in.

Passover Brownies

5000 YEARS IN THE KITCHEN   SISTERHOOD TEMPLE EMANU-EL   DALLAS, TEXAS

2 eggs
1 cup sugar
½ cup matzo cake meal
¼ cup unsweetened cocoa
¼ teaspoon salt
½ cup peanut oil
1 tablespoon orange juice
  concentrate
½ teaspoon grated orange
  peel*
½ cup chopped nuts

Preparation time: 10 minutes
Baking time: 25 minutes
Makes about 24

1. Preheat oven to 325°.

2. Beat eggs and sugar until thick and fluffy. Add cake meal, cocoa, and salt and stir well. Blend in remaining ingredients and spread in a well-oiled 9 x 9 baking pan. Bake for 25 minutes. Cut into squares while still warm.

Mocha Pudding (Passover)

PASSOVERAMA TEMPLE BETH HILLEL-BETH EL SISTERHOOD WYNNEWOOD, PENNSYLVANIA

4 ounces semi-sweet
  chocolate
2½ cups milk
½ cup very strong coffee
½ cup sugar, or to taste
¼ cup potato starch
Dash salt

Preparation time: 10 to 15 minutes
Chilling time: 1 hour
Serves 6

1. Cut chocolate into pieces.

2. Place all ingredients in a saucepan and place over medium heat. Cook until thickened, about 10 minutes, stirring constantly.

3. Pour into sherbet glasses and chill.

Note: Tastes best the same day.

Passover Banana Sherbert

PASSOVERAMA SISTERHOOD OF TEMPLE BETH HILLEL-BETH EL WYNNEWOOD, PENNSYLVANIA

⅔ to 1 cup sugar
3 bananas
1 cup orange juice
1 tablespoon lemon juice
1 egg white

Preparation time: 5 minutes
Freezing time: 3 hours
Serves 6

Food processor

1. Insert metal blade and process sugar until very fine (powdered sugar). Add remaining ingredients to work bowl and process until smooth, scraping bowl several times. Pour into individual ice cube molds and freeze until solid, 3 to 4 hours.

2. Empty cubes back into food processor and process until very thick and fluffy (do not overprocess). Serve immediately.

Index

Contributors

The following cookbooks are represented in *Quick & Easy*. Many organizations will fill orders for their cookbooks by mail; the price and mailing address for each of these is also listed.

ARIZONA. TUCSON. *Salt and Pepper to Taste,* Sisterhood Congregation Anshei Israel.

CALIFORNIA. ENCINO. *Shabbos the Rabbi Ate Late,* Maarev Temple. NORTH HOLLYWOOD. *Flavored With Love,* Adat Ari El Sisterhood. Send $5.00 plus $1.50 shipping to: Adat Ari El Judaica Shop, 5540 Laurel Canyon Boulevard, North Hollywood, CA 91607. SAN DIEGO. *One More Bite,* Temple Beth Israel Sisterhood. Send $4.50 plus $1.00 shipping to: Adele Honchor, 4787 Cather Avenue, San Diego, CA 92122. SANTA CRUZ. *Apples All Ways,* Santa Cruz Chapter of Hadassah. Send $5.00 plus $1.00 shipping to: Santa Cruz Chapter of Hadassah, 230 Felix St. Apt. M, Santa Cruz, CA 95060. TARZANA. *Delectable Collectibles,* Sisterhood of Temple Judea.

CANADA. ST. LAURENT, QUEBEC. *Second Helpings, Please!* Mt. Sinai Chapter, B'nai B'rith Women. Send $15 (subject to change) to: Mt. Sinai Chapter, B'nai B'rith Women, 867 Alexis Nihon Blvd., St. Laurent, Quebec H4M2B8.

CONNECTICUT. WEST HARTFORD. *Passover Made Easy,* Emanuel Synagogue. Send $5.50 plus $1.00 shipping to: Emanuel Synagogue c/o Mrs. L. Beck, 28 Brightview Drive, West Hartford, CT 06117.

FLORIDA. HALLANDALE. *Do It in the Kitchen,* Women's American ORT, VI. Send $6.00 plus postage to: 2101 East Hallandale Blvd., Hallandale, FL 33009. HOLLYWOOD. *Family Favorites,* Temple Solel Sisterhood. HOLLYWOOD. *Noshes, Nibbles and Gourmet Delights,* Temple in the Pines. Send $6.00 plus $1.00 shipping to: Temple in the Pines, 9730 Stirling Road, Hollywood, FL 33024. MIAMI. *All This and Kosher, Too.* Beth David Sisterhood. ORLANDO. *Cook's Delight,* Congregation Ohev Ahalom. 5015 Goddard Street, Orlando, FL 32810. SATELLITE BEACH. *Our Favorite Recipes,* Sisterhood of Beth Shalom.

GEORGIA. ATLANTA. *Reading, Writing & Recipes,* Gateway School. Send $8.00 plus $1.00 shipping to: Gateway School, 3686 Peachtree Road, Atlanta, GA 30319. ATLANTA. *The Happy Cooker.* Temple Sinai. Send $6.50 to: 5645 Dupree Drive, N.W., Atlanta, GA 30327. AUGUSTA. *All That Schmaltz,* Augusta Chapter of Hadassah. Send $10.00 plus $1.00 shipping to: Linda Cohen, Augusta Chapter of Hadassah, 3119 Edinburgh Drive, Augusta, GA 30909.

ILLINOIS. CHICAGO. *Portal to Good Cooking, Vol. 2.* (paperback), Women's American ORT, VIII. Send $6.00 plus $.95 to: 111 N. Wabash Avenue, Chicago, IL 60602. *Portal to Good Cooking, Vol 4* (hardcover), Send $10.00 plus $.95. HIGHLAND PARK. *Tradition in the Kitchen,* North Suburban Beth El Sisterhood. Send $6.95 plus $.95 shipping to: 1175 Sheridan Road, Highland Park, IL 60035. WILMETTE. *World of our Flavors – Certified Ta'am,* Beth Hillel Sisterhood. Send $8.00 plus $1.50 shipping to: Jackie Rosenwasser, 444 LaVergne, Wilmette, IL 60091.

IOWA. WATERLOO. *Jewish-American Favorites,* Sisterhood of Sons of Jacob Synagogue.

KENTUCKY. LEXINGTON. *Taste of Tradition,* Sisterhood of Temple Adath Israel. Send $7.50 plus $1.00 shipping to: 124 North Ashland Ave., Lexington, KY 40502.

MARYLAND. POTOMAC. *Pot of Gold,* Sisterhood Congregation Har Shalom. Send $5.00 plus $1.50 shipping to: Congregation Har Shalom Gift Shop, 11510 Falls Road, Potomac, MD 20854. ROCKVILLE. *Jewish Creative Cooking,* Jewish Community Center of Greater Washington.

MASSACHUSETTS. BOSTON. *Specialty of the House,* Sisterhood Temple Israel. Send $7.95 plus $1.00 shipping to: Paula Ligums, 2 Shaw Road, Chestnut Hill, MA 02167. LEXINGTON. *Food for Thought,* Temple Emunah Sisterhood. NATICK. *From the Balabusta's Table,* Sisterhood of Temple Israel. Send $7.00 to: Elaine Marmer, Gift Shop Chairman, 145 Hartford Street, Natick, MA 01760. NORWOOD. *Creative Cookery,* Sisterhood Temple Shaare Tefilah. Send $6.75 plus $1.25 shipping to: 556 Nichols Street, Norwood, MA 02062. PEABODY. *Cook Along With Us,* Sisterhood of Temple Beth Shalom. Send $3.00 to: 489 Lowell Street, Peabody, MA 01960. SUDBURY. *In the Best of Taste,* Congregation Beth El. Send $8.50 to: Congregation Beth El Judiac Shop, Hudson Road, Sudbury, MA 01776.

MICHIGAN. ANN ARBOR. *Cook with Temple Beth Emeth,* Temple Beth Emeth Sisterhood. Send $6.50 to: B. Heilveil, 2455 Placid Way, Ann Arbor, MI 48105. DETROIT. *Fiddler in the Kitchen,* National Council of Jewish Women. Send $8.50 plus $1.50 to: National Council of Jewish Women, 16400 West Twelve Mile Road, Southfield, MI 48076. FLINT. *Eat Darling — And Enjoy!,* Beth Israel Sisterhood. Send $8.95 plus $1.50 shipping to: Idelle Binder, 1321 San Juan Drive, Flint, MI 48504. SOUTHFIELD. *Glennwood's Gourmets,* Women's American Ort-Glennwood Chapter. Send $8.00 plus $1.00 shipping to: Women's American Ort, 21540 W. 11 Street, Southfield, MI 48076.

MINNESOTA. MINNEAPOLIS. *Food for Show, Food on the Go,* Mt. Sinai Hospital Auxiliary. Send $9.95 plus $1.25 shipping to: Mt. Sinai Hospital Auxiliary — Cookbook, 2215 Park Avenue, Minneapolis, MN 55404. ST. PAUL. *Palate Treats,* Mt. Zion Temple Sisterhood. Send $5.50 plus $1.25 shipping to: 1300 Summit Avenue, St. Paul, MN 55105.

MISSOURI. COLUMBIA. *Favorite Recipes from Hadassah,* Mid-Missouri Deborah Chapter of Hadassah. Send $6.00 to: Barbara Haines, 1107 University Ave., Columbia, MO 65201. ST. LOUIS. *From Generation to Generation,* B'nai Amoona Sisterhood. Send $8.95 plus $1.00 to: Charlotte Teicher, 9512 Laguna Drive, St. Louis, MO 63132.

NEW JERSEY. CLARK. *Garden of Eating,* Sisterhood Temple Beth O'r. Send $7.00 plus $.50 shipping to: Temple Beth O'r, attn: Marcia Schulman, 111 Valley Road, Clark, NJ 07090. FAIR LAWN. *To Serve with Love,* Sisterhood of Temple Avoda. Send $6.50 to: Temple Avoda (Polly Lewis), 10-10 Plaza Road, Fair Lawn, NJ 07410. HIGHTSTOWN. *Essen 'N Fressen,* Congregation Beth Chaim. Send $8.00 to: Sisterhood c/o Congregation Beth Chaim, P.O. Box 128, Hightstown, NJ 08520. RED BANK. *Quick Quisine,* Greater Red Bank Section NCJW. Send $6.00 to: Maxine Klatsky, 12 Sheraton Lane, Rumson, NJ 07760. ROCKAWAY. *Seasoned With Love,* White Meadow Temple Sisterhood. Send $8.50 to: White Meadow Temple, 153 White Meadow Road, Rockaway, NJ 07866. SOUTH ORANGE. *Love Jewish Style,* Temple Sharey Tefilo/Israel. Send $5.00 plus postage to: Mrs. W. Milford, 46 Boyden Parkway, Maplewood, NJ 07040.

NEW YORK. AMHERST. *The Kosher Kitchen,* Sisterhood Temple Shaarey Zedek. Send $8.95 to: Sisterhood Cookbook Chairman, Temple Shaarey Zedek, 621 Getzville Road, Amherst, NY 14226. BALDWIN. *The Wonderful World of Cooking,* Baldwin Hadassah, Namal Group. BINGHAMTON. *Cookie Cookbook,* Temple Israel Sisterhood. Send $2.50 to: Deerfield Place, Binghamton, NY 13903. BROOKLYN. *The Spice and Spirit of Kosher Jewish Cooking,* Lubavitch Women's Organization. Send $16.95 to: 852 Eastern Parkway, Brooklyn, NY 11213. BROOKLYN. *Sisterhood Cook Book,* Sisterhood of Brooklyn Heights Synagogue. Send $4.50 to: Belle Huffman, 117 Remsen Street, Brooklyn, NY 11201. KINGSTON. *To Stir With Love,* Sisterhood Ahavath Israel. Send $7.45 to: Florence Gossett, 88 Watson Lane, Kingston, NY 12401. MT. VERNON. *Inspirations ... from Rena Hadassah,* Rena Group Hadassah — Mt. Vernon Chapter. Send $4.00 to: Linda Wildman, 125 Longview, Scarsdale, NY 10583. NEW ROCHELLE. *A Book for the Cook,* Brandeis University National Women's Committee. Send $6.75 to: Hannelies Guggenheim, 110 Bon Air Ave., New Rochelle, NY 10804. NEW YORK. *Kosher Cookery Unlimited* and *Manual for Holidays,* Women's League for Conservative Judaism. Send $2.75 to: 48 East 74th Street, New York, NY 10021. NORTH BELLMORE. *Kosher Gourmet II,* Temple Beth-El of Bellmore. Send $8.00 to: 1373 Bellmore Rd., N. Bellmore, NY 11710. NORTH WOODMERE. *Add a Dash of Love,* Woodmere Hadassah. PLAINVIEW. *Kosher Cooking for Everyone,* Sisterhood Plainview Jewish Center. WEST HEMPSTEAD. *With Love and Spice,* Shoshana Chapter, American Mizrachi Women. Send $6.25 plus .75 shipping to: Mrs. Rita Berkowitz, 558 Langeley Avenue, West Hempstead, NY 11552.

OHIO. CANTON. *Sharing Our Best,* Canton, Ohio Chapter of Hadassah. Send $7.95 to: Hadassah, 329 36th St. N.W., Canton, OH 44709. CINCINNATI. *Cook Unto Others,* Hillel Jewish Student Center. Send $6.95 plus $1.00 to: 2615 Clifton Ave., Cincinnati, OH 45220. CINCINNATI. *In the Beginning* and *Beginning Again,* Rockdale Temple Sisterhood. Send $8.85 per title to: Rockdale Ridge Press, 8501 Ridge Rd., Cincinnati, OH 45236. CLEVELAND. *Fairmont Temple Cookbook,* Fairmount Temple. Send $7.50 plus $1.50 shipping to: 23737 Fairmount Blvd., Cleveland, OH 44122. CLEVELAND. *The Sport of Cooking,* Women's American ORT, VII. CLEVELAND. *Artistry in the Kitchen,* Temple Women's Association. PEPPER PIKE. *From Our Kitchens,*

Brith Emeth Sisterhood. Send $8.00 to: Barbara Kahn, 25527 Bryden Road, Beachwood, OH 44122. TOLEDO. *Under the Chef's H.A.T.*, The Hebrew Academy of Toledo. Send $6.00 plus $1.00 shipping to: 2727 Kenwood Blvd., Toledo, OH 43606. WARREN. *Super Chef*, Beth Israel Temple Sisterhood. Send $6.00 plus $1.00 shipping to: 2138 E. Market Street, Warren, OH 44483.

OKLAHOMA. TULSA. *The Cook's Book*, Temple Israel Sisterhood. Send $7.00 plus $1.00 shipping to: Temple Israel Sisterhood Judaica Shop, 2004 East 22nd Place, Tulsa, OK 74114.

PENNSYLVANIA. CARLISLE. *Cooking With Chutzpah*, Jewish Women's Council of Carlisle. Send $5.00 to: Kay Freiberg, 40 Meadowbook Road, Carlisle, PA 17013. ELKINS PARK. *Our Cookbook*, Beth Sholom Congregation. Send $12.00 to: Beth Sholom Congregation—Cookbook, Old York & Foxcroft Roads, Elkins Park, PA 19117. LANSDALE. *Joy of Fressing*, and *Why is this Cookbook Different – Because It's for Passover*, Beth Israel Sisterhood. LEBANON. *Not for Noshers Only*, Beth Israel Sisterhood. Send $7.00 to: Beth Israel Sisterhood, 411 S. 8th Street, Lebanon, PA 17042. WASHINGTON. *The Way to a Man's Heart*, Beth Israel Congregation. Send $5.00 to: 265 North Avenue, Washington, PA 15301. WYNNEWOOD. *Quick and Easy Cookbook*, Main Line Reform Temple Sisterhood. Send $3.00 to: 410 Montgomery Ave., Wynnewood, PA 19096. WYNNEWOOD. *Passoverama*, Temple Beth Hillel-Beth El Sisterhood. Send $9.95 plus $1.50 shipping to: Remington Rd. & Lancaster Ave., Wynnewood, PA 19096.

SOUTH CAROLINA. CHARLESTON. *From Charleston With Love*, Synagogue Emanu-El Sisterhood. Send $8.20 total to: 5 Windsor Drive, Charleston, SC 29407. CHARLESTON. *Historically Cooking – 200 Years of Good Eating*, K. K. Beth Elohim Sisterhood. Send $6.50 plus $1.50 to: 85 Hasell Street, Charleston, SC 29401. COLUMBIA. *The Stuffed Bagel*, Columbia, S.C. Hadassah Chapter.

TENNESSEE. BLOUNTVILLE. *Recipes by Request*, B'nai Sholom Sisterhood. Send $6.25 to: Mrs. Leonard Supman, 1300 Bel Meade Drive, Kingsport, TN 37664. MEMPHIS. *The MJCC Presents Our Favorite Recipes*, Memphis Jewish Community Center. Send $9.00 to: MJCC Cookbook, 6560 Poplar, Memphis, TN 38138.

TEXAS. BELLAIRE. *The Cookie Cookery*, Brith Shalom Sisterhood. CORPUS CHRISTI. *The Legacy of Good Cooking*, Temple Beth El Sisterhood. Send $8.95 plus $1.50 shipping to: 1315 Craig Street, Corpus Christi, TX 78404. DALLAS. *5000 Years in the Kitchen*, Sisterhood of Temple Emanuel. Send $8.00 plus $1.50 shipping to: 8500 Hillerest, Dallas, TX 75225.

VIRGINIA. DANVILLE. *Favorite Recipes From Our Best Cooks*, Temple Beth Shalom Sisterhood. Send $4.25 to: Mrs. Walter Feibelman, 418 Linden Place, Danville, VA 24541. FALLS CHURCH. *From Soup to Nosh*, North Virginia Chapter of Hadassah, Fairfax, VA. HAMPTON. *Collectable Delectables*, Rodef Sholom Temple Sisterhood. Send $7.95 plus $1.00 shipping to: 318 Whealton Rd., Hampton, VA 23666. RICHMOND. *Made to ORTer*, Day, Evening, James River Chapters of Women's American Ort. Send $7.95 to: 8808 Overhill Road, Richmond, VA 23229. RICHMOND. *Try It, You'll Like It*, Temple Beth El Sisterhood.

WEST VIRGINIA. CHARLESTON. *Mrs. Cooper's Encore*, B'nai Jacob Synagogue Auxiliary. Send $8.50 plus $1.50 to: Mrs. Samuel Zacks, 3809 Kanawha Ave., Charleston, WV 25304. HUNTINGTON. *A Matzo Ball is NOT Another Dressup Dance!*, Bnai Sholom Sisterhood. Send $7.95 plus $1.00 shipping to: 949 10th Ave., Huntington, WV 25701.

▪▪

Title of Book _____

No. Copies _____ Price, incl. shipping _____

Ship to _____

Address _____

City, State, Zip _____

▪▪